Thomas Hood and nineteenth-century poetry

Manchester University Press

Thomas Hood and nineteenth-century poetry

Work, play and politics

Sara Lodge

Manchester University Press

Manchester and New York

distributed exclusively in the USA by Palgrave

PR
4799
.L63
2007

The right of Sara Lodge to be identified as the author of this work has been asserted by her in accordance with the Copyright, Designs and Patents Act 1988.

Published by Manchester University Press
Oxford Road, Manchester M13 9NR, UK
and Room 400, 175 Fifth Avenue, New York, NY 10010, USA
www.manchesteruniversitypress.co.uk

Distributed exclusively in the USA by
Palgrave, 175 Fifth Avenue, New York,
NY 10010, USA

Distributed exclusively in Canada by
UBC Press, University of British Columbia, 2029 West Mall,
Vancouver, BC, Canada V6T 1Z2

British Library Cataloguing-in-Publication Data
A catalogue record for this book is available from the British Library

Library of Congress Cataloging-in-Publication Data applied for

ISBN   978 0 7190 7626 8   *hardback*

First published 2007

16 15 14 13 12 11 10 09 08 07   10 9 8 7 6 5 4 3 2 1

Typeset
by SNP Best-set Typesetter Ltd., Hong Kong
Printed in Great Britain
by Biddles Ltd, King's Lynn, Norfolk

For my parents, Isobel and John Lodge

Having already done honour to 'the only true and lawful Boz,' . . . it is now beseeming and proper that we should speak of the works of Thomas Hood. To do this intelligently is not an easy task. Paradoxical as our assertion may appear, it is nevertheless true that there are few writers extensively popular who are so little known or so imperfectly understood as our friend of the thousand-and-one crotchets. His works, indeed, have been largely enjoyed, but enjoyed, as some author quaintly says of the winecup, 'without respect.'

H.F. Chorley, *London and Westminster Review*,
29 (April 1838), p. 119

Contents

Figures

Preface

Our first love of language is playful. Sounds fascinate us with their capacity to divert, to tease, and to tickle. If we come to care for reading, we do so because of the pleasure the words afford: we trace the patterns of words on the page like ladders and snakes delivering us to unforeseen yet familiar destinations, via bends that are often as entertaining as their ends. The playfulness of our verbal interaction remains throughout adulthood an index of intimacy, solicitude, and self-disclosure: far from being marginal, play is the home base of our free communicative lives. All too often, however, as academics we are paid to marginalize play. Literature becomes our work. Academics are compelled to frame reading and writing as work to allow their jobs and their students' degrees to hold the value accorded to difficult labour. To maintain our claim to be taken seriously, those of us who teach and research in the academy valorize seriousness. To maintain our claims to professionalism, we eschew language that might be deemed insufficiently professional. Moreover, to meet ever-increasing demands for productivity, we praise the text's productivity, emphasizing its complexity – the freight we are paid to explicate – its 'importance', which underwrites ours. We forget to critique the implicit assumption that 'importance' is the central criterion for judging literature.

This book is about Thomas Hood, a nineteenth-century writer and illustrator whose work is characterized by play. I was drawn to comic poetry as a subject because my own love of poetry began with Edward Lear, Hilaire Belloc, and later Dorothy Parker, e e cummings, and Ogden Nash. Comic verse constitutes a large proportion of the poetry people buy, enjoy, and remember. Yet, outside the specialized field of children's literature, it is under-represented in the academy. There can be genuine difficulties in approaching comic poetry from an academic perspective. Seen as too local, too ephemeral, too available to require interpretation, it is frequently tacitly regarded as sub-academic. In fact much comic poetry is counter-academic. Its typically small scale and overt, sensory pleasures mount a challenge to scholars whose status depends on the assumption that literature needs professional analysts, a challenge we routinely repress. I wanted to write about Hood because he had been loved by readers but disdained by scholars and I wondered what his play could tell us about their mismatched priorities. But another motive shone through the paper I was writing on as time went by, like a watermark. I felt oppressed by current trends in the way that writing, within the academy, is conceived, incentivized, and valued. Like Virginia Woolf, doodling on the margins of her notes in *A Room of One's Own*, I discovered, in looking at my attraction to cartoon, that I was angry.

Over the last twenty years dramatic changes have swept faculties of Arts and Humanities throughout the United Kingdom, some positive and necessary, but many tending to lower morale and a sense of the intrinsic value and delight of literary study, as opposed to its 'measurable' outcomes. While academic salaries have, in real terms, fallen some fifty percent behind non-manual average earnings, academics have faced insistent pressure to justify their jobs. The only quantifiable way in which they are permitted to do this is by publication. Books, which once were written *ad libitum* after years of scholarship and teaching, are now increasingly the only acceptable evidence that a young academic merits a post, that an established one merits promotion, and that an older one deserves to escape the sack. Not since De Gaulle demanded that French-women breed as a matter of government injunction has something that ought to be voluntary and pleasurable become so anxious and forced. Dubbed 'research', scholarly writing about literature is now primarily conceptualized as the expert mining and analysis of fresh data. Lecturers are encouraged to think of themselves as more like chemists than like musicians, their job a matter of winning and administering the largest possible sums in funding and producing the largest number of measurable outputs to a given standard, rather than of participating in a form of live social experience, performance, interaction that is profound partly because its outcomes, among them pleasure, cannot readily be measured.

In the race to seek large sums of funding (often not needed to write books but to please institutions) *big* projects – on high-profile and prolific authors and subject areas with scope for future expansion – acquire added cachet. Those choosing a project, whether at PhD or at lecturer level, ignore the systemic hierarchies that favour 'major' bids at their peril. Despite brave talk, and some progress, on expanding the canon, the pressure to publish, and the pressure on publishers to sell books about authors who feature widely and centrally in syllabuses, tends to reinforce the distinction between 'major' and 'minor' authors; in various senses, the system works to maintain its margins. Despite notional potential equality between types of written product, in practice, as UK universities compete to maximize their government funding, which is based on 'research output', enormous pressure has been exerted upon individuals to up the ante: to produce full-length single-authored monographs as often as possible, to write books not 'just' papers, and to publish what they publish with the most 'prestigious' journals and presses. Oddly, the most commercially viable and socially wide-reaching forms of publication – textbooks, popular editions – are often rewarded less than those based on 'pure research' (in chemistry, where 'pure research' may lead to profitable applied product, this makes long-term economic sense: in English, where books are the applied product, it is puzzling). Desperately looking to discover and create difference, national audit has driven wedges between colleagues and has, in many cases, led to intra-departmental bullying, as institutions have become nervous about projects (the slow, the unworldly, the small-scale) that could 'drag down' their collective score. Each work, and each academic, is labelled with a grade ranging from 'unstarred' to 'four stars' ('international importance'). The claims of 'importance' and 'productivity', then, have worked tacitly to underwrite continuing hierarchies not only between 'major' and 'minor' subjects of literary study but also between 'major' and 'minor' forms of output, and ultimately between 'major' and 'minor' academics. In such an environment, play and pleasure have little place.

The 'outcomes' of this process are obvious. Academics, like Western farmers, caught in a nexus where production rather than profitability has become an end in itself and the onus is on them to seek ever-larger institutional grants to maintain their own livelihoods, are increasingly estranged from the generous and co-operative social basis of the profession. Teaching is undervalued, because there is no competitive economic scale by which to measure it, as are other forms of pastoral and collegial contribution. Pressed into the service of work, academic liberalism in English studies routinely manifests itself only in digging up the buried radicalism of a slighted author. I am not immune to this charge. But my advocacy of Hood is grounded in an explicit claim for the literary value of play, and of the notionally 'minor' (authors, works, and academics). I hope that, as a result of reading this book, readers will encounter or re-encounter Thomas Hood's work and will be as entertained and stimulated as I have been. But I also hope to suggest to academic readers that we should rediscover the centrality of play and pleasure to the best part of what we do and, collectively, renegotiate the terms and structures by which we count how and why we count, and by whom and for what we are paid.

Acknowledgements

It is a pleasure to thank the many people who have helped and supported me in writing this book. Peter F. Morgan, the editor of Hood's *Letters*, shared the fruit of many years of work on Hood and, with extraordinary generosity, gifted me parts of his library. Dinah Birch first convinced me that 'there needs to be a book on Hood' and shared her enthusiasm for Hood and for this project over several years. John Strachan and Greg Dart gave invaluable advice and encouragement. Tim Milnes patiently bore multiple drafts and regular despondency. My fellow Victorianists at St Andrews, Emma Sutton and Phillip Mallett, quietly did chores that would otherwise have fallen to me, while I was in the last stages of completing the manuscript. Jon Ralls calmly dealt with the illustrations. Tim Chilcott, Simon Alderson, and Oliver Sacks cheerfully and promptly responded to offbeat queries. The Carnegie Trust awarded me a grant that enabled me to visit libraries I could not otherwise have consulted. The Trustees of the National Library of Scotland kindly gave me permission to reproduce illustrations from material held in its collection. The staff and readers of Manchester University Press have been unfailingly friendly, helpful, and patient. Finally, for generous hospitality during research trips and for cheering the weary researcher I am deeply grateful to Lesel Dawson, Rob and Stefanie Hamlyn, Ben and Barbara Madley, Gerald Montagu, Tom and Erin Moore, and, last but not least, my parents.

Abbreviations

CW = *The Complete Works of Thomas Hood*, ed. Tom Hood and F.F. Broderip, 10 vols (London: Moxon, 1869–73).

Letters = *The Letters of Thomas Hood*, ed. Peter F. Morgan (Edinburgh: Oliver and Boyd, 1973).

Memorials = F.F. Broderip and Tom Hood, *Memorials of Thomas Hood*, 2nd edn (London: Moxon, 1869).

PW = *The Poetical Works of Thomas Hood*, ed. Walter Jerrold (Oxford: Oxford University Press, 1906).

For ease of reference I have chosen in most instances to direct readers to the *Complete Works* and *Poetical Works* above, which remain the most comprehensive sources for Hood's poetry and prose. Neither is, however, wholly satisfactory and readers are encouraged to consult *Selected Poems of Thomas Hood*, ed. John Clubbe (Cambridge, Massachusetts: Harvard University Press, 1970), and *Selected Poems of Hood, Praed and Beddoes*, ed. Susan Wolfson and Peter J. Manning (London: Penguin, 2000), both of which provide excellent notes and discussion of textual variants.

Introduction

Thomas Hood was one of the best known and best loved of nineteenth-century poets. A humorist, in verse and prose, hailed as 'the best punster in or out of England',[1] Hood would long be remembered as the author of the *Comic Annual* (1830–9), a yearly magazine of comic poems and vignettes, illustrated with lively woodcuts designed by Hood himself, that broke new ground in the nineteenth-century periodical market and gave pleasure to thousands of readers of all ages. Hood's comic poetry tickled Coleridge, who enjoyed the puns.[2] Goethe recommended it.[3] Alfred Tennyson, according to his son, recited Hood's verse for the benefit of friends, 'laughing till the tears came'.[4] Thackeray, travelling as a student in Germany, wrote letters home requesting copies of the *Comic Annual*.[5] Indeed, the *Comic Annual* found a place in the bookcases of admirers from Ruskin to Poe, from Dickens to the Duke of Devonshire.[6]

Many of those readers were also familiar with Hood's early lyric poems, two of which – 'The Deathbed' and 'I Remember, I Remember' – were included in the most successful poetry anthology of the Victorian era, *Palgrave's Golden Treasury* (1861). In a 1997 radio survey that asked the British public to name its hundred favourite poems of all time, Hood's 'I Remember, I Remember' polled twenty-eighth: it was more popular than any poem by Shelley, Blake, or T.S. Eliot.[7] Hood's lyrics of the 1820s reflect the fact that, becoming the companion and then brother-in-law of John Hamilton Reynolds, who had just lost his last close friend and collaborator – Keats – Hood had access to notebooks containing Keats's poems and became one of the first writers to respond in poetry to Keats's legacy. Dante Gabriel Rossetti, whose brother William edited Hood's *Poetical Works* in the 1870s, deemed Hood 'a *great* poet . . . whose first volume is more identical with Keats's work than could be said of any other similar parallel'.[8] Other readers revelled chiefly in the grotesque energies of Hood's narrative poems, which submerge the reader in the fantastical world of nightmare. Poems such as 'The Dream of Eugene Aram', 'The Last Man' and 'The Haunted House' impressed writers including Robert Browning and Robert Louis Stevenson.[9]

All who knew Hood's work also knew his 'protest' poems, 'The Lay of the Labourer' (1844), 'The Bridge of Sighs' (1844), and, above all 'The Song of the Shirt' (1843), a ballad about sweated labour among seamstresses, which reputedly tripled the circulation of the magazine *Punch* and stimulated an unprecedented popular response, inspiring paintings, plays, and charitable donations for the relief of the women Hood depicted. 'The Song of the Shirt' is described in William Morris's utopian *News from Nowhere* as a 'revolutionary song'; Hood's protest verses occupy a place in Condition of England novels including Elizabeth Gaskell's *Mary Barton* (1848) and Charles Kingsley's *Alton Locke* (1850), they were lauded by the Chartist poet Gerald Massey, remarked by Friedrich Engels, and became popular in Russia.[10] In America, both Longfellow and Abraham Lincoln enjoyed Hood's work.[11] On Hood's death, his surviving family was awarded a pension by Prime Minister Robert Peel who had, the year before, sent Hood a letter assuring him 'there can be little, which you have written and acknowledged, that I have not read'.[12]

Hood's life (1799–1845) spanned the tumultuous first half of the nineteenth century; his fame survived the second. A *Complete Works* in ten volumes and a biography, both issued by his children, Tom and Fanny, in the 1860s, familiarized a new audience with the pathos of Hood's life, which was dogged by persistent illness and financial struggle, and kept the memory of his writings green. Between his death in 1845 and Queen Victoria's in 1901, there was barely a year in which Hood's works were not reprinted in some form. In the 1860s Harrow sixth-formers were set Hood alongside Keats, Byron, Worthsworth, and Arnold for translation into Latin.[13] Conjuring up Hood's special charm on April Fool's Day 1871, twenty-six years after his death, J. Fraser could still write in the *Westminster Review*:

> Tom Hood is one of ourselves, an intimate friend, a member of our family; with whom we can laugh and be merry, and to whom we can tell our secrets, and chat in a pleasant, homely fashion. We are at home in his company, as if we had been intimate with him since boyhood, and can fancy at times that we hear his quiet laugh, his merry quip, and see the pleasant smile that lit up his pale, solemn face.[14]

The fact that Hood remains one of 'ourselves', assimilated to the realm of friend and family, attests to his central place in Victorian popular literary culture. The rhythms of his verse influenced poems as disparate as Lewis Carroll's 'The Walrus and the Carpenter' and Oscar Wilde's 'The Ballad of Reading Gaol'. In the twentieth century Hood's select but stalwart band of supporters included the war poets Edward Blunden and Siegfried Sassoon, who was, as he recalls in his autobiography, inspired to become a poet by the epiphany of reading Hood's 'The Bridge of Sighs'.[15] It also included W.H. Auden, who championed Hood as 'a major poet' in the introduction to his 1967 edition of *Nineteenth Century Minor Poets*.[16]

How is it, then, that Thomas Hood is not a part of teaching syllabuses or scholarly discussion about nineteenth-century poetry now? Given the richness and diversity of his output, the range and breadth of his readership, his cultural prominence and literary legacy, Hood's near-total absence from academic analysis of nineteenth-century literature is curious and striking. Although Hood's verse continues to be widely anthologized and Carcanet (1992) and Penguin (2000) have published modern *Selected Poems*, there is, remarkably, no modern critical study of Hood. A survey (Jeffrey 1972), two biographies (Reid 1963; Clubbe 1968), a *Collected Letters* (Morgan 1973), and a handful of journal articles comprise the Hood scholarship of the last four decades.[17] This book aims to restore Hood to view after half a century of unwarranted critical neglect.

More than merely examining Hood's inherent interest and prowess as a writer and illustrator, however, this book argues that looking closely at Hood illuminates three areas of nineteenth-century cultural production that modern scholarship has yet fully to explore: the output of the years 1824–40; comic poetry; and the grotesque. These three areas of discomfort are linked: each of them threatens boundaries that are convenient for literary criticism. Hood, as a figure who straddles the eras traditionally identified as 'Romantic' and 'Victorian', and as an author who is drawn to unstable subjects – the tragi-comic; the part-human; the pun; the grotesque – both embodies and articulates amphibology: unresolved energies and ambivalence in nineteenth-century literature. Responding to Hood necessitates responding to these energies and, potentially, to our own critical ambivalence about aspects of that literature and the culture in which it was produced. A master of punmanship, Hood himself became during his lifetime and has remained a socio-literary pun: a figure evoking class tensions that express themselves in anxiety about his 'vulgarity' or his 'bourgeois' limitations, a figure inspiring unease about the strength and direction of his political commitments – like Dickens, he has been described as a 'sentimental Radical';[18] a figure associated with amusement, but also with equivocation and the apparently self-cancelling impulses that the pun can momentarily fuse: acuity and vacuity, extravagance and economy, delight and disgust. Examining the mixed feelings that Hood inspires, I hope to investigate the cultural politics that inform Hood's production and reception and to suggest that a better understanding of Hood can not only illuminate the popular literature of this period but shed reflexive light on current critical preoccupations. Although I draw frequent connections between Hood's liberalism and the comic devices with which he criticizes aspects of political governance, from taking tithe to banning begging, my use of the terms 'politics' and 'play' in this book is deliberately broad. As James English argues, the intervention of comedy consists as much in the processes it enjoins as in the views it espouses:

> What the joke *does* is to intervene in a particular system of social relationships, putting into circulation a 'mutilated and altered transcript' of certain of the system's elements, a 'most strange revision' of the problems or contradictions that bind those elements within the system. And this intervention must always entail certain shifts in subjective alignment or identification, momentary adjustments along the axes of hierarchy and solidarity.[19]

Hood's writing and illustration is not all comic, but it constantly actuates and solicits this kind of mobility. One can bring a Derridean conception of play to bear upon Hood's treatment of language as a series of indeterminate signs in flux. Yet play in Hood's oeuvre is also a willed event that can embrace the resonances of childhood games, the performative, transactional pleasures of theatre, and respite from labour in an economy dominated by work. I hope, in different chapters, to explore different aspects of Hood's play, making a virtue of the very susceptibility to plural interpretation in which the delight of play for Hood consists.

A biographical sketch

Thomas Hood was born in 1799, one of six children of a Scottish bookseller-publisher in the heart of the City of London. Like Charles Lamb, he was educated into his early teens, after which, and following his father's untimely death, he began work as a clerk in a counting-house. The work suited neither his already fragile health nor his temperament and he began training to be an engraver, his uncle's profession, while practising writing and joining a local literary society. Hood's lucky break came when, in 1821, he was invited to become a sub-editor for the *London Magazine*, run by John Taylor, who had served his apprenticeship as a publisher in the firm of Vernor and Hood and must have seen an opportunity to return a favour to the son of his old employer. Contributors to the *London Magazine* whom Hood would meet professionally and socially in a period he later recalled with delight included Thomas De Quincey, William Hazlitt, Bryan Waller Procter, Allan Cunningham, John Clare, John Hamilton Reynolds, and Charles Lamb, who became 'almost a father' to him. His editorial position at the *London Magazine* enabled Hood to experiment with writing and publishing anonymously short pieces in a variety of styles. His first book of poetry, *Odes and Addresses to Great People* (1825), written with John Hamilton Reynolds, capitalizes on that variety and anonymity to try out comic accounts of prominent personalities from Elizabeth Fry to Joseph Grimaldi. Its success led to two self-illustrated volumes of *Whims and Oddities* (1826–7): often blackly comic poems and vignettes, some of which had first appeared in the *London*, and which display Hood's wonderful facility for word-play. Meanwhile, a selection of 'serious' poems including odes, sonnets, and narrative verse appeared as *The Plea of the Midsummer Fairies* (1827), a volume dedicated to Lamb, who valued it highly, but which was commercially unsuccessful, as was a prose volume of *National Tales* (1827). During this period Hood also worked briefly as a theatre reviewer for the *Atlas*, and wrote several comic pieces for the stage. In 1828 he edited the *Gem* for 1829, an annual anthology of poems, tales, prose sketches and illustrations by well-known authors, including, in the *Gem*'s case, work by Scott, Lamb, Procter, Reynolds, Clare, and a posthumous sonnet by Keats. The *Gem* also included Hood's extraordinary 'The Dream of Eugene Aram', a poem about an eighteenth-century murderer, who, undetected, worked as a school usher for over a decade until finally incriminated by an accomplice. Beautifully presented and packaged as gift selections, annuals were the most successful commercial form for poetry from the mid-1820s to the late 1830s. Hood's editorship of a conventional poetic annual gave him the experience and the insight to develop his own, trademark *Comic Annual* (1830–9, 42), which, containing a variety of humorous poems, prose pieces, and illustrations similar to those he had created for *Whims and Oddities*, was enormously popular and widely imitated.

In the early 1830s, with sales of the *Comic Annual* flourishing, Hood felt sufficiently confident to move with his wife out of London and to take a house at Wanstead, Essex where he could dabble in country pleasures. Here he wrote his only completed novel, the three-decker *Tylney Hall* (1834). Sadly, also in 1834, following the collapse of a firm in which he had invested, Hood's ever-precarious finances collapsed. To retrench and pay off creditors, he accepted self-imposed exile in Germany and Belgium, whence he continued to conduct the *Comic Annual* and wrote a successful humorous travelogue, *Up the Rhine* (1839). Returning to England with his wife and two children in 1840, he edited the *New Monthly Magazine* (1841–3) and *Hood's Magazine* (1844–5), publishing poems that, increasingly, drew attention to the social effects of exploitative capitalism. These included 'Miss Kilmansegg and Her Precious Leg', 'The Workhouse Clock', and, most famously, 'The Song of the Shirt'. Among the contributors to *Hood's Magazine* were Charles Dickens, Hood's friend since 1840 and a fellow campaigner for changes in copyright legislation that would give greater protection to writers and their estates, and Robert Browning, who 'loved Hood heartily'[20] and furnished poems, including 'The Flight of the Duchess' and 'The Bishop Orders his Tomb at St Praxed's Church' when the magazine lacked copy during Hood's last illness.

Between the acts: 1824–40

Recent scholarship has done much to recover the work of individual writers prominent during the later 1820s and 1830s and Richard Cronin's *Romantic Victorians: Literature 1824–1840* offers a salutary survey.[21] Yet these decades remain undervalued. A brief consideration of the above biographical sketch will suggest the difficulties that critics have faced in comprehending Hood. Editor, illustrator, dramatist, travel writer, journalist, novelist, humorist, and poet, Hood does not fit neatly into the divisions of genre and period that tend to shape university courses and their attendant course-readers. Yet his multifarious output was not untypical for professional urban writers between the 1820s and the 1840s: a fact that suggests that our preference for studying literature as discrete, single-authored volumes distorts our view of early nineteenth-century production. A glance at the curricula vitae of Charles Lamb, Charles Dickens, William Thackeray, Mark Lemon, or Douglas Jerrold would produce a similar list of activities: miscellany fosters the play with multiple voice, genre, and style that energizes the work of all these writers. As Edward Bulwer Lytton remarked in 1833, 'It is a great literary age – we have great literary men – but where are their works? a moment's reflection gives us a reply to the question: we must seek them not in detached and avowed and standard publications, but in periodical miscellanies. It is in these journals that the most eminent of our recent men of letters, have chiefly obtained their renown.'[22] It was an age of reform in politics and revolution in commercial print culture. The primacy of the periodical in this revolution cannot be overstated. Hood, born and apprenticed into the dynamic, newly diversifying world of print, was from childhood surrounded by the multiplicity of forms that publication took. My first chapter is concerned with the effects of this context on Hood's remarkably pluralistic approach to words, texts, and readers, both as material entities and as imaginative projections. Hood's upbringing in the book trade, and his training as an engraver and editor, gives him a facility for construing word and picture as inseparable forms of plastic visual sign that invite multiple reading. Moreover the dissenting culture of his father's publishing firm and education at Nicolas Wanostrocht's liberal Camberwell Academy, a school attended also by James and Horace Smith, fosters his tolerant, social worldview, where recreation is central to creativity.

The second chapter explores Hood's early career at the *London Magazine*, restoring the dynamic context in which he began experimenting with voice and genre and reading his work against that of fellow contributors including Charles Lamb, John Hamilton Reynolds, and Thomas Griffiths Wainewright. It examines the connection between the *London*'s liberal politics and its culture of play. It argues that periodicals of this era, and particularly the *London*, both develop the terms (major/minor; genius/talent) that define the Romantic canon and, by drawing attention to the secondary and inauthenticable nature of all texts, expose the fictional status of those terms ('originality', 'authenticity') by which 'major' and 'minor' authors are distinguished. Our understanding of Hood's relation to his literary environment has been limited by a simplistic and sometimes derogatory construction of his early work as 'minor Romantic'. In fact Hood establishes a dialectical relationship with Romantic authorship that is by turns deferential and deflationary, sometimes inviting us to see him as a 'minor' or 'belated' figure, yet simultaneously undermining the values that underlie such distinctions. Hood draws on topoi of loss, of introspection, of isolation that respond to Romantic models and absences, but he also delights in comic transposition of those tropes to concrete, commercial, and class-conscious situations in which they appear doubtful or ludicrous. Hood plays with limitation, makes it a critical conduit, and uses it to position himself closer to the reader. Looking at his work should encourage us to reconsider the 'minor' as a deliberate stance and a quality to be celebrated, rather than redeemed.

In my third chapter I explore Hood's work in relation to the so-called 'minor' or 'illegitimate' theatre of the 1820s and 1830s, contending that his writing and illustration, with their overt performativity, characteristic genre mixing, and emphasis on physical spectacle, draw on the rich traditions of the unlicensed stage. Hood's work similarly plays out the possibilities of an emergent cultural democracy. It is part of a trend shared by early nineteenth-century periodical and theatrical culture toward representing the city's social variety to its inhabitants: turning the mirror on the audience and blurring divisions between reader and writer, actor and spectator. Hood's experience of theatre, as a writer and reviewer, informs his multiple use of voice and his sense of all social interaction as role play; his acute depiction of social 'feinting' draws attention to class itself as an effect of performance. Hood has been largely absent from discussion of the dramatic monologue, yet his monologues, which frequently counterpoise repressed and expressed aspects of the speaking self, deserve to be considered in accounts of the development of the form and recall its connections with popular theatre.

Horrid Hood: the grotesque and its mirrors

Michael Hollington rightly notes in *Dickens and the Grotesque* that 'if one figure can be said to create and disseminate the taste for the grotesque in the 1830s it is Thomas Hood'.[23] The grotesque is central to Hood's vision as a writer; indeed, the visuality of Hood's work enables its grotesquerie, for the grotesque is a highly visual mode of expression: its imagery is predominantly somatic – body-based – and deliberately provokes pre-rational, visceral responses. Hood's illustrations feature the potential strangeness and malleability of the body, its capacity to vary, to break, to reconfigure, to assimilate its components to those of other creatures and objects. At the primary level of word, letter, and line, Hood's work is similarly characterized by proliferation, metamorphosis, and unstable doubles that draw attention to the body of language itself: its visual shape-shifting and aural relationships to forms similar but diverse.

In Chapter 4 I consider the grotesque as a richly fruitful axis for understanding Hood's work across different genres. Hood has long been identified as an exponent of the grotesque: Ruskin, Poe, and Hood himself use the term 'grotesque' to describe his art. Remarkably, however, existing accounts of the Victorian grotesque do not dwell on Hood.[24] I consider textual and iconographic influences upon Hood's grotesquerie and reflect on the traditionally demotic and often radical connotations of the grotesque idiom. I also consider features of the early nineteenth-century context that contribute to an environment often depicted in grotesque terms: from revolutionary and evolutionary anxieties to the reifications of a market in which, Ruskin argued, the 'mind *plays* with *terror*' in reaction to the increasingly mechanical nature of work.[25] It is tempting to mirror the unresolved tensions of the grotesque back on to the figure of Hood himself, who becomes accordingly a tragic jester or a grinning death's head, but this approach under-represents Hood's deliberate choice of the grotesque as a shared contemporary aesthetic mode. The singularity and 'morbidity' of Hood's grotesquerie have too often been stressed at the expense of exploring their typicality and topicality: I hope to redress that balance.

One feature of Hood's style, more than any other, has exasperated critics: as Karl Kroeber puts it, 'those hideous puns!'[26] Punning is a habit of thought for Hood, as it is for James Joyce; words, for him, are not fixed and closed entities but are forever alluding to and morphing into their verbal and visual relatives. Chapter 5 is devoted to considering Hood's puns, their effects, their detractors, and the cultural politics of punning in the nineteenth century. Punning, I contend, is itself a form of grotesque art, an 'aesthetic of the irreconcilable' in miniature. Like the duck-rabbit famous in psychology, puns disconcert by drawing attention to the process of reading and the potential co-existence of incompatible readings; they delay arrival at the sentence's end, and disrupt linear models of reading's 'end'. In Hood's writing they are an engine of mobility, generating energetic verbal fusions and fissions mirrored in the physical metamorphoses and dismemberments, exchanges and reforms that proliferate in his subject matter. Hood was fully aware that his puns were critical irritants; his persistent allegiance to this trope above all others is significant. The teasing verbal mobility that puns effect between high and low, concrete and abstract, subject and object has levelling social implications. Pitting the robust, punning inheritance of Swift against the literary snobbery of Johnson, Hood deliberately chooses to ally himself with a tradition of literary humour that is suspicious of genteel sublimation and linguistic regulation. Punning also vividly expresses the values of pluralism, tolerance, and recreative leisure that are central to Hood's political vision. The endlessly recombinant energies of the pun embody the free play of a populace that cannot forcibly be contained in any church, nor deterred from reproduction by Malthusian admonitions.

The paradox of comic poetry: the familiar and the marginal

If periodization and the fairground mirror of the grotesque are two of the barriers that have hindered modern critical appreciation of Hood, the third hurdle is deceptively simple. Nineteenth-century comic poetry excites little academic interest. Romantic satire is still taught in universities; Lear and Carroll are known as children's authors; but the bias of most anthologies, courses, and textbooks is serious. In 1988, in the last issue of *Victorian Poetry* devoted to comic verse, Donald J. Gray ironically entitled his essay, 'Victorian Comic Verse; or, Snakes in Greenland' – the joke being that there are no snakes in Greenland. In fact the list of writers producing comic poetry in the nineteenth century is long and lively, and includes William Aytoun, Hilaire Belloc, C.S. Calverley, Lord Alfred Douglas, Alfred Henry Forrester, W.S. Gilbert, A.E. Housman, Theodore Martin, William Mackworth Praed, Louisa Henrietta Sheridan, Robert Louis Stevenson, and William Thackeray, as well as many anonymous authors. A contemporary anthology, *The Comic Poets of the Nineteenth Century* (1876), lists fifty-four different writers, and it draws only from living poets.[27] There is a danger in teaching predominantly of nineteenth-century poetry's cultural work that we under-represent its culture of play – and the intricate connections between them.

My final chapter examines the politics of Hood's play in relation to nineteenth-century debate about labour and leisure. Tracing connections between his early poems about vagrancy and the workhouse, his anti-Sabbatarianism, and his best-known 'protest' songs, it argues that Hood's writing resists increasingly rigid labour discipline and its attendant social controls by offering a counter-discourse that both mimics the repetitive forms of work and disrupts them, insisting on the transformative power and restorative value of play. Hood is not primarily a children's writer, yet his playfulness allies him with the adult reader's memories of childhood, drawing on codes of intimacy and shared experience that enable him to make common cause with a wide and varied audience. Hood's poetry can also fruitfully be read against didactic evangelical nursery verse: as I show for the first time, his trenchant poem 'A Lay of Real Life' is a parody of Ann Taylor's 'My Mother'. Where Taylor voices the litany of a child's debts to its parent, Hood voices the litany of a child's neglect by every relation who ought ordinarily to supply its wants. His writing opposes itself to the authoritarian rhetoric associated with preaching the virtues of industry over the vices of idleness and with legislation inimical to working-class pleasures. Indeed, Hood asserts that he is, in a literal sense, 'of the working-class': his unusual insistence on representing the writer as a worker among others involved in producing the book as material object is central to his participation in contemporary protest about the conditions of labour.

Hood ought to be an easy writer to reclaim. His language and style are not abstruse. There is nothing recondite about him. But the very availability of his work poses a subtle challenge to academic critics. Juliet John has recently demonstrated that previous academic approaches to Dickens have been limited by their insistence on reading him 'in terms of cultural assumptions to which he was opposed', refusing to recognize the ideological coherence and significance of his 'scepticism about "depths"' and 'refusal to valorize interiority'.[28] In *Nicholas Nickleby* the acting troupe encounters a man who has devoted his life to considering the question of whether the Nurse's husband in *Romeo in Juliet* was or was not 'a merry man': this worrier of literary loose ends, the proto-academic, can never in Dickens's writing be anything other than a figure of fun – failing, unlike the actors, to embrace the shared performative interaction that constitutes 'reading', his lone studiousness entails misconstruing not only the letter but the spirit of the text. Academic critics of Hood, as of Dickens, need to beware that, judging his writing via strategies and values antithetical to its own, they do not merely report mutual dissatisfaction. Hood depicts his scepticism about the interiority of intellectual analysis in 'The Logicians':

> See here two cavillers,
>   Would-be unravellers
> Of abstruse theory and questions mystical,
>   In tête-à-tête,
>   And deep debate,
> Wrangling according to forms syllogistical.
>
>   Glowing and ruddy
> The light streams in upon their deep brown study,
> And settles on our bald logician's skull:
> But still his meditative eye looks dull
>   And muddy,
> For he is gazing inwardly, like Plato;
>   But to the world without
>   And things about,
> His eye is blind as that of a potato:
>   In fact, logicians
> See but syllogisms – taste and smell
>   By propositions;
> And never let the common dray-horse senses
>   Draw inferences.[29]

Hood's comic verse, like much comic writing, deliberately prefers the concrete to the abstract, the physical to the metaphysical. Likewise, it typically draws attention to its own material form, preferring the expected 'punch-rhyme' to more self-effacing modes of closure; blatantly italicizing puns, themselves often ostentatiously 'forced'; enjoying the flourish of the exclamation mark; flirting with ineptitude – several of Hood's poems pretend to be by contributors ignorant of the 'rules' that govern poetry, in the process casting doubt on what those rules are. Where most non-comic poetry seeks to conceal its art, Hood's comic verse revels in the recognizable, foregrounding the openness and availability of its mechanics, the familiar repetitions of its rhythmic and rhyming patterns, which allow readers to anticipate, memorize, and 'own' his poems. Predictable pattern, echoing the 're-counting' of intimate childhood routine, is, indeed, as essential to Hood's comic verse as it is to hopscotch, snap, or skipping – an analogy he himself highlights in 'Skipping: A Mystery':

> Little children skip,
> The rope so gaily gripping,
>   Tom and Harry,
>   Jane and Mary,
>   Kate, Diana,
>   Susan, Anna,
> All are fond of skipping!

> . . . But oh! how Readers skip,
> In heavy volumes dipping!
> ***** and *****
> ***** and *****
> ***** and *****
>   ********
> All are fond of skipping![30]

Like Christina Rossetti's better-known 'Winter: My Secret', this is poetry as game, its ellipses teasing the reader: it invites us into a joke of which we may be the butt. That is, however, part of its appeal. Looking at Hood entails looking at ourselves, our own reading processes, the balance we negotiate, in literature and outside it, between work and play. At a time when anti-social models of competition, productivity, and labour discipline increasingly dominate academic life, that is one of many good reasons to read him again.

Notes

1 Anon, 'Literary Intelligence', *Edinburgh Literary Gazette*, 26 September 1829, p. 66.
2 For Coleridge's admiring response to *Odes and Addresses to Great People* (1825) see Samuel Taylor Coleridge, *The Collected Letters of Samuel Taylor Coleridge*, ed. Earl Leslie Griggs, 6 vols (Oxford: Clarendon Press, 1971), vol. 5, pp. 472–3.
3 Johann Wolfgang von Goethe, 'Whims and Oddities 1827', reprinted in *Sämtliche Werke: Schriften zur Literatur III*, 40 vols (Stuttgart and Berlin: Gotta'sche, 1902), vol. 38, pp. 134–5.

4 Hallam Tennyson, *Tennyson: A Memoir*, 2 vols (London: Macmillan, 1897), vol. 1, p. 37.

5 William Thackeray, *The Letters and Private Papers of William Makepeace Thackeray*, ed. Gordon N. Ray, 4 vols (Oxford: Oxford University Press, 1945), vol. 1, p. 132.

6 For John Ruskin's encomia on Hood see *The Library Edition of the Works of John Ruskin*, eds E.T. Cook and Alexander Wedderburn, 39 vols (London: Allen, 1903–1912), vol. 6, p. 471; vol. 19, p. 158; vol. 29, p. 223. Poe's thoughtful assessment is in Edgar Allan Poe, 'Thomas Hood', *Broadway Journal*, 9 August 1845, reprinted in *Essays and Reviews of Edgar Allan Poe* (Cambridge: Cambridge University Press, 1984), pp. 274–88. Dickens's friendship with Hood and admiration for his work is expressed in *The Letters of Charles Dickens*, ed. Madeline House, Graham Storey and Kathleen Tillotson, 12 vols (Oxford: Clarendon, 1965–2002), for example vol. 3, p. 341. The Duke of Devonshire, appreciative dedicatee of the 1831 *Comic Annual*, commissioned Hood to create punning titles for a false bookcase at Chatsworth, which can still be seen. For a discussion of the bookcase see pp. 170–1 below.

7 *Classic fM: One Hundred Favourite Poems* (London: Hodder & Stoughton, 2001). The British radio station Classic fM has some five million listeners and this anthology has sold over fifty thousand copies. In a similar anthology, *The Nation's Favourite Poems* (London: BBC Worldwide, 1996), based on a 1995 poll organized by the television programme, *The Bookworm*, to coincide with National Poetry Day, Hood's 'I Remember, I Remember' came 55th, suggesting that the Classic fM result was no fluke. In the BBC survey, Keats, Yeats, and Auden proved to be the nation's most popular poets.

8 Dante Gabriel Rossetti quoted in T. Hall Caine, *Recollections of Dante Gabriel Rossetti* (London: Stock, 1882), pp. 179–80.

9 For Robert Browning's affection for 'The Last Man' see his letter to Alfred Domett, 23 November 1845, in *The Brownings' Correspondence*, ed. Philip Kelley and Ronald Hudson, 10 vols (Kansas: Wedgestone, 1987), vol. 11, p. 193. Robert Louis Stevenson's copy of Hood's *Poems* (1867) is held in the Beinecke Library at Yale. 'The Dream of Eugene Aram' is marked 'Best' in his handwriting – a preference that may reflect the Jekyll-and-Hyde qualities that Aram foreshadows.

10 See William Morris, *News from Nowhere and Other Writings*, ed. Clive Wilmer (Penguin, 1993), pp. 99–100; Gerald Massey, 'Thomas Hood: Poet and Punster', *Hogg's Instructor*, 4 (1855), pp. 326–7; Friedrich Engels comments in *The Condition of the Working Class in England* (Oxford: Oxford University Press, 1993), p. 219, that 'Hood, the most talented of all the English humourists now living. . . . published . . . a beautiful poem, "The Song of the Shirt", which drew sympathetic but unavailing tears from the daughters of the bourgeoisie'. On Russian translations of Hood see J.C. Reid, *Thomas Hood* (London: Routledge & Kegan Paul, 1963), pp. 262–3.

11 Dickens, letter to Hood of 13 October 1842, reprinted in *Letters of Dickens*, vol. 3, p. 341, states: 'I will bring . . . if you will let me, Professor Longfellow of Boston (whose poetry you may have seen) who, admiring you as all good and true men do, wants to know you'. On Lincoln see John Clubbe, *Victorian Forerunner: The Later Career of Thomas Hood* (Durham, North Carolina: Duke University Press, 1968), p. 75.

12 Robert Peel, letter to Hood of 10 November 1844, reprinted in *Memorials*, p. 437.

13 Richard D. Altick, *The English Common Reader* (Chicago: University of Chicago Press, 1952), p. 181.

14 J. Fraser, 'Thomas Hood', *The Westminster and Foreign Quarterly Review*, 1 April 1871, p. 337.

15 Siegfried Sassoon, *The Old Century and Seven More Years* (London: Faber, 1938), pp. 217–19.

16 W.H. Auden, *Nineteenth Century Minor Poets* (Faber, 1967), p. 19. While dubbing Hood a 'major poet', Auden included him in the anthology. His assessment and selection stress the value of Hood's comic poetry, where previous critics often privileged Hood's lyrics and later protest poems.

17 Mention should also be made of the scholarly contribution represented by John Clubbe's *Selected Poems of Thomas Hood*, ed. John Clubbe (Cambridge, Massachusetts: Harvard University Press, 1970); Peter F. Morgan's doctoral study *Thomas Hood's Literary Reading, as Shown in His Works*, University of London (1959); and Roger Henkle's *Comedy and Culture 1820–1900* (Princeton: Princeton University Press, 1980).

18 V.S. Pritchett, *The Living Novel* (London: Chatto and Windus, 1946), p. 64.

19 James English, *Comic Transactions: Literature, Humor, and the Politics of Community in Twentieth-Century Britain* (Ithaca and London: Cornell University Press, 1994), pp. 15–16.

20 Robert Browning, letter to Frederick Oldfield Ward of 22 May 1844, reprinted in *The Brownings' Correspondence*, vol. 8, p. 318.

21 Recent scholarship on writers active during this period includes Jane Aaron, *A Double Singleness: Gender and the Writings of Charles and Mary Lamb* (Oxford: Oxford University Press, 1991); Glennis Stephenson, *Letitia Landon: The Woman Behind L.E.L.* (Manchester: Manchester University Press, 1995); David Bradshaw, *Resurrection Songs: The Poetry of Thomas Lovell Beddoes* (Aldershot: Ashgate, 2001); and a renaissance of work on John Clare, such as Alan Vardy, *John Clare, Politics and Poetry* (Basingstoke: Palgrave, 2004).

22 Edward Bulwer Lytton, *England and the English*, 2 vols (London: Bentley, 1833), vol. 2, p. 61.

23 Michael Hollington, *Dickens and the Grotesque* (London: Croom Helm, 1984), p. 35.

24 Isobel Armstrong's chapter on grotesque as a 'radical aesthetic' in *Victorian Poetry: Poetry, Poetics and Politics* (London: Routledge, 1993) is chiefly

devoted to Morris and Ruskin. The excellent Colin Trodd, Paul Barlow, and David Amigoni (eds), *Victorian Culture and the Idea of the Grotesque* (Aldershot: Ashgate, 1999) does not discuss Hood.

25 John Ruskin, *The Stones of Venice*, 3 vols (London: Allen, 1906), vol. 3, p. 138 (original emphasis).

26 Karl Kroeber, 'Trends in Minor Romantic Narrative Poetry', in James V. Logan, John Jordan and Northrop Frye (eds), *Some British Romantics: A Collection of Essays* (Columbus, Ohio: Ohio State University Press, 1966), p. 290.

27 *The Comic Poets of the Nineteenth Century: Poems of Wit and Humour by Living Writers*, ed. William Davenport Adams (London and New York: Routledge, 1876).

28 Juliet John, *Dickens's Villains: Melodrama, Character, Popular Culture* (Oxford: Oxford University Press, 2001), p. 16.

29 'The Logicians', *PW*, p. 431. Hood's humour at the expense of the overly intellectual has elements of irony. The rhyme on 'Plato/potato' is used by Byron in *Don Juan* (canto 7, stanza 4).

30 'Skipping. A Mystery', *PW*, pp. 637–8.

1

Material backgrounds: print, dissent, and the social society

How did Hood become a writer and illustrator whose every utterance is liable to play? Answering this question means looking afresh at Hood's background and the route he followed into the literary profession. The first two chapters of this book are particularly concerned with three aspects of Hood's upbringing and apprenticeship: his early exposure to the burgeoning marketplace of printed products, the culture of dissent that shaped his family life and schooling, and the social and political community within which he produced his first works. Unusually amongst authors, Hood was born into the publishing industry. He grew up in the midst of typefaces, burins, books and broadsides, political cartoons and advertisements. Trained as an engraver, his intimate relationship with words as signs is distinctive. In a letter of May 1833[1] Hood writes to fellow-engraver John Wright about a seaside holiday that he is enjoying (Fig. 1.1).

Exuberantly breaking the formal rule of line, the sentences on the page have become the waves that they describe, an ideogram as well as a description. Individual words are also in flux: abstract mythology becomes personal my-thology, as Neptune materializes in Ramsgate. Hood's approach to writing is energized by constant awareness that language is a shifting assemblage of unreliable characters – as he puts it in his late poem, 'A Tale of a Trumpet', where a deaf old lady is seduced by the offer of a magical hearing aid: 'Filthy conjunctions, and dissolute Nouns, / And Particles pick'd from the the Kennels of towns, / With Irregular Verbs for irregular jobs, / Chiefly active in rows and mobs, / Picking Possessive Pronouns' fobs'.[2] To Hood, words are like people, with a lively tendency to mingle and misbehave, so that meaning is inherently multiple, constructed, an effect of social reading where intention and reception may be hilariously at odds. In the preface to his German travelogue *Up the Rhine* (1839) he tells the story of 'a plain Manufacturer of Roman Cement, in the Greenwich road', who 'was once turned by a cramped showboard' into a 'MANUFACTURER of

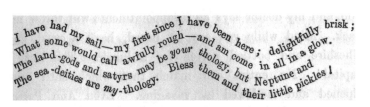

I have had my sail—my first since I have been here ; delightfully brisk ;
What some would call awfully rough—and am come in all in a glow.
The land-gods and satyrs may be your thology, but Neptune and
The sea-deities are my-thology. Bless them and their little pickles !

1.1 Lines from a letter by Hood to John Wright (1833)

ROMANCEMENT' and quips that 'a Tour up the Rhine has generally been expected to convert an author into a dealer in the same commodity', but his own account will be heretically prosaic.[3] Roman cement is a type of cement made of lime, water, and sand, which was patented at the turn of the nineteenth century and was used chiefly as a render for the outside walls of buildings. Hood, with his quick eye for public signs and advertisements, instantly notes unintended coalescence between the most prosaic of building materials and the most ethereal of literary fabrics. His upbringing in a world of print makes Hood hyper-aware of the porousness of language and its susceptibility to plural readings within the marketplace of competing representations. This awareness informs a remarkably democratic view of literature as a commodity: purveyors of render and renderers of narrative turn out to be working the same stall; the 'Literary and Literal' (the title of one of Hood's poems) can never be kept apart, when a cramped showboard will always suggest their fundamental identity.

Hood's play with the idea of 'Romancement' as a commodity is also a direct consequence of the steam-driven literary landscape he inhabits. As the preface to *Up the Rhine* continues:

> Since Byron and the Dampschiff, there has been quite enough of vapouring, in more senses that one, on the blue and castled river, and the echoing nymph of the Lurley must be quite weary of repeating such *bouts rimés* as – the Rhine and land of the vine – the Rhine and vastly fine – the Rhine and very divine. As for the romantic, The Age of Chivalry is Burked by Time, and as difficult of revival in Germany as in Scotland. A modern steamboat associates as awkwardly with a feudal ruin, as a mob of umbrellas with an Eglintoun 'plump of spears.'[4]

Hood's attraction to the prosaic, the material, and the humorous, and his frequent exposure of the tension between them and 'poetic' sensibility, reflect his consciousness of the irony that, as the 'romantic' has become widely prized and imitated, it has contributed to fuelling commercial developments at odds with its ostensible vision. There is a direct connection between lyrical vapouring and the tourist steamboat retracing the journey described in the third canto of *Childe Harold's Pilgrimage*. Industrialization and poetry, apparent enemies, are actually sleeping partners. The years following the Napoleonic wars saw a marked rise in the number of works being published.[5] New technologies brought larger print runs and a wider range of publications with new kinds of format, illustration, binding. The status of literature as an industrial product had never been so obvious. The commercial reach of the print trade and of the literary lion were greater than ever before. Yet the growing ubiquity of the printed word and of authorship created a situation where different kinds, forms, and genres of text were no longer securely separable and the increasing prominence of competing indexes whereby a text might hold value (as autograph, as advertisement, as gift, as aesthetic object) threatened literary hierarchies. In one sense Hood is a typical writer of the 1820s and 1830s. As Richard Cronin remarks in *Romantic Victorians*, these decades are marked by authors' increasingly open engagement with the commodified status of their own writing: in Silver Fork novels, in Newgate novels, in journalism.[6] But Hood is atypical in that as a poet, raised and supremely at home in the new print culture, he brings its fortuitous mixing and creative exploitation of textual materiality into poetry itself. His play revels in the susceptibility of words to be recomposed, as they might be by a proofreader or a typesetter, but also in shop fronts, newspapers, letters, as sites of competition and conversation between the 'literary' and the 'literal'.

A world of print

Hood was born the second son of Thomas Hood, a partner in the bookselling and publishing firm Vernor and Hood (later Vernor, Hood, and Sharpe). As he joked in his 'Reminiscences', he had 'ink in his blood'. His maternal grandfather, James Sands, was an engraver, as was his uncle Robert Sands, and Hood would as a teenager go through the apprenticeship that permitted him to work as an engraver within the print industry. This training enabled him to illustrate his writing with comic woodcuts, making his *Comic Annuals*, like Edward Lear's later books of nonsense, wonderfully composite texts in which word and image have an unusually fluid relationship. Hood learned, minutely, to copy backwards, in a format where letters are just one form of malleable sign: skills that underwrite his gift for parody and his sensitivity to the 'doodle' and 'babble' qualities of words, their susceptibility to morph into visual and aural relations. The premises of Vernor and Hood at 31 The Poultry were centrally located in the heart of the City, amidst a panoply of trade, close by the Guildhall and the Exchange. They published poetry, most notably the works of the shoemaker-poet Robert Bloomfield, but also plays, some fiction, travelogues, atlases, a variety of religious, educational, and discursive works, and periodicals – the *Ladies Monthly Museum* and the *Monthly Mirror* – a multiplicity of textual forms mirrored in Hood's own writing. Moreover, Hood and one of the new technologies that would transform the print industry arrived almost simultaneously: Vernor and Hood were reputedly responsible in 1804 for the second book ever stereotyped in England.[7] His quotidian experience of the practical logistics of book and periodical manufacture infuses Hood's understanding of the page as a microcosm of the marketplace.

From the beginning of his career Hood's eye is joyfully alive to the variety of forms that print can take. In his 1825 engraving *The Progress of Cant*, Hood depicts the London street as a crowded mêlée of competing texts. There are sixty people in this imaginative scene, but they are far outnumbered by the printed materials that surround them, primarily the banners individuals carry to indicate their partisanship of particular causes, but also the books, pamphlets, and other papers they trample underfoot; the boards and flags that identify the buildings underneath which they are passing; and the multiple layers of posters and bills attached to walls and fences. Hood does not allow any conventional hierarchy or fundamental distinction between these different kinds of text. Indeed the books scattered on the ground are lowest in the visual field, whereas the signs that hang from the walls and buildings are highest. A Meeting of Operatives, an entertainment at Drury Lane, Patent Pumps and a Prayer Meeting compete equally on a wall for the attention of passers-by, much as people in the crowd compete for an audience on an equal footing. The purveyor of concrete goods and services (a bank) and of spiritual salvation (Whitfield and Wesley) promote their goods in a proximity that generates a pun on 'saving'. Everyone is advertising something, and the effect is not only to erode difference between different textual media, but also between material and abstract commodities. People and signs are identified with one another, as almost all persons bear a legend, the text carried on a banner or an apron, a hat-band or a collar: the crowd of figures and letters is ultimately inseparable. The street becomes a page in which words encounter each other, jostle, debate, fight and flirt: forced to exist in constant relationship, with the result that their intended meaning is subject to contextual disruption and potential subversion. A good example of this play is the kite that a naughty boy from the Seneca House Academy has made out of the school's prospectus. The educational prospectus becomes its own commentary on the 'Universal Erudition' and 'Church of England

1.2 Detail from Hood's engraving, *The Progress of Cant* (1825)

morals' the school claims to instil: language intended to perform a particular kind of work proves always liable to play, in the related senses of plasticity and of entertainment.

The Progress of Cant, as Charles Lamb recognized in his appreciative review of the engraving, pays explicit homage to Hogarth.[8] The urban composition of the picture, with buildings on each 'wing' of the scene pointing upstage toward a central backcloth and a crowded chorus of figures occupying the foreground, but also erupting from windows and doors, recalls Hogarth's famous print 'Southwark Fair' (1732). Hood's title, too, gestures towards Hogarth's famous series, 'The Rake's Progress' and 'The Harlot's Progress'. Strikingly, Hood the engraver approaches emblem in the same way that Hogarth does, making each inn sign, each banner, and each miniature interaction frame its own commentary. Letters and other kinds of visual sign mingle freely within a theatrical spectacle that cannot be assimilated at a single glance. The viewer is invited to choose his or her own non-linear reading route, to enjoy the lengthier process of deciphering the picture's multiple areas and layers of textual joke. Thus the textual play and pluralism within the picture also influence the playful model of reading it proposes, a model which is pertinent to the reading of Hood's work in general. Many of the jokes necessitate reading texts against one another, in ironic conjunctions that are made to appear an accidental consequence of the competing mass of signs. An upright piano is advertised upside down. A banner reading 'Fry for Ever', extolling Elizabeth Fry's prison education, flutters suggestively close to the devil, but also to a poster advertising 'The Complete Cook' and one reporting a 'Distressing Fire'. 'The Church in Danger', partially obscured, becomes 'The Church in Anger'. A barber shop sign proclaiming that, by order of the magistrates, there shall be no shaving on the Sabbath has developed a hole, so that it now proclaims that there shall be no saving. (Already Hood is having a dig at the Sabbatarians – a group that will be the butt of his criticism for the next twenty years.) Even the name of the pub, the 'Angel and Punch Bowl', proprietor T. Moore, perpetrates a sly joke at the expense of Moore the poet, recent author of an oriental fantasy, *The Loves of the Angels*.

The 1820s and 1830s are remarkable for the extent to which writers begin to engage creatively with the status of writing as a commodity. Hood is in the vanguard of this creative engagement: ideally positioned to see the multiplication of printed materials, forms, and subjects and to explore the literary consequences of the increasing ubiquity of writing in the marketplace, the competitor yet also the servant of other kinds of article. Hood's engraving is indebted to the tradition of Hogarth, who was also born to a dissenting family within the City of London some three streets away from Hood's birthplace, yet the difference between the eighteenth-century London of Hogarth's prints and the early nineteenth-century London of Hood's is also marked: in Hogarth's engravings, words form a commentary on the relentless market of human affairs; in Hood's picture, words have become the market's central medium and product. In his first book of poems, *Odes and Addresses to Great People*, written in collaboration with John Hamilton Reynolds and published like *The Progress of Cant* in 1825, one of the most creative pieces is Hood's 'Ode to the Great Unknown', the author of the Waverley Novels, whose identity as Sir Walter Scott was not yet common knowledge. Hood revels in the theatrical coup by which the absent author becomes himself 'The Master Fiction of fictitious history', a blank text compelling because the reader is obliged imaginatively to supply the ellipsis of its central character. Hood compares the Great Unknown to The Invisible Girl, the Cock-Lane Ghost, Frankenstein's monster, and the Man in the Iron Mask. Perhaps, Hood speculates, the author was 'born / To be unknown', having been abandoned as an infant pinned to an illegible ticket. Perhaps he is a scholar who stumbled on 'a dusty pack / Of Rowley novels in an old chest hidden'. Whoever he is, Hood congratulates him as a 'mystery-monger / Dealing it out like middle cut of salmon, / That people buy and can't make head or tail of it; / (Howbeit that puzzle never hurts the sale of it;)'. Hood celebrates the author as showman and huckster, but he is also perceptive about the ways in which the author's material success and cultural power constitutes a loss of control, as the tantalizingly indeterminate sign that represents his 'self' is increasingly constructed and owned by others; he becomes his own product:

> . . . thou might'st have thy statue in Cromarty –
>   Or see thy image on Italian trays,
> Betwixt Queen Caroline and Buonaparté,
>   Be painted by the Titian of R.A.'s,
> Or vie in sign-boards with the Royal Guelph!
>   Perhaps have thy bust set cheek by jowl with Homer's,
> Perhaps send out plaster proxies of thyself
>   To other Englands with Australian roamers –
>   Mayhap, in Literary Owhyhee
>   Displace the native wooden gods, or be
> The China-Lar of a Canadian shelf![9]

The celebrity cult surrounding figures like Scott and Byron helped to create the self-awareness about self-representation that is evident in this poem: Hood would later joke that, if asked for a specimen of his hand, Byron would likely have sent a plaster cast.[10] But Hood's playful voice, itself theatrical in address, and his confident weaving amongst diverse street-level attractions – Constable, sign-boards, and the Invisible Girl – reflect his City background and his particular delight in evoking the commercial juxtapositions that see the modern author competing with scandalous royals, fallen dictators, and false idols.

Hood is fascinated by the language of advertising and is one of the first writers ever to consider advertising as a form of literature with its own stylistic rules and criteria of excellence. His article 'The Art of Advertizing Made Easy. With Specimens of the Most Approved Kinds For the Use of Tradesmen and Others. By A Lover of the Fine Arts', which appeared in the *London Magazine* in February 1825, is humorous, but full of curiosity and pleasure in advertisement as a genre. Hood presents numerous specimens of newspaper advertisement, inviting his audience not merely to glance over their subject matter but to close-read their prose. Lawton, purveyor of the Patent Anti-Peculator Lock, is judged 'almost sublime, where he states how the case would be, "if the whole of the keys that were ever yet made, could be collected"'.[11] Mr. Tayler, the breeches-maker, is observed to 'speak . . . like Mr Hume, in figures' (Tayler's figures are, however, numeric). Hood enjoys the theatrical bravura of the advertisement, its dire warnings and hyperbolic promises. Not everyone, he warns, can be guaranteed to excel in the genre: 'it is pretty well known, that a celebrated prose writer of the present day was induced by Bish to try his hand at . . . the Lottery puffs; and that his productions were returned upon his hands as being too modest for use'. Hood even compiles an honour list of those he considers the best advertizement writers of the present age:

> Russia Oil – Prince; Macassar – Rowland; Fluid or Fluent – Atkinson; Anchovy – Burgess; Minor-periodical – Colburn; Cape-Madeira – Wright; Symmetry – Wallace; Jet-black – Day and Martin, and Cat-reflected – Warren.[12]

Henry Colburn, the publisher notorious for 'puffing' his firm's novels in his own periodicals, is placed by 'The Art of Advertizing' on precisely the same level as manufacturers of corsets and purveyors of anchovies, hair-oil, ink, and shoe-polish.

The publicity campaign for Warren's blacking (shoe-polish), and that of their rivals Day and Martin, changed the face of commercial advertising in Britain at the turn of the century. Warren kept poets as copywriters, and the ubiquity of his trademark advertisement, involving a cat which, fooled by its image in a pair of boots treated with Warren's blacking, begins to fight its reflection, brought instant brand recognition. Mark Lemon, future editor of *Punch*, wrote his first successful farce in 1836, entitled 'The P.L.; or 30 Strand' on the subject of Stamper Jingle, the Poet Laureate of Warren's Blacking. Hood's 'The Art of Advertizing' followed an article in the *Westminster Review* of July 1824 by his friend John Hamilton Reynolds, which observed that Poetry had dashed for sanctuary into Warren's blacking manufactory 'as a scared pigeon flies down a lawyer's chimney'.[13] Reynolds, in turn, was responding to William Deacon's *Warreniana* (1824), a delightful collection of parodies of authors including Wordsworth, Coleridge, and Byron, couched in the form of advertisements for blacking purportedly composed by these poets. As John Strachan rightly argues, the cleverness of Deacon's parodies lies not only in their stylistic critique but in their exposure of the fact that poets and advertisers are engaged in the same strategies.[14] Dickens became a copywriter for Warren's Blacking during his better-known career as a parliamentary reporter. Jennifer Wicke notes: 'Dickens is a phenomenon of mass culture, a writer who is present at the creation of advertising as a system, and whose work and personal career participate in shaping that system.'[15] Hood, too, belongs to this moment in the development of mass culture, where distinctions between 'high' and 'low' cultural forms and audiences are shifting and eroding. Hood's work is studded with brand names: Double X Ale, Pickford's removal vans, Chubb's locks, McAdam's tar, Fry's chocolate, Chappell's sausages, Ingram's rustic chairs. The fact that several of these brands are still familiar today is an indication that in Hood's mass culture lies the beginning of our own: a shared yet foreign space that makes Hood's output both accessible and potentially disconcerting to the modern reader. The fact that these brand names appear in Hood's *poems* suggests the gauntlet that his work openly throws down to anyone who considers the poem a literary form properly defined by its immunity from shoppiness.

Hood's upbringing and apprenticeship within the literary marketplace shapes his approach to textuality. It makes his vision of what might be considered to be 'literature' exceptionally broad. It heightens his interest in encounters between different kinds of literary medium, genre, and style. And it makes him constantly aware of literature's place in a chain of convertible consumables. He knows from daily experience that writing that doesn't sell for its literary content will be turned into more mundane paper products. In August 1821, as a sub-editor at the *London Magazine*, he commented wryly that the death of Napoleon would be the death of the editor, for he was up to his middle in mourning verses: 'We have elegies enough to paper all the tenements in Saint Helena, and should be very glad to contract for furnishing linings to any respectable builder of bonnet boxes.'[16] Typically, heroic elegy morphs into anti-heroic comedy via the grounding force of commerce. Remaindered poems, to Hood, are wallpaper or lining-paper in the making. He bought up the unbound sheets of his own commercially unsuccessful volume of poems *The Plea of the Midsummer Fairies* (1827), his family remembered, to save them from the butter shops. Hood sees in a book the composite work of multiple trades, which may revert to its constituent products. He not only makes transaction a central concern of his writing but highlights the transactionality of writing itself, whether he is imagining a poor gentleman's 'Fugitive Lines on Pawning My Watch', penning an 'Epigram on the New Half-Farthings', or satirizing a socialite's scavenging diary: 'The poor, dear dead have been laid out in vain / Turn'd into cash, they are laid out again.'[17] Through Hood's punning play, the reader, too, participates in a form of pleasurable, yet guilty, exchange: the tightly rhymed couplet foregrounds equivalence and repartee, teasing us with the sense in which the dead may be both 'poor' and 'dear' and hinting at the transaction (bodies/money) at the heart of the commercial cycle. Emphases on linguistic and textual materiality underline the economic frame within which all narrative operates.

Roger Henkle rightly suggests that Hood 'is close to being the first poet laureate of the consumer culture'[18] and that his poems are commodities that contain within their sign system a construct of the desires and anxieties of their consumers. Henkle, however, is inclined to read in Hood's work a lingering Romantic resistance to the 'denaturing' of 'individual subjectivity' produced by the 'compulsion toward commodification of the poetic sign system', and a definitively petit-bourgeois sensibility that circles around class inequity but ultimately punishes the parvenu, directing its truest aspirations toward home and the private realm. This reading seems to me limiting, in that it is itself deeply inflected by a post-Romantic assumption that subjectivity and commerce are at odds and that the class from which Hood emanated (but for which he did not exclusively write) is particularly defined by its material desires and its awkwardness in either transcending or incorporating them into a 'cultural' sphere. In fact the centrality of material commerce and exchange to Hood's conception of all writing is, in my view, individually liberating, and socially democratic; it calls transcendence into question.

This was a period of genre slippage and conversation in which class boundaries within literature, as within society, were destabilized under pressure of economic and political movement. Hood enjoys playing on the boundaries of genre and his delight in the possibilities of mistaking one kind of writing for another reflects the social freedom implied in the difficulty of securely differentiating one class of writer from another. In 'The Spring Meeting', an entertainment written by Hood in 1828 for the actors Charles Mathews and Frederick Yates, one character reads aloud newspaper articles in which advertisement masquerades as reportage:

On Thursday last, as a poor labouring man was at work on the top of a ladder at Holborn bars, he was, by a sudden gust of wind, blown to the door of No. 20, Hatton Gardens, where you can purchase the celebrated Macassar Oil – poo, poo! It's a puff; I hate puffs . . . Portugal; ah, this is something interesting, no doubt; we state, on the very best authority, notwithstanding the appearance of affairs in Portugal, that Don Miguel declares it to be his fixed determination, in opposition to the advice of his faithful followers, to use no other than Warren's blacking; to be had at No. – oh! nonsense! why that's a puff![19]

Advertisement has melded with journalism to the point where the two are indistinct. (Thackeray makes a similar point in the 1840s when he presciently imagines a novel wholly based on product-placement.[20]) There is no sphere of literature or of life that can claim immunity from the commercial: but this, in Hood's eyes, far from being a recent or threatening development, is an age-old truth that time has simply magnified. In 'The Advertisement Literature of the Age' (1843) he wryly asserts that 'the advertisement has long since become an independent department of literature, subject to its own canons of criticism, having its own laws of composition, and conducted by a class of writers, who though they may (we do not assert they do) acknowledge their inferiority to the great historians, poets, or novelists of the day, would nevertheless consider themselves deeply injured were we to hesitate to admit them into the corporation of the *gens de lettres*'.[21] The copywriter for Guinness, he insists, is merely for his product what Homer was to Achilles, Tasso to Godfrey, Camões to Vasco da Gama, or Milton to Cromwell. Emphasizing such common ground subjects the advertisement as text to a new kind of reading; it also forces a reconsideration of the way we read Classical literature, revealed as equally shaped by material and commercial interests.

The difficulty of establishing secure boundaries between different kinds of text, and of controlling the way in which texts are read, is also politically challenging at a time when government censorship and fear of the seditious potential of journalism and correspondence made written words suspect as the swell mob of 'bad characters' to which Hood often playfully likens them. Both Hood and Dickens stage incidents where one kind of writing is mistaken for another, with inflammatory results. In Hood's novel, *Tylney Hall* (1834), the Cockney merchant Twigg is incensed by a document that he takes to be a blackmail threat, but which is actually a quite innocent letter about a horse. In 'The Corresponding Club' (*Comic Annual*, 1839), intercepted letters exchanged by residents of Stoke Poges create panic about what seems an impending revolutionary riot, but turns out to be merely conversation between members of the 'Free and Easy' of the inadequate local pub about how they will dispense with the 'Queen's Head'.[22] More famously, in Dickens's *The Pickwick Papers* (1837), Pickwick is sued by his landlady for breach of promise on the basis of two notes, one requesting chops and tomato sauce and the other refusing a warming pan. In each case, prosecution and imprisonment looms (Pickwick, of course, does go to jail) but comedy finally triumphs and the writer is vindicated. The play inherent in language and its susceptibility to misconstruction becomes here a vehicle for exploring suspicion between classes. In Hood's work that suspicion proves groundless: the blurring of boundaries between different types of writing adumbrates the desirable possibility of increasing freedom in literary power relations and cross-class social discourse.

The line between the poetic and prosaic links various disputed territories of the 1820s and 1830s and Hood is its forgotten ropedancer. Wordsworth had notoriously claimed in the 1800 preface to *Lyrical Ballads* that many of the best lines of poetry might be written as prose: the language and diction of poetry ought not to be specialized in such a way that they distorted the rhythms of feeling naturally expressed and the elemental connections between people, words, and familiar objects. Yet Wordsworth was deeply suspicious of the enervating effects of commercialization on language and literary taste: the prosaic, in his poetry, is associated with the rustic. Hood, raised and working in an urban, journalistic environment where, as the *London Magazine* put it in February 1820, poetry and prose play into each other's hands 'as is the fashion now-a-days',[23] treats 'prosaic' matter in poetry and 'poetic' matter in a prosaic manner that constantly reflects back upon the shared commodity status of all words. Like his close friends Charles Lamb and John Hamilton Reynolds, Hood worked for a time as a clerk: the lower middle-class first experience of professional writing was often closely linked with accounting. In a poem remembering his time as a clerk, Hood joked about the tendency of his pen to move from trade figures to poetical ones:

> Now double entry – now a flowery trope –
> Mingling poetic honey with trade wax –
> Blogg, Brothers – Milton – Grote and Prescott – Pope –
> Bristles – and Hogg – Glyn Mills and Halifax –
> Rogers – and Towgood – Hemp – the Bard of Hope –
> Barilla – Byron – Tallow – Burns – and Flax![24]

Nouns are in this poem insistently material objects and poets (indistinguishable from their works) stand on equal terms with other physical commodities in the ledgers of trade: the poem is about mixing poetry and prose and it performs the action it describes. Later, in 'Poetry, Prose, and Worse' (1836), Hood draws on a recent article in the *Athenaeum*, which claimed that the Turks once conducted government business in poetry, to imagine the consequences of versified bureaucracy:

The victim cut shorter for treason,
  Though conscious himself of no crime,
Must submit and believe there is reason,
  Whose sentence is turned into rhyme!

... A tax would the Lord of the Crescent?
  He levies it still in a lay,
And is p'rhaps the sole Bard at this present
  Whose poems are certain to pay.

Anticipating Gilbert and Sullivan's later treatment of government as operetta, Hood makes game not only of the relationship between poetry and prose but of the relationship between poetry and authority. The poem is about poetic rule, but it also queries the rules that define poetry, as Hood frequently does, whether experimenting with unusual metrical forms or presenting joke articles such as 'A New Plan for Writing Blank Verse in Rhyme'.

In 'Poetry, Prose, and Worse', as elsewhere, Hood dwells on the problem of making poetry profitable, making the tension between poetry's aesthetic and commercial value a topic of the poem itself. The commercial vulnerability of poetry from the 1820s to the 1840s laid the ground for such self-referential teasing, which interrogates poetry's situation in a crowded market; Hood was better placed than most to know how supply exceeded demand. But Hood's schooling in print amounts to more than an insider's understanding of what books cost and which books sell. His writing and illustration are illuminated by appreciation of the mobile, performative nature of all texts; the persistent possibilities of conversation and slippage between one kind of text and another. The materiality and convertibility of the text in his work is creative, not denaturing, emphasizing its connection with the multiplicity of other objects that surround it. In this sense, and in a wider social framework, Hood's play involves acknowledging the constitutive and liberating force of relationship, the impossibility of writing alone.

A culture of dissent

Hood's father was a dissenter. He hailed from Dundee, which, having completed an apprenticeship to a bookseller, he quitted in the early 1780s to go to London and make his way in the book trade. He joined, as an assistant, the bookselling/publishing business of Thomas Vernor, who was so pleased with his performance that after a few years Hood became his partner. This successful work placement was not merely fortuitous. Vernor was a member of the Glasite sect, which followed the teachings of the breakaway Perthshire Presbyterian minister John Glas.

He became a prominent member (a Deacon in 1765 and an Elder in 1766) of the London Glasite congregation and Glasite records show that his house in London was a base through which young Dundonian Glasites found their way into the metropolis, supported by the nonconformist network.[25] It seems highly probable that Hood's father was sent from Dundee to meet up with Vernor and that the Glasite faith was the bond that initially brought them together. Glasites did not proselytize,[26] but it is hard to believe that Vernor would have chosen to make Hood his business partner had he held views that differed markedly from his own: Hood was certainly a Presbyterian, if not a Glasite. Vernor and Hood's publication list retained strong Scottish connections; they reissued work by Scottish authors including Boswell, Smollett, and Ramsay, they became the London outlet for many books otherwise printed only in Scotland, and a good number of the discursive works they published were by Scottish Presbyterian ministers. Argument fell on both sides of the revolution debate, but the framing perspective in either case was that of dissent. For example, Vernor and Hood took the chance of publishing in 1793 the account of Thomas Fyshe Palmer, a Dundonian Unitarian minister, of his trial for seditious libel, for having distributed at a meeting of the Dundee 'Society of the Friends of Liberty' a petition calling for citizens to break the chains that bound them and to demand the universal franchise and an end to war in France, which involved 'THE DESTRUCTION OF A WHOLE PEOPLE MERELY BECAUSE THEY WILL BE FREE'.[27] Vernor and Hood, however, also (and more typically) published essays in 1794 by John Young, Presbyterian minister at Hawick, preaching loyalty and submission, and evidently nervous about the fact that 'by the active part which some dissenters, both in England and Scotland, have taken in the present disputes, – an odium has been brought upon the dissenting interest, in the eyes of Government and its adherents, which will not easily be wiped off'.[28] Given the established status of Presbyterianism within Scotland, it is easy to forget that Presbyterians were part of a dissenting culture that was at this time the subject of discrimination and government anxiety: but they were, and Hood's upbringing within the culture of dissent made him alert to the exclusionary forces of politics in a way that underpins his writing.

Hood's birth went unregistered until he was a teenager, when he needed documentation to seal his apprenticeship. The papers were then lodged in Dr Williams's Library: the repository created in the late eighteenth century in order for dissenters – excluded from the parish record system – to have an independent archive for the records of their births, marriages, and deaths. Hood later in life elected to downplay this heritage. He proved, however, a very infrequent churchgoer, preferring throughout his life a private and informal relationship with God, expressed through Christian charity, to the forms of public worship. His children, somewhat embarrassed by the doubts which hung over the precise complexion of Hood's faith, felt the need to stress in their memoirs of him that despite 'the impression that exists, not in one instance, but in twenty, as to [my] father's disbelief and scepticism',[29] he was a devout Christian whose '*practical* faith and Christianity'[30] suffused his life and work. The fact that a proportion of his audience was prepared to ask the question Hood jokingly relates – 'Mr Hood, are you an Infidel?' – is suggestive of the noncomformist signals he gave out by declining membership of a Church and by waging verbal war against 'the Evangelical and Elect', 'Tartuffes, Maw-worms, Cantwells, Puritans', asserting that 'if they be the Righteous, I am content to be the Leftous of the Species'.[31]

Though Hood as an adult did not become a Glasite (and indeed the sect itself was small and short-lived), his own principles echo palpably with the resonance of his dissenting heritage. The Glasites were a small, close-knit Presbyterian sect that placed a high value on social contact and affection. A central element of their meetings was the 'love feast', designed to bring rich and poor together, when all dined together and each member saluted the person sitting next to him or her on each side: 'we account the grand central duty of Christians . . . BROTHERLY LOVE for the truth's sake'.[32] Looking literally upon the precepts of the New Testament as binding modern commitments, they stressed the importance of alms-giving ('we reckon it unlawful to lay up treasures on earth, by setting them apart for any distant, future, uncertain use'[33]) and other acts of charity: washing each other's feet was a regular practice. They had strongly egalitarian principles of participation and officiation, electing a plurality of elders 'not objecting to any for want of human learning, or any such acquirements, as are commonly thought necessary' nor objecting to engagement in any trade or merchandise as a hindrance. They deemed unanimity necessary for all decision-making. Glasites declared themselves 'loyal subjects . . . submitting themselves in civil concerns', but regarded Church and State as distinct, subjecting themselves to no human authority on matters of conscience and opposing themselves particularly to the doctrine of election, and to egotism and self-righteousness. Hood's lifelong distaste for religious intolerance, aggressive proselytizing, and the aggrandisement of church privilege, such as taking tithe, reflect his nonconformist roots. Perhaps most tellingly, the Glasites' emphasis on social intimacy as an expression of Christian love and their assertion that 'as we cannot find where DIVERSION public or private is forbidden; we account any amusement lawful that is not connected with circumstances really sinful'[34] is salient to Hood's own belief in the constructive value of recreation and his vocal opposition to attempted Evangelical prohibition of various public and private diversions.

Hood's secondary schooling, like Keats's, took place in a liberal academy: one of those establishments identified by Nicholas Roe in *Keats and the Culture of Dissent* as offering an inspiring counter-curriculum to the Classicism of traditional public schools such as Eton.[35] The name of the school was Alfred House Academy, Camberwell, and its proprietor was Nicolas Wanostrocht, a Flemish émigré. Interestingly, James and Horace Smith, comic writers who were part of Hood's social and professional circle, also attended Alfred House Academy. The Smiths' mother was a Presbyterian, and their late-Victorian biographer, Arthur Beavan, makes it clear that the reason for the choice of Alfred House was its suitability to nonconformist parents seeking a liberal education for their children. James Smith attended Alfred House Academy (1790–1) after spending a year at Hackney New College (1789–90), a better-known dissenting school, where Joseph Priestley lectured. Horace Smith attended Alfred House between 1791 and 1795. They would therefore have been gone before Hood began. But the fact that Hood attended the same school is suggestive of the cultural ties that bound writers born to nonconformist families in the early nineteenth century. Horace and James wrote for the *Monthly Mirror*, published by Hood's father and owned by the eccentric bibliophile and former dry-salter Thomas Hill, whose Sunday salons were attended by other *Mirror* contributors, including Leigh Hunt. Both Horace Smith and Hood con-tributed to the *London Magazine* and Horace would later contribute to Hood's *Comic Annual*. Hunt, the Smiths, and Hood were connected via a social and political network that predated Hood's writing career.

Beavan reports that 'The proprietor of this school [Alfred House Academy], a Mr Wanostrocht, had been strongly recommended to Robert Smith by his friends in Paris. French was the current language of the school, and Italian, German, and Spanish were taught, together with drawing, fencing, dancing, and music, in addition to the usual course of Latin, Greek, writing, arithmetic, and book-keeping.'[36] This curriculum is practical, as was usual for schools whose pupils were assumed to be passing directly to commercial jobs, but it is also strik-ingly broad, particularly in its emphasis on the arts and on modern languages. At a time of war with France, the fact that French remained the 'current language' of the school is suggestive. Schools run by émigrés, such as Alfred House and the London lycée attended by the young Mary Russell Mitford and Letitia Landon offered their pupils unusual opportunities to develop literary creativity, multilingual fluency, and an international perspective, at a time when more traditional schools concentrated on rote learning and heavy-handed corporal punishment. Beavan also quotes the Alfred House Academy prospectus, which promised that:

> according to the custom of every academy, there are two half-holidays a week, viz. Wednesdays and Saturdays. On these occasions, the master himself always accompanies the young gentlemen, sometimes in the fields; and by pointing out to them the most useful productions of nature, endeavours to lead their young minds into a habit of observation and attention. In every little country excursion, a variety of objects, both in the vegetable and animal kingdoms, present themselves, and furnish numerous subjects of conversation, and it is the master's employment so to direct his inquiries as to excite the curiosity and improve the understanding of his pupils.[37]

The emphasis on 'exciting curiosity' and stimulating 'conversation' through spontaneous rambles, rather than drumming in facts in the schoolroom, was a distinguishing feature of the academy system that reflected the pedagogic ideas of liberal theorists such as Thomas Day.[38] Hood's education undoubtedly left him, as the prospectus intended, with a curious and observant eye for the broad world outside the school's boundaries. Equally, it validated the idea of the 'half-holiday' as a day of discovery, not idle mischief. The positive value of recreation was at the heart of the Academy ethos and it permeates Hood's writing, as it does the work of the Smith brothers. As Horace Smith would write in his 1831 account of *Festivals, Games, and Amusements, Ancient and Modern*, 'it is in our diversions, where we follow the spontaneous impulse of the mind, that its genuine qualities are revealed'.[39]

The social society

After the end of his formal schooling, as an apprentice engraver with literary aspirations, Hood joined a local 'Social Literary Society' whose membership, he remembered, included Quakers and Methodists. Such amateur societies were a significant means whereby those excluded from university education, including women, could share their ideas and writing with a supportive mixed audience. One of Hood's fellow members was Hannah Lawrance, a Congregationalist, who became a journalist and historian, writing revisionist biographies of English queens. She recalled that Hood's first address to the Society was on 'The Plurality of Worlds'. The title recalls De Fontenelle's *Conversations on the Plurality of Worlds* of 1686, where a scientist discusses with a marquise the possibility of moon-dwellers visiting earth, capturing a human, and flying away.[40] Hood's title also has a wider resonance: raised, as we have seen, in an urban environment of multiple discourses, Hood was from the beginning of his career attracted by the idea of pluralism. The 'addresses' he composed for the Literary Society are written in end-stopped couplets influenced by Pope and Christopher Anstey, whose *New Bath Guide* Hood had parodied as a boy, transposing the comic description of fashionable Bath to the less glamorous Dundee, where he holidayed with his paternal relatives. Hood's addresses effect a similar translocation between traditional poetic territory and the quotidian environment of London. In 'The Departure of Summer' Hood describes the Cockney summer and the Cit's desire for rustic pleasures with gentle humour:

> All Cockney beauties are to Cockneys sweet,
> So Canonbury seems a country seat.
> The pale New River is as bright a stream,
> As mighty Tiber – the proud Roman's theme.
> Nor Italy's sweet groves are half so good
> As that green labyrinth at Hornsey Wood;
> And say, what garden e'er was plann'd or penn'd
> Like that of Fleecy Hosey – at Mile End?
> ... The Cit invests a sum in Purple Stocks,
> And from his window hangs his Country Box.
> There strives the smells of London to forget,
> Snuffing the fragrance of the Mignonette[41]

Hood's writing, from the first, delights in familiarity: linguistically, thematically, and in terms of the relationship it solicits between author and audience. Reading out compositions within the Social Literary Society doubtless helped to shape that voice. Hood was himself a literal Cockney, born within the sound of Bow Bells. As such, he registers the cultural distance between 'Italy's sweet groves' and Hornsey Wood: but the smile of recognition he solicits is affectionate, not contemptuous. Hood relishes the counterpoint of concrete London place names – Canonbury, Fleecy Hosey, and Mile End – with destinations celebrated in ancient literature. The downscaling represented by the poem has the same charm and validity as the businessman's window box, whose poetry lies paradoxically in its stubbornly prosaic limitations. The linguistic and imagistic juxtaposition that Hood sets up here between the Classical and the metropolitan, the epic and the homely, shows early kinship to other Cockney landscapers (Leigh Hunt, Charles Lamb, John Hamilton Reynolds) and foreshadows a lifelong interest in playing a formal off against a more informal descriptive vocabulary. Often the two fuse in puns – 'Purple Stocks' – that force the language of work and the language of recreation to shake hands. In this address Hood praises his fellow members individually by name and looks forward to shared merriment in the autumn: 'When jolly farmers their October brew – Then, this Society shall meet anew. / Then Social Harmony shall take the Chair . . . And smiling Mirth shall mingle with the rest, / A welcome, nor an uninvited guest'. The quasi-tautological name of the Social Literary Society highlights the value of sociability as a literary end in itself, a value communicated in all Hood's later work.

Sociability and playfulness were also at the heart of Hood's family life. In 1804 Vernor and Hood took on a twenty-two-year-old assistant, the son of a nonconformist printer-bookseller in Nottinghamshire, who had been working with a friend, James Hessey, for 7s 6d a week at James Lackington's 'Temple of the Muses', an enormous book emporium in Finsbury Square. The ambitious young assistant was John Taylor, the future publisher of the *London Magazine*, and of Hunt's, Keats's, and Clare's poems. Two of Taylor's formative years learning the book trade were spent in the Hood household. Letters he wrote home reveal that:

> I am more than ever attached to Mr. and Mrs Hood . . . I can say anything to them, & feel as much at ease as with you – Mr. Hood so entirely divests himself of all care when in the midst of his Family and Friends that he is always playful, & merry – and looks more like a laughing Lad than a Man of Business.[42]

Familiarity and playfulness were clearly part of the way the elder Hood did business. It is interesting to speculate how much Taylor's own approach in managing the social circle of contributors that formed the *London Magazine*, and indeed the personal relationships he formed with writers he published, including Leigh Hunt, John Hamilton Reynolds, John Keats, and John Clare, was influenced by what he learned from the Hoods. (In a letter of 1804 Taylor tells his father that he held 'a Levée of Engravers, Designers, and Authors, in imitation of my Master'.[43]) Taylor knew what it was to be an underling in an industry whose less glamorous chores involved working from 9am until 10 or 11pm a couple of nights a week to see the periodicals to bed.[44] At best, however, this kind of shared labour could cause the boundaries between co-worker, friend, and family to blur. It is telling that Taylor feels he can 'say anything' to Thomas Hood's parents. Sharing a dissenting background, he also finds within the Hood household a familiar ease, a congenial company where merriment and play cement social bonds.

Jeffrey Cox has argued in *Poetry and Politics in the Cockney School: Keats, Shelley, Hunt and Their Circle*[45] that sociability, revealing itself in habits of collaborative reading, discussion, writing, and publication and in work that foregrounds the building of the good community through social literary practices, is a uniting feature of Cockney discourse: a manifestation of political liberalism in socio-literary form. Although Hood was a late arrival to the Cockney milieu and his work, less threatening and less overtly political, did not attract the bitter attacks that other Cockney writers faced, the continuity between the sociability Cox describes as integral to the Keats–Reynolds circle and that practised by Hood is very striking. Hood took Keats's place as John Hamilton Reynolds's boon companion, marrying his sister, and inheriting, along with some of Keats's manuscript material, a network of friends and literary colleagues, many of whom had been part of that earlier circle. The Keats–Reynolds Commonplace Book, a notebook designed for the self-taught writer (produced by the firm of Taylor and Hessey) in which Keats and Reynolds recorded details of the poems they were working on, which later passed to Hood and contains examples of his own draft poems, is a symbolic reminder of this continuity.[46] Looking at Hood's and Reynolds's collaborative comic poems; their puns and other verbal expressions of shared play; their performative letters, full of intimate badinage; and their habit of writing in periodicals where one work frequently played off another, it is easy to see that, while Hood's writing develops in different directions, its ludic qualities are rooted in the same liberal discourses that brought Keats and Reynolds together.

Hood's playfulness, then, is not merely an accident of character or, as Victorian critics sometimes guessed, a forced response to the vicissitudes of ill-health and the exigencies of a market whose demand for amusement was lamentably greater than its appetite for lyric. His upbringing in a changing print culture makes him unsually alert to and appreciative of the play of language, the serendipitous intertextuality of the street where signs are in constant dialogue with one another. His play with form and genre, at a time of shifting literary class boundaries, expresses delight in the social freedoms implied by such mobility. His upbringing, meanwhile, in a culture of dissent, is significant to the value that Hood places on recreation and its association with ideas of sociability strongly connected in this period with political liberalism and tolerance.

Notes

1 *Memorials*, p. 65.
2 'A Tale of a Trumpet', *PW*, p. 608.
3 Preface to the second edition of *Up the Rhine* (1839), reprinted in *CW*, vol. 7, p. 3.

4 Ibid., p. 4. 'Dampfschiff' is German for 'steamboat'. The Lorelei rock is a tourist attraction on the river Rhine: the nymph Lorelei, celebrated in poetry by Heinrich Heine, was supposed to lure boatmen to their death with her siren song. Hood's prosaic account of this myth is typical of his ambivalent approach to mermaids, which, as I suggest in Chapter 2, is emblematic of his suspicions about romantic idealism. Edmund Burke's *Reflections on the Revolution in France* (1790) famously asserts that 'the age of chivalry is gone. That of sophisters, economists, and calculators, has succeeded'. Hood, punning on the verb 'burke' (meaning 'murder'), presents this as a comic inevitability, rather than a tragic threat. See his poem 'A Lament for the Decline of Chivalry' (1828) for the development of this idea.

5 Simon Eliot, *Some Patterns and Trends in British Publishing 1800–1919* (London: Bibliographical Society, 1994) notes that publication figures before 1840 are much less reliable than those after 1840, by which time copyright legislation was enforced and methods of listing works were becoming standardized. After 1814 annual publication figures more than double, but this reflects the Copyright Act and changes in recording as much as expansion in the industry. Still, the trend is inexorably upward, with steeper rates of increase in book production in the 1830s as it caught up with technology that had revolutionized periodical production in the 1810s and 1820s. The 1830s saw the impact of powered presses but also the external stimulus of social and cultural debate on increased publication levels (p. 19).

6 Richard Cronin, *Romantic Victorians: English Literature 1824–1840* (Basingstoke: Palgrave, 2002), p. 11 and his chapter 4 passim.

7 Peter Thorogood, 'Thomas Hood: A Nineteenth-Century Author and His Relations with the Book Trade to 1835', in *Developments of the English Book Trade 1700–1899*, ed. Robin Myers and Michael Harris (Oxford: Oxford Polytechnic Press, 1981), p. 117. Stereotyping was a new printing press using moulds from the original type to print larger editions.

8 See Lamb, 'The Progress of Cant', reprinted in *The Works of Charles Lamb*, ed. E.V. Lucas, 6 vols (London: Methuen, 1912), vol. 1, p. 431.

9 'Ode to the Great Unknown', *PW*, p. 15.

10 'An Autograph', Hood, *CW*, vol. 8, p. 129.

11 Hood, 'The Art of Advertizing Made Easy', *London Magazine*, 11 (February 1825), p. 248.

12 Ibid., p. 247.

13 John Hamilton Reynolds, 'Professor Wilson's Danciad', *Westminster Review*, 2 (July 1824), pp. 213–24.

14 Graeme Stones and John Strachan (eds), *Parodies of the Romantic Age*, 5 vols (London: Pickering and Chatto, 1999), vol. 4, p. xxxv.

15 Jennifer Wicke, *Advertising Fictions: Literature, Advertising and Social Reading* (New York: Columbia University Press, 1988), p. 19.

16 Hood, 'The Lion's Head', *London Magazine*, 4 (August 1821), p. 120.

17 'Epigrams Composed on Reading a Diary Lately Published', *PW*, p. 223. Hood is critiquing Charlotte Campbell, *Diary Illustrative of the Times of*

George the Fourth, Interspersed with Original Letters from the late Queen Caroline and from Various Other Distinguished Persons, 2 vols (London: Colburn, 1838). In this composite text of letters and diary entries the rickety carriages, dirty apartments, and dull conversation of the nobility are unsparingly treated. Caroline, in particular, is portrayed as a bloated ball, surrounded by hangers-on who bear her no genuine affection.

18 Roger B. Henkle, 'Comedy as Commodity: Thomas Hood's Poetry of Class Desire', *Victorian Poetry*, 26 (1988), p. 312.

19 Hood, *Mathews and Yates at Home* ('The Spring Meeting' and 'Harlequin and Mr Jenkins – a Monopolylogue') (London: Duncombe, 1829), p. 9.

20 William Makepeace Thackeray, 'A Plan for a Prize Novel', in *Novels by Eminent Hands, and Character Sketches* (London: Bradbury and Evans, 1847).

21 'The Advertisement Literature of the Age', CW, vol. 9, pp. 1–2.

22 As John Clubbe points out in *Victorian Forerunner*, pp. 82–3, 'The Corresponding Club', despite its anticlimactic ending, raises some serious political issues: universal suffrage and schooling and reforms to the legal, church, and corporate systems are all discussed.

23 'Poetry and Prose by a Member of Parliament, &c &c &c', *London Magazine*, 1 (February 1820), p. 121.

24 'Literary Reminiscences', *PW*, p. 303.

25 Records in Dundee University Library Glasite archive note on 10 March 1772, for example, that 'There is taken for Mr R Lyon a House near to Bunhill Row not far from Morefields – it is within 5 minutes walk of Mr Vernors' and later 'Mr Thomas Vernor Bookseller St Michaels Alley Cornhill London. David Walker is with him.' Acc. M/409 6/22, pp. 2–3.

26 An 1832 account of Glasite beliefs and practices states that 'we are utterly against aiming to promote the cause we contend for, either by creeping into private houses . . . or by obtruding our opinions upon others in conversation'. *An Account of the Christian Practices Observed by the Churches called Glasites in Scotland and Sandemanians in [England and] America* (Galashiels: Fair, 1832), p. 26.

27 Thomas Fyshe Palmer, *An Account of the Trial of Thomas Fyshe Palmer Unitarian Minister, Dundee, Before the Circuit-Court of Justiciary at Perth, on the 12th and 13th days of September 1793 For Sedition* (Perth: Morison; and London: Vernor and Hood, 1793), p. 5. Palmer was found guilty and sentenced to seven years' transportation. Vernor and Hood, in publishing his account of the trial, were walking a fine line: on the one hand, they could be seen to be publicizing the harsh judgement that would be visited on 'seditious' publishing; on the other hand, their text reprints the seditious address whose publication and dissemination constituted the original crime.

28 John Young, *Essays on the Following Interesting Subjects: viz. Government, Revolutions, The Br Constitution etc* (Glasgow: Niven; Edinburgh: Creech; London: Vernor and Hood, 1794), p. 3.

29 *Memorials*, p. 458.

30 Ibid., p. 457.

31 Ibid., pp. 350–2.

32 *An Account of the Christian Practices*, pp. 24–5.

33 Ibid., p. 13.

34 Ibid., p. 15.

35 Nicholas Roe, *John Keats and the Culture of Dissent* (Oxford: Clarendon Press, 1997). See pp. 27–46 (on Enfield Academy) and p. 66 (on Eton).

36 Arthur H. Beavan, *James and Horace Smith: Joint Authors of 'Rejected Addresses'* (London: Hurst and Blackett, 1899), p. 50.

37 Ibid., p. 51.

38 One wonders whether school excursions to the Grove, where pupils were told – on the site of the crime – the story of George Barnwell, the apprentice who murdered his uncle, gave the young Hood a grisly thrill that would influence poems such as 'The Dream of Eugene Aram'.

39 Horace Smith, *Festivals, Games, and Amusements, Ancient and Modern* (London: Colburn and Bentley, 1831), p. 1. Smith's declaration suggestively prefigures Virginia Woolf's more famous dictum 'it is in our idleness, in our dreams, that the submerged truth sometimes comes to the top': Virginia Woolf, *A Room of One's Own* (London: Grafton, 1977), p. 32.

40 Hannah Lawrance, 'Recollections of Thomas Hood', *British Quarterly Review*, 46 (1867), p. 324. In a later poem, 'A Flying Visit' (*Comic Annual*, 1839), Hood would explore this scenario in the opposite direction – having the man in the moon descend to earth and narrowly escape kidnap by the proprietors of a show-caravan.

41 *Memorials*, p. 16.

42 John Taylor, quoted in Tim Chilcott, *A Publisher and His Circle: The Life and Work of John Taylor, Keats's Publisher* (London: Routledge, 1972), p. 9. I have pursued the manuscripts of Taylor's early letters home, when he was working for Hood senior, without success. When Tim Chilcott saw them, they were part of the private 'Bakewell' collection, owned by R.W. Cockerton, a descendant of Taylor's brother James. Most of the 'Bakewell' letters have now passed to the Derbyshire Record Office at Matlock, but, alas, these letters are not among them. I am grateful to Tim Chilcott for his helpful correspondence on this matter.

43 Thorogood, 'Thomas Hood: A Nineteenth-Century Author', p. 116. See previous note.

44 Ibid., p. 115. Taylor's normal hours at Vernor and Hood were 9am to 8pm – an eleven-hour day.

45 Jeffrey N. Cox, *Poetry and Politics in the Cockney School: Keats, Shelley, Hunt and Their Circle* (Cambridge: Cambridge University Press, 1998). See pp. 38–81.

46 The Commonplace Book, now in Bristol Public Library, was consciously designed as a tool for autodidactic writers who, by recording and studying their thoughts, would be enabled to improve their writing and reasoning skills.

2

Hood and the minor: at the *London Magazine* and after

Originality only takes a tithe of mankind – the rest are merely homographs – men that only multiplicate each other ... Next to a man with a soul, I like a man with a self: not always the same, but changing colours, like a cameleon, in different lights ... As for L—, he is but a semi-original; for he is always making fac-similes of himself. (COGIN, 'On Imitation', *London Magazine* (January 1822))[1]

The Echo, we fear, will not answer. (Hood, 'The Lion's Head', *London Magazine* (July 1822))[2]

Hood's professional writing career began at the *London Magazine*: an innovative, inspired, independent liberal monthly that published Charles Lamb, William Hazlitt, John Hamilton Reynolds, John Clare, and a roster of other supremely gifted writers of the 1820s. The dynamics of the *London* and its culture of play provide vital clues to Hood's literary development and the relationship between his writing and that of his contemporaries, which this chapter will explore.

The later 1820s and 1830s were once routinely depicted as a literary doldrums, a graveyard shift characterized by loss, transition, and translation of the Romantic into derivative, diminished, domesticated forms. That picture is changing, with new work on writers such as Thomas Beddoes, Felicia Hemans, Leigh Hunt, Charles Lamb, Mary Russell Mitford, Thomas De Quincey, and Letitia Landon, and Richard Cronin's valuable *Romantic Victorians: English Literature 1824–1840*, which surveys this temporal 'no-man's land that no one is fighting for'.[3] Yet the shadow of secondariness lingers on decades sometimes described as a British *Biedermeierzeit*.[4] As Virgil Nemoianu argues in *The Taming of Romanticism*, the Biedermeier reaction to Romanticism, in which he groups writers as diverse as Hazlitt, Lamb, Peacock, De Quincey and Hood, is marked by its need to defuse the 'existential force' of high Romantic themes, by miniaturization, populism, and pragmatism: 'the romantic vision ... was being assimilated or bent and melted in dozens of little forges'.[5] His metaphor suggests precious metals alloyed and turned into coin; the Biedermeier model of Romanticism 'tamed', which tends to associate smaller scale with lesser scope and commercialization with the compromise of higher aesthetic aims, can never quite hide its dislike of the rising power of the petit-bourgeois reader and writer, whose 'nervous' tastes are often coded feminine. However, viewed on their own terms, the developments of this era appear more exuberant, expansive, and experimental. The smaller scale of poetry like Hood's answers the demands of a changing market that favoured the publication of individual poems in periodicals; such poems were accessible to large, new audiences and the mixed company in which they appeared stimulated new kinds of literary and visual dialogue. Thematic, as well as actual, literary downsizing is often also a deliberate riposte to predecessors' evocation of sublimity and grandeur: the reduced scale of Hood's poem 'The Last Man' (1826), for example, is crucial to its humorous, critical engagement with work by Thomas Campbell, Byron, and Mary Shelley. The domestic, likewise, is not, in poetry of these decades, merely the plainer, housebound married cousin of the wild wood nymph of liberty; as Herbert Tucker notes, the powerful charm of home in poetry of this period 'derived in great measure . . . from certain mystifications that were inherent in the Romanticism to which it seems to be opposed.'[6] The domestic in Hood's work, as in Hunt's and Lamb's, is a liberating, rather than a confining space, a portal for confidences, daydreams, and games. Contemporary commercial developments, too, enable the emergence of the professional journalist and illustrator and abet creative experimentation with textual form.

More than this, periodicals, as the primary literary vehicles of these decades, both participate in establishing the terms (major/minor; genius/talent; inspiraton/imitation) by which their contributors' relation to Romantic writing will subsequently be read and expose the insubstantiality of those terms and their dependence on ideas of authenticity and originality whose status as fictions the anonymous periodical article highlights by foregrounding its own unreliability. As Margaret Russett observes in *De Quincey's Romanticism: Canonical Minority and the Forms of Transmission*, 'periodical writing typically and explicitly "emphasize[s] the secondary or staged quality of literary discourse . . . Magazine production *dialectically* negates book-market discourses of authenticity"'.[7] Like his colleagues at the *London Magazine*, De Quincey, Hazlitt, and Lamb, Hood establishes a relationship with Romantic writing that is by turns deferential and deflationary, sometimes inviting us to see him as a 'minor' or 'belated' figure, yet simultaneously undermining the values that underlie such distinctions.

In looking at examples of Hood's early work in the *London Magazine* and beyond, I hope to show how the *London*'s sophisticated heteroglossia and insistent self-reflexivity shape Hood's approach to persona and the synchronous emergence of his lyrical and comic voices. Hood's output was once parsed by genre: his 'Keatsian' odes and sonnets billed under the rubric of 'late' Romanticism, while his parodic ballads and comic sketches were cited as examples of 'early Victorian' humour. In fact Hood's comedy and his dialectical relationship to Romantic authorship are intimately connected.[8] Hood draws on imagery of loss, of introspection, of isolation that responds to Romantic models and absences, but he also takes pleasure in transposing such imagery to concrete, class-driven and commercial contexts that compromise and implicitly critique it. In 'The Mermaid of Margate', for example, where the protagonist is a fishmonger and his seductress is seeking revenge for the shrimps he has eaten, the introspection and poetic idealism implicit in mermaid poetry of the period (including Hood's own 'The Water Lady') is countered by the drier lure of the social and the real. As in Lamb's 'On Witches and Other Night Fears', where Elia describes a dream of riding in Neptune's train only to make an inglorious inland landing at the foot of Lambeth Palace, his flight self-confessedly curtailed by the prosaic bounds of his imagination, the relation between the oceanic depths of Romantic poeticism and the pedestrian surfaces of the post-Romantic littoral is teasing and ironized. On the one hand, Elia appears to announce his own limited and secondary status, an admission also connected with social class; on the other, by relocating the scene and terms of romantic loss and longing, Elia both undercuts the metaphysical fantasizing of Coleridge and De Quincey and presents himself as an alternative autobiographer and (anti-)hero. Hood, similarly, blends homage with critique; in depicting a minor 'last man', he apparently confesses the small and secondary nature of his work, yet his disreputable protagonist also sends up the solipsism of previous treatments of 'lastness' as an aesthetic condition, undermining contemporary visions of an artistic landscape defined by loss.

Hood's imitative-parodic engagement with the 'Romantic' is simultaneously self-deprecating and sharp: like Edward Lear, he plays with limitation (his own, his characters', his verses') and uses it to position himself closer to the reader. In a witty yet sympathetic poem, 'There's no Romance in that' (1833), his imaginary speaker laments that:

No Bandits lurk – no turban'd Turk
To Tunis bears me off –
I hear no noises in the night

Except my mother's cough, –
No Bleeding Spectre haunts the house;
No shape, – but owl or bat,
Come flitting after moth or mouse –
There's no Romance in that!

Her fiancé, likewise, is regrettably neither dark, pensive, nor forbidden:

He wears no plumes or Spanish cloaks,
Or long sword hanging down;
He dresses much like other folks,
And commonly in brown;
His collar he will not discard,
Or give up his cravat,
Lord Byron-like – he's not a Bard –
There's no Romance in that![9]

Although he learns much from Byron, Hood is not a Bard, either, and he wears his 'collar' knowingly. Using Lamb's own theory of imperfect sympathies, Hood approvingly described Lamb as in philosophy the opposite of Kant and in poetry the opposite of Byron.[10] His self-portraiture is likewise anti-Byronic. In 'The Life of Zimmermann (By Himself)', a prose sketch in the 1832 *Comic Annual* whose tag is Byron's 'This, this, is solitude', Hood has Zimmermann lovingly recount the growth of his own egotism. Zimmermann as a student hates the society of the University of Göttingen and is punished for his noncompliance by being forced to share a cell. Of his co-detainee Zimmermann says:

> I had no alternative but to endeavour to make him a convert to my principles, and in some days I succeeded in convincing him of the individual independence of man, the solid pleasures of solitude, and the hollow one of society, – in short, he so warmly adopted my views, that in a transport of sympathy we swore an eternal friendship, and agreed to separate for ever, and keep ourselves to ourselves as much as possible.[11]

Hood is an anti-recluse, spoofing writers who dwell 'at Number One, in Wilderness Street'.[12] Connecting writing that is ostentatiously 'by oneself' to the misanthropic desire to be 'by oneself', he finds the idea of autobiography itself embarrassing: he confided, when preparing his 'Literary Reminiscences' for *Hood's Own* (1839) that 'he never wrote anything with more difficulty from a shrinking nervousness about egotism'.[13] His essay 'An Autograph' (1840) typically turns the question of writing the self outward to embrace ordinary readers, playing with transitory signs of their identities:

Some persons chalk them on walls; others inscribe what may be called auto-lithographs, in sundry colours, on the flag stones. Gentlemen in love delight in carving their autographs on the bark of trees ... Amongst various modes, I have seen a shop-boy dribble his autograph from a tin of water on a dry pavement ... Our grandmothers worked their auto-graphs in canvass samplers ... I have seen something like a very badly scribbled autograph made by children with a thread of treacle on a slice of suet dumpling. Then it may be done with vegetables. My little girl grew her autograph the other day in mustard and cress.[14]

'Autograph', meaning 'a sample signature', is a coinage of the first decade of the nineteenth century.[15] One of the consequences of Roman-tic emphasis on tracing the self and evidence of interiority as a mark of authentic feeling was a new interest in reproducing famous signatures and facsimiles of original work. Yet, paradoxically, the success of the cult of authenticity was self-undermining, as forms and technologies designed to showcase the authentic drew attention to their own com-mercial self-consciousness and reproducibility.[16] Hood, imbued in that commercial print culture, from the beginning of his career casts doubt on the value of 'originality'. In an early pseudonymous piece 'On Imita-tion' for the *London Magazine*, he reflects, as we have seen, that:

Originality only takes a tithe of mankind – the rest are merely homographs – men that only multiplicate each other ... Next to a man with a soul, I like a man with a self: not always the same, but changing colours, like a cameleon, in different lights; – a man that is shot, – like my aunt Tabitha's gown; not dyed, but tinted in the warp and woof of his original fab-ric ... As for L—, he is but a semi-original; for he is always making fac-similes of himself.[17]

Hood's 'cameleon' reflects Hazlitt's ideas about genius and perhaps a memory, through Reynolds, of Keats's now-famous idealization of the 'camelion poet'.[18] Yet the essay makes its own play around the dialectic between originality and imitation, wittily announcing itself as imitative (the title of the essay recalls Hazlitt's essay 'On Imitation' in *The Round Table*) and telling an anecdote about the author's failure to imitate R— (presumably Reynolds), but also suggesting that those most con-scious of man's derivative nature, form their 'own contradiction'. The description of L— (presumably Lamb) as 'semi-original', for he is 'always making fac-similes of himself', exposes to ridicule the autoge-nous rhetoric of originality – you cannot be *semi*-original – while expos-ing tensions between the commercial reproducibility of print and the concept of single selfhood: Lamb's persona is both the source of his originality and its negation.

Looking at Hood's work, like looking at Lamb's and De Quincey's, should encourage us to reconsider the category of the 'minor'. As James Najarian has suggested, 'minor' can be a deliberate stance rather than an imposed status and a quality to be celebrated rather than regretted.[19] It may be that the freshest interpretation of nineteenth-century poetry will not involve 'expanding the canon' but reconsidering the alternative claims of those works that apparently solicit their own deselection:

> Minor poets ask us to look differently at Romantic and post-Romantic notions of originality. From that investigation we might see a set of alternative literary histories or narratives that endorse the unoriginal, the imitative, the echoing, and the belated.[20]

Hood often chooses a small, ephemeral, collaborative, or relative framework for his poetry. In 'There's no Romance in that', Hood contrasts the plumed Byronic lover and the speaker's fiancé who 'dresses much like other folks'. The poem, like its anti-hero, provokes and delights by its ordinariness. Hood, too, prefers cheaply available forms and sites of transmission. He reports in 1826 that he has 'never been vainer of any verses' that of his part in the comic ballad 'Faithless Sally Brown':

> Dr. Watts, amongst evangelical muses, has an enviable renown – and Campbell's Ballads enjoy a snug genteel popularity. *Sally Brown* has been favoured perhaps, with as wide a patronage as the Moral Songs, though its circle may not have been of so select a class as the friends of *Hohenlinden*. But I do not desire to see it amongst what are called Elegant Extracts. The lamented Emery, drest as Tom Tug, sang it at his last mortal Benefit at Covent Garden; – and ever since, it has been a great favourite with the watermen of Thames, who time their oars to it, as the wherrymen of Venice time theirs to the lines of Tasso. With the watermen, it went naturally to Vauxhall: – and, overland, to Sadler's Wells . . . Cheap printers of Shoe Lane, and Cow-cross, (all pirates!) disputed about the Copyright, and published their own editions . . . it has cost, but has never brought me, a half-penny.[21]

Hood's desire for a common audience can be framed within Romantic aspirations toward entering the folk tradition as a national poet (Tasso is celebrated by Byron). Yet his depiction of anonymous dissemination via penny sheet, comic opera, and water taxi as the ultimate sign of poetic success and his distaste for the 'snug gentility' of 'Elegant Extracts' signals an aversion to the class-driven selectivity involved in creating literary canon that has affected his position in it. J.S. Fraser commented in 1871 that:

> We give short names to those we love best. It would sound as oddly to talk of Sir Richard Steele or Mr Hood as to call Milton 'Jack' or Browning

'Robert' ... Steele, Lamb, and Hood ... are more like ourselves; we love them for their intense humanity – for the very failings that help to draw them within the circle of our affinities.[22]

A Victorian audience was not as comfortable as we have become with discussing eminent writers on first-name terms. The fact that Hood is alluded to in this way is simultaneously a mark of affectionate intimacy and disrespect. The seeming 'failings' of Hood, as of Lamb, however, deserve reconsideration as they reflect strategic choices about genre, tone, and persona. Shortcomings, like short names, invite a specific kind of dialogue. The familiar address that Hood prompts in his Victorian audience – he is Tom or even Tommy, in a way that Browning can never be Bob – establishes a lesser status correlative with the child or servant. But the readily patronized persona paradoxically also confers independence: Hood, like Lamb, punctures the gravitas of authorship, playing with the reader on terms that elude 'adult' hierarchies. Later in this chapter I consider the uses to which Hood puts loss, the lesser and the later, and why his 'minor-ness' is enabling, both for him and for his readers.

Hood at the *London Magazine*

When Hood became in the summer of 1821, at the age of twenty-two, a sub-editor at Taylor and Hessey's *London Magazine*, the move that established his writing career, it was no accident: John Taylor was repaying the Hood family's kindness to him, but he also knew both that Hood would be familiar with the practicalities of producing a monthly periodical and that his views would accord with the tone of a publication that pitched its metropolitan counter-chorus against the Tory trumpeting of *Blackwood's Edinburgh Magazine*. The *London Magazine* was a year and a half old when Taylor took it on: it was the brainchild of John Scott, a brilliant journalist who, like Hood's father, was a Scot – a secessionist Presbyterian – who had come to London to make his fortune.[23] Scott quickly became involved in the liberal press, forming friendships with William Hazlitt and Leigh Hunt, to whose newspaper *The Statesman* he contributed before founding his own unsuccessful weekly *The Censor*. Scott then moved to Lincolnshire, where he edited a liberal weekly, *Drakard's Stamford News*, which advocated electoral reform, the abolition of slavery, Catholic emancipation, and press freedom, undergoing a prosecution for seditious libel for its criticism of military flogging. After three years Scott returned to London as owner of *Drakard's*, the London edition of his Stamford paper, and renamed it *The Champion*, attracting contributors including William Hazlitt,

Charles Lamb, and John Hamilton Reynolds. He abandoned *The Champion* in 1817, but when in 1820 he launched his new venture, *The London Magazine*, Hazlitt, Lamb, and Reynolds joined its enviable pool of writing talent. The *London Magazine* incorporated writers of different political hues and resisted identification with any party interest. Hood would adopt the nonpartisan stance held by the *London* as his own official literary position on politics throughout his career. In both cases, however, this assertion was far from apolitical: Hood is in essence a liberal writer and the *London* a liberal monthly. Mark Parker, in *Literary Magazines and British Romanticism*, depicts aspects of the *London*'s editorial practice as morally conservative, stressing Scott's distaste for radical agitation and his preference for upholding institutions and trusting to 'wisdom without reflection' in the absence of viable political alternatives.[24] Under John Taylor, Parker argues, the *London* becomes more politically evasive, replacing a conscious 'programme of displacement' with an unconscious displacement of politics that reflects the escapist desires of a bourgeois audience. There is some truth in this portrait. Yet Parker's account tends to underplay the *London*'s liberalism.

Under Scott's editorship, the *London* distanced itself from radical violence and disorder, yet it was strongly committed to a reform agenda within a constitutional framework. The politicians cited by Scott with approval are Sir Francis Burdett, leader of the independent radical MPs within Westminster, but described by Scott as 'an English oppositionist . . . such as existed in the best days of English history'[25] and Sir John Russell, leader of the Whig campaign in the Commons for parliamentary reform. Horace Smith's poem 'Farewell in England', in the London's first number, warns against radical demagogues but also observes that 'at home the fierce struggle is not yet begun' and that:

> From the thinking, the wise, and the good,
>   Old and youthful, the cautious and warm,
> A cry has gone forth, that will not be withstood,
>   For a safe and a sober Reform.
> Like a column of steam is the national breath;
> Resisted, – it scatters destruction and death.[26]

Building pressure for political change is not always so explicitly imaged in the *London*, yet reformist energies work beneath the surface of articles such as Bryan Waller Procter's 'On May Day' (May 1820), which recalls the ancient customs associated with Robin Hood's Day and public assemblies held for the distribution of law, when Justice was not 'cribbed and confin'd' in rooms or 'masqued' in wigs, but 'showed her fair face abroad'.[27] 'On May Day' was part of the same issue that covered the Peterloo. trial. Scott's commentary on that process is circumspect, yet he implicitly compares Britain with Spain where a peaceful revolution, in which the king was obliged to yield to the wishes of the nation, recently ended with 'a great national change for the better'.

Although under Taylor the magazine eschewed such 'Historical and Critical Summaries of Public Events', Hood's introduction to the *London* marked his allegiance with a group of writers, including Hazlitt, Lamb, and Reynolds, associated with 'oppositionist' politics. Charles Wentworth Dilke, a lifelong radical and fellow contributor to the *London*, became one of Hood's tightest inner circle of friends. In a letter of 1838 to Dilke, written in the heat of disgust about politicians' nepotistic abuse of free postage franks, Hood teased:

> But I'm a low-lived, ungenteel, villainous, blackguard Radical. There is a deep stigma on the Have-nots trying to take from the Have-somethings, but what ought to be the stigma on the Have-everythings trying to take from the Have-nothings? Chorley has proclaimed me a '*Liberal*'. I don't mind being called at once a Moderate Republican.[28]

This was an exceptional outburst; in his public writing Hood emphasizes his painstaking determination to avoid identification with any party. The writers and periodicals with which he identifies himself, however, testify eloquently to the fact, privately acknowledged, that he has 'favoured liberal principles'.[29] His most direct contributions to politics would be his 'open letters' in support of the Copyright Bill repeatedly introduced to Parliament by Thomas Noon Talfourd, another *London Magazine* writer, who joined the radical wing of the Liberal Party and later acted as Edward Moxon's defence lawyer in his trial for publishing Shelley.

There is a strong relationship between the *London*'s liberal politics and its culture of play. Contributors were given unusual freedom to express views that were not those of the editor and to pursue a wide and eclectic range of subjects. As Thomas Noon Talfourd put it, the editorial policy was 'not to hold a despotic rule over subject contributors', the *London*, unlike *Blackwood's*, fostered a 'little commonwealth of authors'.[30] Stylistically, although there was some shared ground between *Blackwood's* and the *London* in terms of format, audience, and contributors there was also self-consciously articulated difference. The *London*, famously, defended the poetry and aesthetics of the 'cockney' school of writers: Leigh Hunt, John Keats, and others, against *Blackwood's* defamatory attacks, which accuse these authors of overreaching their limited socio-cultural status, breeding, and ability. The *London* takes an interrogative approach to 'cockneyism', redefining an aesthetic in which *Blackwood's* had sought to mesh conservative contempt for the commercial, the vulgar, the urban, and the puny. Moreover, to *Blackwood's* cavalier, hurtful and exclusive wit, the *London* opposes a deliberately gentler, more transparent and inclusive humour.

Mark Parker has argued that the difference between the *London* and *Blackwood's* lies in their approach to rhetoricity:

> Scott's program – direct, sober, respectful of boundaries between the facetious and the serious – is directed to an audience that reads with the expectation that what is said is said straightforwardly and unironically . . . the bias of Scott's *London* is toward representation; that of *Blackwood's* is toward performance.[31]

Again, this reading tends to make the *London* seem a more straight-laced magazine than it is. Much of the *London*'s writing is overtly performative. Thomas Griffiths Wainewright, who had at least three different interactive personae in the *London* (Egomet Bonmot, Cornelius van Vinkbooms, and Janus Weathercock), was outrageously louche with an arch absorption in all his unreliable selves unmatched till the appearance of Oscar Wilde. When not inviting the reader to join him in explicitly masturbatory acts of composition in his boudoir, he is smothering his face in a bed of cow-slips, wet with May-dews, 'rolling under a hedge, like a little boy, or a cow!!!'.[32] Charles Lamb's essays involve a similarly multi-layered tissue of irony: 'Elia' invites and resists unwrapping with a humour ambiguously sober and riotous. But while *Blackwood's* is full of private jokes, masks, and serious insults to which the reader is not privy, the *London*'s play is much more amiable, open, and generous. The overtness with which it handled the fiction of the authorial subject paradoxically enabled intimacy: as Elia teased, 'Reader, what if I have been playing with thee all this while – peradventure the very *names*, which I have summoned up before thee are fantastic'.[33] The *London*'s sustained interest in play and recreation need not be read as evidence of political 'displacement'. When John Hamilton Reynolds, writing as 'Edward Herbert', invites readers to join him on the September holiday taken alike by 'master and clerk . . . knight, gentleman, and apprentice', he appeals to experiences many Londoners could recognize they held in common.[34] Focusing on shared metropolitan experience, the *London* acted out the conviction that between the failures of both ministerial party and opposition, between the threats of despotism and anarchy, there was common ground for agreement both on the value of

English tradition and on the need for parliamentary, legal, and social reform. Making its own production central to its subject matter, the magazine invited readers to join the society created through its liberal discourse.

'The Lion's Head'

Through the mask of 'The Lion's Head' at the *London*, Hood began to experiment with the freedoms of printed voice, learning from the examples of Lamb, Reynolds, and Wainewright. The Lion, once played by Scott himself, commanded the first page of the *Magazine*, flirting with the Public, accepting and rejecting readers' literary submissions. Part of the joke was that readers could not know whether the submissions discussed on this page were from 'inside' contributors or 'outside' contributors, or were wholly imaginary. Indeed, 'The Lion's Head' foregrounds the metafictional status of the *Magazine* as a whole and celebrates the absence of referent as a source of textual pleasure. As one of Hood's tartest 'responses' to contributors announces: 'To Y. and Y. No. A word to the *Ys!*'.[35] The impossibility of identifying the authorship of work submitted anonymously, or of securely attaching any text to any body, with the likelihood of deliberate and unconscious plagiarism, create rich material for editorial humour. The September 1822 'Lion's Head' comments drily that:

> We should have preferred seeing 'the *original* production' of Gallus, before we decided upon its originality; – and if we had then been convinced of its 'genuineness,' it would not have been unpleasant to us to find that it was the work of 'An eccentric Frenchman.'[36]

Elsewhere, the Lion quips that 'The writer of "the following Lines", (which do *not follow*) has sent us his "*second* thoughts," which rather too closely resemble the *first* thoughts of some other Author'; 'T. says that his tale is out of his own Head: is he a tadpole?'; and 'The Echo, we fear, will not answer'.[37] Hood's comments reflexively highlight the secondariness of all writing – lines always do *follow* – quizzing equally the purportedly original and the nakedly derivative composition. 'The Echo', a probably imaginary work, neatly captures the ellipsis that made the periodical such fun to read: the presence of its voice depends on authorial absence; the voice points to its own inauthenticity and yet simultaneously to the liberty afforded by verbal 'bouncing', as apparently communicative statements announce the dependency of their meaning on unrecoverable origins. Since 'inside' contributors used the space offered by 'The Lion's Head' to respond to 'correspondents', particularly – in the case of Lamb and De Quincey – to provide teasing answers to queries about their identity and its relation to their quasi-autobiographical work,[38] the 'Head' knowingly raises doubts about originality and authenticity in the apparent act of assuaging them, appropriately presenting a reading model for the body of the text that follows.

Writing as the Lion's Head put Hood in the position of exposing the periodical text as fundamentally inauthenticable; by the same token the emotions and sentiments expressed in work submitted by contributors were subject to perpetual suspicion and deflationary critique. As he remarks punningly in September 1822, 'W's "Tears of Sensibility" had better be dropped'.[39] Hood's pithy comments form a deliberate foil to the effusions of the 'naïve' contributor, whose 'The First Kiss' and 'Sonnet on a Cluster of Snowdrops' are, he gleefully reports, '(to use a tender word) rejected'. Inundated with weakly conventional amateur verse, he quickly developed a withering eye for the overblown. In the March 1822 'Lion's Head', he observes that 'G.R.'s diction would inflate a balloon. He should remember that a "power of fine words" is not poetic power' and ' "Lines to a Friend," on her departure to Antigua, show more sympathy than poetry. Some of them are almost long enough for log lines.'[40] (A log line was a piece of wood attached to a long cable, used to measure how fast a ship was travelling.) Hood's own work, when he begins placing it, anonymously, either in the masked space of 'The Lion's Head' or in the body of the *Magazine*, reflects his self-consciousness about the problems of 'authenticity' and 'sincerity' and the pleasure of playing with the reader's inevitable uncertainty regarding the identity of text, author, and genre.

Loss and imposture: 'The Sea of Death' and 'Faithless Sally Brown'

All Hood's insertions in the *London*, in one way or another, present themselves as found writings whose 'true' origins are obscured. Just as Thomas Griffiths Wainewright appeared as Egomet Bonmot, Janus Weathercock, and Cornelius Van Vinkbooms – characters who insulted one another's style – so Hood contributed to the *London* as 'T.', 'H', 'Ovid', 'INCOG', 'COGIN', '***', 'Printer's Devil' and, in 'The Lion's Head', 'Anthony Rushtowne' and a variety of other imaginary correspondents. Materials accompanying the work also suggest its prior existence. 'To a Critic' and 'The Fall of the Deer' (printed in Gothic type) appear as if they might possibly be examples of 'ancient' writing ('The following is taken, as Nimrod assures us, from a real "Old Poem," upon hunting, and indeed it has the appearance of never having been young'[41]), though the puns give the game away; 'Faithless Sally Brown' is labelled 'An Old Ballad' and is accompanied by a note that queries what we are to think of it. 'Lycus the Centaur' is 'from an unrolled manuscript of Apollonius Curius', while 'The Sea of Death: A Fragment' and 'Presentiment: A Fragment' both pose as relics of longer works. All are associated with the lost – but presented in textual circumstances that convey the likelihood that the figured loss may be fictitious: they thus simultaneously advertise and dissemble their own secondary status.

'Presentiment: A Fragment', for example, a peculiar but evocative prose piece of December 1822, is an account of an ambiguous vision. In it the narrator goes into 'a little land of graves' where there are many monuments with 'sunshine on one side and shade on the other', through whose 'black frowning letters' one can hear 'the dead speaking silently and slow'.[42] Watching a tableau of children weeping over their father's grave, he gradually recognizes the children as his own and believes himself to be dying. On returning home, however, he finds that it is his children who have died and he remains alive. The tale conjures up a quasi-allegorical limbic landscape, where figures are 'shadowless', and both ghosts and relicts are equally insubstantial. It is never wholly clear whether the presentiment is fulfilled or whether the fragment is all dream and thus represents events that may occur. Hood imagines the anguish of bereavement, but his narrator's condition is uncertain: does he belong to the superseded or the surviving generation; is it the author or his productions that have perished? As in Lamb's 'Dream-Children, a Reverie' in the January 1822 *Magazine*, the figuration of loss is poignant, conferring upon the narrator the patina of the bereft, but the loss itself is imaginary: in both pieces the children are created by the prose that erases them. The dream of 'failed' authorship (dead or unborn offspring) postulates a self-conscious belatedness with suggestive literary overtones, yet ultimately dispels the vision of belatedness it temporarily entertains.

The nebulous atmosphere of 'Presentiment: A Fragment' is shared by several of Hood's lyrics in the *London Magazine*, which also deal with prior literary voices equivocally through verbal echoes and images of absence and silence. In 'Ode: Autumn' (February 1823), Hood pays poetic homage to Keats; he is one of the first writers to do so. His 'Ode' wears its indebtedness to Keats on its sleeve, audibly echoing, as Susan Wolfson and Peter J. Manning note, 'To Autumn', 'Ode to a Nightingale', 'La Belle Dame Sans Merci', 'Ode on Melancholy', the opening of *Hyperion*, and perhaps even 'When I have fears', which Hood's sister-in-law (after 1825), Charlotte Reynolds, had transcribed in manuscript.[43] But Hood's 'Ode: Autumn' also deliberately stakes out its difference from Keats's 'To Autumn', placing its allegorical description of the season at a later point, where the languid voluptuousness of Keats's loaded vines has ceded to a violent 'wither'd world' of 'bitter fruits' where birds have fled 'lest owls should prey / Undazzled at noon-day, / And tear with horny beaks their lustrous eyes'.[44] Hood pictures 'old Autumn in the misty morn / Stand shadowless like Silence, listening / To silence' and the figure of Autumn melancholy 'amongst the sunless shadows of the plain', who, alone, 'sits and reckons up the dead and gone': Keats himself is incorporated into the losses that the poem catalogues. Hood positions himself, in various senses, *after* Keats, deferentially figuring in his poem the testamentary 'reckoning up' of past glory. But the recurrent motif of the 'shadowless' form of personified Silence also suggests the power of the memorialist to define presence and absence, which here trade properties. (Silence, normally an absence, is embodied, but the body, normally solid, casts no shadow.) 'Ode: Autumn' asserts the possibilities of poetic succession in the act of representing Keats's work through layers of recession: 'like a dim picture of the drowned past / In the hush'd mind's mysterious far away / Doubtful what ghostly thing will steal the last / Into that distance, grey upon the grey'.[45]

In his clever, haunting 'Sonnet: Silence', also printed in the *London Magazine* for February 1823, but with a different signature, Hood differentiates between 'silence where hath been no sound', which one might find under the sea or in uninhabitable deserts, and the 'green ruins . . . where man hath been', where silence has a different meaning because it constitutes not absolute vacancy but knowing contrast:

Though the dun fox, or wild hyena, calls,
And owls, that flit continually between,
Shriek to the echo, and the low winds moan,
There the true Silence is, self-conscious and alone.[46]

'Sonnet: Silence', like 'Ode: Autumn', deliberately echoes Romantic poetics (the 'antique palaces' recall Shelley and Byron) but incorporates its own 'lateness' into a vision where apparent deficit is richly sonorous. Again the owl looms large: its echoing call predatory rather than subdued. The lines, 'no voice is hush'd – no life treads silently' anticipate the movement of Hood's famous 'comic' poem 'No!' ('No shade, no shine, no butterflies, no bees, / No fruits, no flowers, no leaves, no birds, – / November!'[47]), where multiplying negatives triumphantly total their sum in a positive noun. Richard Cronin rightly portrays the 1820s and 1830s as a time when many writers were preoccupied by the subject of loss – both in and of their literary predecessors.[48] Yet Harold Bloom's oedipal model of 'greatness' as a gauntlet (he describes Clare's poetry as 'a postscript to Wordsworth's, even as Beddoes, Darley, and Thomas Hood are *epigoni* in their poetry to Shelley and Keats'[49]) fails to capture the liberties afforded by inheritance and the ways in which poets like Clare and Hood develop a language unencumbered by debt. Hood, in his early work, deploys the imagery of desolation, invoking night and winter and Time's ravages, but, as a young writer enjoying every moment of a new career in illustrious literary company, he turns absence into a vehicle for his own voice: a voice often elusive, self-cancelling, but simultaneously assertive and self-aware.

Hood's fellow writers at the *London Magazine* constantly play with the trope of their own insubstantiality. Elia, Janus Weathercock, and Edward Herbert were all, at one time or another, reported to be dead. Lamb, writing as 'Phil-Elia' was thus, notoriously, enabled to write the obituary of his own persona. Since, however, the editors were naturally in on the joke, they could make teasing allusions to the characters' survival. Hood hinted that:

> Elia's ghost . . . cannot sleep in its grave, for it has been constantly with us since his death . . . his *ghost-ship* has promised us very *material* assistance in our future Numbers.[50]

The (faked) death of the author allows the *London*'s writers to explore the freedom of ghosting: indeed, to suggest the perpetually floating nature of the signifier. Posing as their own successors, they pre-empt and undermine assessment of their literary immortality. Loss and imposture are woven together, such that the pathos of memory is continually punctured by the ebullience of counterfeit: a movement that celebrates the inconstancy of the periodical as a strength and a pleasure.

The March 1822 *London*, where Hood publishes 'The Sea of Death: A Fragment' in the body of the magazine, and 'Faithless Sally Brown: An Old Ballad' in 'The Lion's Head', provides a good example of his own equivocal treatment of loss and authenticity. 'The Sea of Death' imagines a landscape, like that of 'Ode: Autumn' or 'Sonnet: Silence' defined by absence:

>   — Methought I saw
> Life swiftly treading over endless space;
> And, at her foot-print, but a bygone pace,
> The ocean-past, which, with increasing wave,
> Swallow'd her steps like a pursuing grave.
> Sad were my thoughts that anchor'd silently
> On the dead waters of that passionless sea,
> Unstirr'd by any touch of living breath:[51]

The purportedly fragmentary poem enacts the process it describes: stalked by loss that will erase its print, it cannot progress any more than the torpid bodies it watches, locked in temporal stasis. One could read the limbo that this poem evokes as symptomatic of the work of a literary generation acutely conscious of its ephemerality. But the 'fragment' is a blind, as is Hood's self-abnegating alias '***' The literary drift of 'The Sea of Death' looks different when read against the lively mischief of Hood's other sea poem in the same issue. A collaboration between Hood and John Hamilton Reynolds, 'Faithless Sally Brown' is a faked 'Old Ballad' where loss and authenticity are triggers for comedy:

> Young Ben he was a nice young man,
>   A carpenter by trade;
> And he fell in love with Sally Brown,
>   That was a lady's maid.
>
> But as they fetch'd a walk one day,
>   They met a press-gang crew;
> And Sally she did faint away,
>   Whilst Ben he was brought to.
>
> The Boatswain swore with wicked words,
>   Enough to shock a saint,
> That though she did seem in a fit,
>   'Twas nothing but a feint.[52]

Sally Brown's grief, indeed, proves questionable. Her lover returns from his enforced naval duty after two years to find that she has another boyfriend. Distraught, his head is turned, so he chews his pigtail till he dies, an event commemorated in perhaps the best-known verse of Hood's comic output:

> His death, which happen'd in his berth,
>   At forty-odd befell:
> They went and told the sexton, and
>   The sexton toll'd the bell.

The neat and unemotional end of the verse gives subversive pleasure because it handles/emulates death so briskly. Telling the sexton and tolling the bell become equivalent acts of communication: alike formal, alike affect-less. The poem pleases not only in overtly faking its literary origins (it is not 'an old ballad', nor an external submission to the magazine) but in undermining its own narrative of emotional excess (tears, fainting, suicide) with measured lines, economical verses and puns that, like Sally, are engagingly fickle. Seen in the context of 'The Lion's Head', 'Faithless Sally Brown' deliberately undercuts the sentiments and language of rejected contributors' work, constituting an acted critique of G.R., whose 'diction', Hood remarks, 'would inflate a balloon' and B., who 'Has the "Cacoethes Rhymendi," and loves the luxury of feeling that attends it'.[53] Saluting the impossibility of determining 'authenticity', 'Faithless Sally Brown' also suggests the ambivalence with which Hood occupies the role of literary mourner, for the poem is partly parodic.

In Matthew Lewis's *The Monk* the doomed heroine, shortly before seeing her mother's ghost, reads the tragic ballad of 'Brave Alonzo and Fair Imogine': Alonzo is a knight who journeys to Palestine, invoking a fatal curse on Imogine should she be false; when he returns to find her faithless, the curse is fulfilled. Lewis reprinted the ballad in *Tales of Wonder* (1801), but accompanied it with a parody, 'Giles Jollup and Brown Sally Green', which he said was stimulated by a spontaneous parody that had appeared in the newspapers. In Lewis's parody, Giles Jollup is an apothecary and his curse upon his faithless lover is that he should administer rhubarb to her as a physic, which he does, in spectral form. Lewis produced a comic version of his own ballad where the material and the commercial supplant the ethereal and the chivalrous; the pleasure of the parody involves a recognition of the kind of class and commercial circumstances that the original represses. Hood's title, 'Faithless Sally Brown', echoes 'Brown Sally Green' as does his plot, but his hero has descended still lower in the social scale. Hood's poem engages in a similar process to Lewis's: it transposes the romantic ballad in geographical, social, and literary terms and, in doing so, creates a work whose knowingness about the way in which prosaic accommodation jilts poetic longing is essential to its charm. 'Faithless Sally Brown' demonstrates the fruitfulness of the periodical as a space that generates dialogue between works and readers, where authorship, genre, and meaning are constantly in question, and the invocation of loss is inseparable from delight in the freedoms conferred by the inauthenticable text.

Poetic transportation: 'The Literary Police Office' and 'The Stag-Eyed Lady'

Hood and Reynolds established a fraternal friendship early in Hood's period at the *London* and their writing shares a delight in parody and in jokes that involve literary translocation. Reynolds's best essays summon up prominent authors, but imagine them in surprising circumstances: in 'Boswell's Visit', he has Boswell appear as a ghost to relate Samuel Johnson's judgements on current literature; in 'Professor Wilson's

Danciad', he deliberately confuses John Wilson, editor of *Blackwood's* and 'Professor' Wilson, a celebrated dancing-master; in 'The Literary Police Office, Bow-Street', which appeared in the *London Magazine* for February 1823, Reynolds describes modern authors as if they were common criminals. Wordsworth, a 'pedlar', 'that hawks about shoe-laces and philosophy' is arraigned for passing himself off as his grand-mother; Tom Moore is accused of 'picking the pocket of the public of nine shillings'; while Lord Byron, 'a young person, apparently of fero-cious habits', is charged with 'violent assault upon several literary gentle-men' after excessive drinking at the Flying Horse and Pan-pipes.[54] The comedy of 'The Literary Police Office' works on various levels: it ridi-cules the critical 'policing' of literature for political ends; it plays with the relationship between writing and imposture; and it relocates 'high' liter-ary figures in 'low' circumstances, where their pretensions appear ridicu-lous: Wordsworth conducts himself so extravagantly, calling himself 'king of the poets', as 'to give an idea that he was not quite right'.

Hood similarly takes pleasure in relocating Romantic poetics in cir-cumstances that undermine their gravitas. The profession of magazine writer was relatively new in the 1820s and, as we have seen, the *London's* contributors turn to their advantage the anonymity, mutabil-ity, and ephemerality that might otherwise be construed as markers of subordinate status. Reynolds, in comically positing the similarity between writers and crooks (the *London's* contributors are amongst those arrested), sets all contemporary poets before a common bar. The Flying Horse and Pan-pipes converts the mythology of poetic inspiration into the concrete, commercial, urban scenery of the public house. Like Reynolds, Hood had gone through a teenage phase of ardent Byronism, penning 'The Bandit', a tragic romance; but, by the 1820s, his response had evolved: he had absorbed the ironic humour of Byron's late style and, like many other readers, lost his awe of the ubiquitous celebrity who 'threw out more heads than Hydra'.[55]

In the May 1822 *London* Hood published 'The Stag-Eyed Lady, a Moorish Tale', which makes game not only of Byron but also of the orientalism of Southey and Moore.[56] Cleverly reviewing the plot of *The Giaour* through the comic ottava rima of *Beppo* and *Don Juan*, it is both openly imitative and opposes its own poetic landscape and vocabu-lary to that of its sources. Ali Ben Ali is a despotic sultan who, enraged that his wife bears him twin daughters rather than sons, has her drowned in a sack:

> Despotic power, that mars a weak man's wit,
>   And makes a bad man – absolutely bad,
> Made Ali wicked – to a fault: – 'tis fit
>   Monarchs should have some check-strings; but he had

No curb upon his will – no, not a *bit* –
  Wherefore he did not reign well – and full glad
His slaves had been to hang him – but they falter'd,
And let him live unhang'd – and still unalter'd[57]

Hood's 'The Stag-Eyed Lady' is deflationary: the power of the sublime,
and hence the sublimity of power, are gently mocked, countered by the
small, the local, the metropolitan. Hood's Ali Ben Ali is such a monster
that he is comparable to: a horse. The pun on 'bit' is echoed by that on
'reign' and a true Cockney pun on 'un[h]alter'd', all of which diminish
his dignity. When his wife is drowned, she's brought to 'a kind of
Moorish Serpentine' and unceremoniously 'shot from off the shoulders
of a black, / like a bag of Wall's-End[58] from a coalman's back'. London
and its own 'blacks' (coal-heavers) supplant the slaves of the harem.
The stag-eyed lady, as a water peri, laments that 'The *Mussul*-man
coming to fish in this water, / Adds a tear to the flood that weeps over
her grave': again, loss is rendered comical, as the language of common
work replaces the language of alien worship. Hood doesn't stage a slave
rebellion against his imaginary despot, but his approach to the topic of
absolute tyranny involves its own acts of insubordination: the language
of power is made absurd, as domestic and commercial imagery continu-
ally undermines it. Indeed, Hood's comic vision of the despotic Ali Ben
Ali is also a parodic vision of Byronic egotism.

  Both Hood and Reynolds learn a great deal of their comic craft from
Byron – the conversational potential of ottava rima; the delayed punch-
rhyme; the insouciance of allowing the strain of the form to be part of
the joke – but both bring to their writing a different class and local
vocabulary. Hood presents Lamb as 'the opposite of Byron' and his own
public persona is likewise anti-Byronic. Hood's illustrations, too, under-
cut the erotic orientalism of Byron and Moore: his 'She Walks in Beauty
Like the Night' depicts a grinning negress with a cabbage-leaf fan, while
Moore's ' "Rich and Rare Were the Gems She Wore" ' becomes a savage
face with a nose ring. To depict this counterpoint as 'taming' is to miss
the nuances of a dialogue where wayward reading exposes the original
to contexts that unsettle its terms and assumptions. The illustrations
(Fig. 2.1) subvert the association between autocratic male power and
the erotic alien female by presenting an unexpectedly robust female
Other.

Mermaids and fishwives: Lamb and Hood

The figure of the mermaid or water sprite in Hood's work nicely
embodies his playful imitative-parodic engagement with romantic forms
and his ambivalence about the lure of introspection. Mermaids were a

"SHE WALKS IN BEAUTY, LIKE THE NIGHT."

"RICH AND RARE WERE THE GEMS SHE WORE.

2.1 Hood's ' "She Walks in Beauty, Like the Night" ' (1830) and ' "Rich and Rare Were the Gems She Wore" ' (1826) reinterpret lines from Byron and Moore respectively.

source of shared humour at the *London*. In the September 1821 'Lion's Head', Hood quips: 'N. of Margate, says he means to send us "A Marine Subject." We hope it will be a Mermaid.'[59] The October issue contains Elia's 'Witches, and Other Night Fears', in which he claims to be 'mortified' by the poverty of his dreams. Coleridge can conjure up 'icy domes, and pleasure-houses for Kubla Khan'. Bryan Waller Procter (a fellow contributor) 'has his tritons and his nereids gamboling before him in nocturnal visions, and proclaiming sons born to Neptune – when my stretch of imaginative activity can hardly, in the night season, raise up the ghost of a fish-wife'.[60] He goes on to describe a dream in which he briefly rides in Neptune's train as a *'leading god'*, but washes up 'safe and inglorious somewhere at the foot of Lambeth Palace'. Lamb, as Elia, is humorously self-deprecating about the pedestrian soul that causes him to 'subside into my proper element of prose': poetry is equated with a scope and depth beyond his inventive capacities. Yet the essay also mocks Coleridge, Procter, and (implicitly) De Quincey, whose serialized *Confessions of an English Opium Eater*, full of exotic visions, had been appearing in the September and October *London*. Lamb, relating dreams to the personality that produces them, hints at the narcissm of visions of power and mermaids (a traditional symbol of vanity): the gentle bump of reality he describes, neatly beaches his fellow-writers' pretensions. The interrupted nature of Elia's dream, meanwhile, creates a 'minor' counter-narrative of romantic loss and longing, where he is the alternative (anti-)hero and autobiographer. Hood, like Lamb, uses the mermaid to conjure both the fascination of an unattainable poetic ideal and its subversively prosaic remainder.

The *London Magazine* offered a stimulus for both kinds of treatment. The May 1821 *London* recounted 'The Water Lady – A Legend', in which Count Albert, driven by curiosity to visit the spirit of the Black Water Vault, fails in his promise to revisit her on the eve of his wedding, and perishes mysteriously along with his bride, a victim of the undine's vengeance. Contrastingly, in the November 1822 'Lion's Head', Hood claimed to have received a letter from a Dr Rees Price attesting to the authenticity of a 'real' mermaid currently being exhibited in St James's Street. The letter, as Hood's ironic treatment makes clear, was an ill-concealed advertisement. An essay, 'The Mermaid', followed in the December 1822 *Magazine*, which is probably by Hood but comes so close to Lamb's style that its attribution is contested.[61] It jokes:

> To use a sporting phrase, the Mermaid has been well *backed* . . . The great surgeons pay a shilling for a peep – and she is weighed in the *scales*, and found wanting . . . One great surgeon thought her to be half a baboon and

half a gudgeon: another vowed she was half Johanna Southcote, with a salmon petticoat.[62]

Hood's poetry draws on the romantic mystery of tales like 'The Water Lady' but also on the mocking realism of prose pieces such as 'The Mermaid'. His brief and evocative lyric 'The Water Lady' (1826) describes an encounter with a water spirit who vanishes beneath the surface of a stream before the enchanted male viewer can hear her sing: he is doomed to 'fade away', pining for the vision that will never recur. The poem recalls Keats's 'La Belle Dame Sans Merci', Reynolds's 'The Naiad', and Allan Cunningham's 'The Mermaid of Galloway'. Hood's 'Hero and Leander' (1827), chaster than Leigh Hunt's version of the story but certainly influenced by it, has Leander seduced by a sea-nymph, Scylla, who 'compels him to her deeps below', not understanding that taking him to share her underwater home will kill him. In all these poems the fatal siren embodies many of the qualities of poetry itself: she sings, she resists capture or interpretation, and the protagonist is ambiguously her slave and her conjurer (as Reynolds writes in 'The Naiad': 'Is it the form he hath lov'd and sought? / Or is it some vision his fancy hath wrought?'[63]). The protagonist alone sees her and his obsessive watching has no end or consummation but death. Ostensible seduction contains strong elements of literary autoerotism, signalled by the narcissistic associations of water.

Hood's comic verse punctures the model of poetry this iconography presents. In 'The Stag-Eyed Lady', the spirit of Ali Ben Ali's drowned wife is transformed into a singing water peri, but Hood undermines the seductive, indeterminate image of the floating female with puns that describe her *aqua*line nose and *bath* cloak. In 'The Mermaid of Margate' (1826), one of Hood's most enjoyable and characteristic comic poems, the man who is seduced is a fishmonger, Peter Fin, and the object of his entranced gaze is out for revenge on behalf of the seafood he has been responsible for consuming. 'The Mermaid of Margate' is, like 'Faithless Sally Brown', a comic rereading of the tragic ballad plot that relocates it in a class-conscious, modern, local environment: the cheap holiday resort. Many readers would have felt instantly familiar with 'Margate beach, where the sick one roams, / And the sentimental reads; / Where the maiden flirts, and the widow comes – / Like the ocean – to cast her weeds, –'.[64] The poem acknowledges the ocean's 'romantic' qualities, which draw the 'sentimental' reader and women seeking romantic attachment, but maintains an ironic distance from them. The 'romantic', situated within the commercial, is revealed as a form of tourism; meanwhile, the widows who come to Margate to 'cast their weeds' suggest a literal equivalent for the mermaid long before she is introduced. The poem constantly links the fantastical to the actual: the mermaid has a mouth like an oyster, she hops like a kangaroo, and she has 'no more feet than Miss Biffen' (a limbless London artist). Roger Henkle chooses to read 'The Mermaid of Margate' as a fable about class transgression, where Peter Fin is punished for straying out of his depth,[65] but its play, I think, is equally about the pleasures and perils of poetry itself. Unlike the protagonists of Hunt's, Keats's, and Reynold's poems, whose obsessive fascination draws them to their deaths, Peter Fin is rescued, 'by a boat, / Of Deal – (but builded of oak.)'. In this tale, the concrete qualities of language and a solidly literal craft pluck the tradesman hero from the fatally indeterminate clutches of the figurative. Hood conjures the lure of the poetic ideal, whose power and inscrutability are inseparable; yet he is also fundamentally suspicious of its attractions: his comic verse, influenced by the *London*'s journalism, grounds the siren, as Lamb does in 'Witches, and Other Night Fears', deliberately counterpointing depths with surfaces, the enigmatic with the candid, the private with the public.

Later 'Last Man': an insolent subject

Hood's poem 'The Last Man' (1826), published in the same collection as 'The Mermaid of Margate', offers another example of his ambivalence about romantic motifs and nuanced response to literary predecessors; this is a poem that advertises its own secondary status, and whose subject is belatedness, yet that also foregrounds its stylistic differences, undercutting treatments of the same theme by Thomas Campbell, Byron, and Mary Shelley. The self-consciously 'minor' frame of the poem works with the lowly and uncouth nature of its protagonist to produce a disconcerting tone, between bleak judgement and black humour, appropriate to the mixed feelings of defeat and triumph that Hood imagines in his solitary survivor.

The subject of The Last Man was popular in literature and art of the first decades of the nineteenth century. As Fiona Stafford discusses in *The Last of the Race*, the possibility of apocalypse, caused by the death of the sun – in Byron's 'Darkness' (1816) and Campbell's 'The Last Man' (1823) – or a plague epidemic – in Shelley's novel *The Last Man* (1826) and Hood's poem – was topical in years dominated by the aftermath of revolution and twenty-five years of war in Europe.[66] The subject also, in Mary Shelley's case, clearly reflects the experience of outliving Shelley and Byron, whose shadows hover around Lord Raymond and Adrian, Earl of Windsor, the central characters in her novel. Hood's

last man, in telling contrast, is not a nobleman but a hangman: the least
appropriate of relicts, since the plague deprives him not only of society
but of *raison d'être*, but also the most appropriate, since, as death is his
livelihood, the extinct world becomes a natural extension of the charnel
that surrounds his gallows.

> 'Twas in the year two thousand and one,
> A pleasant morning of May,
> I sat on the gallows-tree all alone,
> A chaunting a merry lay, –
> To think how the pest had spared my life,
> To sing with the larks that day!
>
> When up the heath came a jolly knave,
> Like a scarecrow, all in rags:
> It made me crow to see his old duds
> All abroad in the wind, like flags: –
> So up he came to the timbers' foot
> And pitch'd down his greasy bags. –
>
> Good lord! How blythe the old beggar was!
> At pulling out his scraps, –
> The very sight of his broken orts
> Made a work in his wrinkled chaps:
> 'Come down,' says he, 'you Newgate bird
> And have a taste of my snaps!' – [67]

Hood's language (old duds, greasy bags, Newgate bird, snaps) is delib-
erately vulgar, in keeping with his last men and in marked contrast to
Campbell's genteel stanzas and the blank verse of Byron's 'Darkness'.
It gives the verbal landscape of the poem a roughness that makes previ-
ous visions of apocalypse seem ludicrously smooth. Hood creates a
verbal and visual picture of grotesquerie, where the 'merry lay' of the
hangman and the 'jolly knave' jar with the decay around them, calling
attention to the dependence of human survival upon others' death and
the constant competition in human interaction between social and anti-
social impulses: a struggle mimicked in the mixed literary response the
poem embodies and the mixed emotional response it solicits.

Hood's apocalyptic scene is also more politically radical than Byron's
or Campbell's. The poem emphasizes the demise of social hierarchy in
a situation where rats leap out of the masters' beds and 'the grandest
palaces in the land' are 'as free as workhouse sheds': the beggar cele-
brates a revolutionary equality when he asserts: 'come, let us pledge
each other, / for all the wide world is dead beside, / And we are brother
and brother'. The hangman is disgusted by the collapse of status repre-

sented by the beggar's social freedoms, culminating in his appearance in a royal crown. Determined himself to be 'king of the earth', he tries and convicts the beggar for theft:

> But God forbid that a thief should die
> Without his share of the laws!
> So I nimbly whipt my tackle out,
> And soon tied up his claws, –
> I was judge myself, and jury, and all,
> And solemnly tried the cause.[68]

The cruelty and absurdity of this show trial in a situation where rank and property have become empty letters is purposely disturbing: it recalls the legal abuses and rife capital punishment of the 1820s. The beggar, 'blinded in his bags', is hung from the gallows: his discarded body is eaten by dogs. Byron's 'Darkness' likewise culminates in a conflict between two remaining survivors, but, using chiaroscuro, he renders the earth's descent into darkness a large-scale dramatic tableau and the human battle is set off by the portrait of a faithful dog that remains true to its dead master. The mean setting and scale of Hood's final conflict form an ironic contrast to Byron's. His ferocious pack of dogs, which eat their former masters, is also a calculated counter-image to that of Byron's trusty hound. Campbell's poem maintains a mood of religious certitude, with versification reminiscent of a hymn:

> This spirit shall return to Him
> That gave its heavenly spark;
> Yet think not, Sun, it shall be dim
> When thou thyself are dark![69]

Although Hood draws on Biblical imagery ('the lion and Adam were company'), God is notably absent from his apocalyptic scene, where all creatures, even normally domestic animals, are at one another's throats. His poem challenges aspects of the social, teleological, and literary order retained in previous approaches to the 'Last Man' theme.

More than one commentator has described Hood's 'The Last Man' as a 'sick'[70] poem: Hood's use of the grotesque idiom (which I explore more fully in Chapter 4) is, however, traditional, critical, and sophisticated. The *London Magazine* cultivated an interest in early writing, and Hood's comic experiments with 'ancient' orthography in 'To a Critic', 'The Fall of the Deer', and 'The Carelesse Nurse Mayd' reflect his reading, latterly under Lamb's tutelage, of Renaissance texts. Occasional archaisms ('chaunt', 'decentlie') and images that recall alliterative and allegorical verse (the hundred hounds that tear the hart's haunches at the gallows' foot) make Hood's belated version of the theme of belatedness ironically seem older than its predecessors. Both beggar and hangman in Hood's 'The Last Man' resemble allegorical figures of Death as a grinning skeleton, of the kind found in Quarles's *Emblems* and Holbein's *Dance of Death*. Here, as in the traditional *moralitas*, Death warns that hierarchy is meaningless in the face of a common end. Hood's woodcut underlines the connection between his work and that of early popular authors. It is a 'low', cheaply available form that consorts with the 'low' lexical and verbal frame of reference to undercut Byron, Shelley, and Campbell.

The Last Man in early nineteenth-century iconography is also a figure for the artist. Mary Shelley, famously, confided to her journal in May 1824: 'The last man! Yes, I may well describe that solitary being's feelings, feeling myself as the last relic of a beloved race, my companions extinct before me.'[71] Again, here, Hood, in presenting the last man as an ignominious churl, whose power of execution is ironically stayed by the excessive success of his own egotism, undermines the dramatic solipsism of 'lastness' as an aesthetic condition. As *Blackwood's Magazine* remarked of Hood's version: 'The Last Man is a sort of absurd sailor-like insolent ruffian who . . . seems to say gruffly, "Don't care the toss of a tinkler's [*sic*] curse for you all".'[72] The insolence of Hood's last man is a vehicle for resistance to prior voices. His 'minor' treatment of the apocalyptic theme, while laying itself open to construction as derivative and diminished, subverts the terms of loss, the lesser and the later, in such a way as to suggest that the post-Romantic literary world is not as depleted as others would have it seem.

Losing Keats: Hood and the annual

Hood's dialectical relationship with Romantic writing and his equivocal treatment of loss as a literary trope are further demonstrated in his work for the literary annuals: his handling of Keats in the *Gem* again shows him simultaneously occupying the position of respectful mute and comic undertaker. The literary annual was the dominant form in which poetry was disseminated during the later 1820s and 1830s. Small, decoratively bound and illustrated compilations of verse and prose, featuring previously unpublished work by celebrity authors, annuals sold as gift books in huge editions of up to fifteen thousand copies. The literary annual, as I have argued elsewhere,[73] is implicated in both the making and the unmaking of the Romantic. The annuals are shrines that pay homage to Romantic writers including the newly dead Keats, Shelley, and Byron, and popularize the Romantic cult of memory; but their memorializing activity is perpetually undermined from within. Periodicals that espouse constancy, mass products that prize uniqueness, gifts that totemize loss; works based on solicited contributions from professional authors that portray literary creation as spontaneous and free, annuals consciously and unconsciously expose ironies, contradictions, and inconsistencies in the aesthetics they apparently promote. Their homage to specific writers is also laced with riposte: the annuals offer multifarious opportunities to editors, contributors, and readers to respond ambivalently to the work of more famous figures within their pages.

In the *Gem* for 1829, a new annual that Hood edited, the central artefact is a previously unpublished sonnet by Keats. Keats gave the sonnet to Jane Reynolds, Hood's wife, in return for a Tassie gem representing Leander drowning in the Hellespont.[74] This was precisely the kind of relic coveted by the annual: offering a glimpse into the private life of the author. In the case of Keats's sonnet, the subject matter also has an aptness conferred by the author's own untimely death:

> Sinking away to his young spirit's night, –
> Sinking bewilder'd 'mid the dreary sea:
> 'Tis young Leander toiling to his death;
> Nigh swooning, he doth purse his weary lips
> For Hero's cheek, and smiles against her smile.
> Oh, horrid dream! see how his body dips
> Dead-heavy; arms and shoulders gleam awhile:
> He's gone; up bubbles all his amorous breath![75]

The sonnet becomes in various senses a memorial to Keats, as does the annual, which identifies itself with the 'gem' that inspired him. Hood, as editor, is the director of this tribute. Yet his response to Keats in the *Gem* is two-faced. On the commanding recto page after Keats's sonnet, Hood prints his own showcase work: 'The Dream of Eugene Aram'. A powerful poem of repressed guilt about a schoolmaster who succeeds in concealing a murder for many years, until the buried narrative, which he has often recounted as a 'dream', is finally discovered to be true, 'The Dream of Eugene Aram' announces its succession to Keats through its placement and through openly borrowed phrasing:

> 'Oh, God! that horrid, horrid dream
>   Besets me now awake!
> Again – again, with a dizzy brain,
>   The human life I take;
> And my red right hand grows raging hot,
>   Like Cranmer's at the stake.

Hood's 'horrid dream' echoes Keats's, yet stylistically his poem is different from anything Keats might have produced: it is a historicized dream poem that incorporates its own analysis, grounding the figurative in the actual. The metre, which Wilde borrowed for *The Ballad of Reading Gaol*, echoes the repeated return to which Eugene Aram is subject: the trimeter lines, with their strong repeated rhyme, catch up on the tetrameter lines with terrible inevitability. Hood constructs a framework of memory in the *Gem* that is both benign and threatening, deferential and irreverent. A further work adds another twist to the memorial. Hood contributed a poem, printed a few pages after 'The Dream of Eugene Aram' entitled 'On a Picture of Hero and Leander'. This poem, which must have been seen as a reponse to Keats's treatment of the same subject within the annual, is provocatively flippant, conclud-ing each quatrain with a vernacular pun:

> Why, Love, why
> Such a Water-rover?
> Would she love thee more
> For coming *half seas over?*

> Why, Lady, why
> So in love with dipping?
> Must a lad of *Greece,*
> Come all over *dripping?*[76]

Hood had already written a 'serious' poem on the theme of 'Hero and Leander'; here, his deflationary approach seems to signal a refusal to mourn the death of youthful promise to the exclusion of poetic high spirits. Like other contemporary authors, Hood as an annual editor and contributor acknowledges the value of literary relics and the literary losses they enshrine, yet the act of tribute also becomes one of riposte, while the commercial viability of the 'authentic' is self-negating. Hood also contributed to the *Gem* 'as' Charles Lamb (an imposture that offended Lamb). The subject, 'A Widow', is resonant:

> Does the satiric spirit, perhaps, institute splenetic comparisons between the lofty poetical pretensions of posthumous tenderness, and their fulfilment? The sentiments of Love especially affect a high heroical pitch, of which the human performance can present at best but a burlesque parody. A Widow that hath lived only for her husband, should die with him. She is flesh of his flesh, and bone of his bone; and it is not seemly for a mere rib to be his survivor. The prose of her practice accords not with the poetry of her pro-fessions. She hath done with the world – but you meet her in Regent-street. Earth hath now nothing left for her – but she swears and administers. She cannot survive him – and invests in the *Long* Annuities.[77]

Hood, like the widow he depicts, refuses to be defined by loss. The fact that here he is posing as Lamb adds further comedy to his sketch of inauthentic regret. The first *Comic Annual*, produced the year after the *Gem*, would, typically of Hood's work, pay tribute to the successful format of the literary annual and create a comic counterweight to its obsequious ethos and tactics. It contained, like the *Gem*, a sonnet by Keats (his 'Sonnet to a Cat'), deploying the commercial power of the Romantic relic. But, tellingly, it also featured 'St Mark's Eve: A Tale of the Olden Time', a comic treatment of a Keatsian subject, in which both members of a quarrelling couple independently hope to see the 'apparition' of their spouse that will mean they are to be widowed in the coming year: retrospection is ironized by positive previsions of absence.

Conclusion

We need to find a way of thinking about Hood vis-à-vis better-known contemporaries that depends neither upon enlisting him as a 'late' Romantic nor upon insisting upon his 'original' departures from his predecessors as the source of his literary interest. As his version of 'The Last Man' suggests, primacy and lastness are related and suspect conditions in his work. Hood's imitative-parodic response to Romantic authorship means that his evocation of loss, memory, and isolation is always double-edged. The form of much of Hood's writing and illustration is deliberately 'minor'; like his fellow writers at the *London Magazine*, however, he uses markers conventionally associated with lesser literary and class status – the small, the ephemeral, the imitative, the overtly inauthentic – and turns ostensible weakness into a critical strength. This dynamic emerges in the periodical, particularly the *London*, as a response to new conditions of professional journalism, whose relation to book-market discourses of authenticity and single selfhood is self-consciously dialectical.

Hood remains throughout his life a periodical writer, and looking at his work, at the *London Magazine* and after, within the periodical format enriches our reading. Even the single-volume *Comic Annual*s retain the form of the periodical, emphasizing their temporal, metropolitan, composite nature: the various poems, prose sketches, stories, 'letters', epigrams, and pictures have an interactive relationship. The dialogue between pieces in different styles and (genuinely or purportedly) by different hands prefigures the anticipated conversation between the periodical and its diverse crowd of readers. The conscious collapsing, in the periodical, of those hierarchies and boundaries implicit in the format of the authored book, makes the era of journalism in which Hood developed as a writer exceptionally lively, experimental, dialogic, self-reflexive and intimate. His playful work reflects that context, and the proposition it entailed, that text and context are mutually constitutive and ultimately undifferentiable.

Notes

1 COGIN, 'On Imitation', *London Magazine*, 5 (January 1822), pp. 51–2. Walter Jerrold, *Thomas Hood: His Life and Times* (London: Alston Rivers, 1907), p. 100, says this article is 'indisputably' Hood's and the *Index to the London Magazine*, ed. Frank P. Riga and Claude A. Prance (New York: Garland, 1978) follows his attribution. While 'COGIN' points to Hood, who masquerades elsewhere in the London as INCOG, and internal evidence is persuasive – the interest in metempsychosis, and probable references to Charles Mathews ('M') and John Hamilton Reynolds ('R') – its authorship remains, appropriately, unverifiable. Despite meeting at the *London* dinners, Hood was not close friends with Charles Lamb until 1823 so, assuming 'L' is Lamb, the air of intimacy is feigned.

2 Hood, 'The Lion's Head', *London Magazine*, 6 (July 1822), p. 3.

3 Herbert F. Tucker, 'House Arrest: The Domestication of English Poetry in the 1820s', *New Literary History*, 25 (1994), pp. 521–2.

4 Virgil Nemoianu, *The Taming of Romanticism: European Literature and the Age of Biedermeier* (Cambridge, Massachusetts: Harvard University Press, 1984). As Nemoianu explains: 'Gottlieb Biedermeier was a character invented by Adolf Kussmaul and Ludwig Eichrodt and introduced to the public in 1855 in the Munich *Fliegende Blätter*; this smug and cozy philistine was a caricature of the old-fashioned petty bourgeois of southern Germany and Austria' (p. 4).

5 Ibid., pp. 74–5.

6 Tucker, 'House Arrest', p. 527.

7 Margaret Russett, *De Quincey's Romanticism: Canonical Minority and the Forms of Transmission* (Cambridge: Cambridge University Press, 1997), p. 118. Russett partially quotes here Susan Stewart, *Crimes of Writing: Problems in the Containment of Representation* (New York: Oxford University Press, 1991), p. 22.

8 A long tradition of criticism, much of it influenced by Adorno, has stressed the dialectic already at work within the 'ideology' of Romantic literature: what Jerome McGann, in *The Beauty of Inflections: Critical Investigations in Historical Method and Theory* (Oxford: Oxford University Press, 1985), p. 61, memorably calls 'the reflexive world of Romantic art'. Marjorie Levinson, in *Rethinking Historicism: Critical Readings in Romantic History* (Oxford: Blackwell, 1989), p. 2, goes so far as to argue that the idea of hermeneutical and historical reflexivity 'might even be described as *the* ethico-epistemological feature subtending our formal use of the category-term Romantic'. It could be argued, however, that it is in the work of writers like Hood, with their more open engagement with the materiality and market-

ability of the topoi of imagination, that the negative dialectic of Romanticism is fully played out.

9 'There's no Romance in that', *PW*, p. 278.

10 'Literary Reminiscences', *CW*, vol. 2, p. 389.

11 Hood, 'The Life of Zimmermann (By Himself)', *Comic Annual* (London: Tilt, 1832), p. 82.

12 Ibid, p. 85.

13 *Letters*, p. 383.

14 'An Autograph', *CW*, vol. 8, pp. 127–31.

15 *OED* gives Isaac D'Israeli's *Curiosities of Literature* (1791–1817), which was concerned with establishing quotation itself as an autodidactic and effective art, as the first text to use 'autograph' meaning 'a person's own signature'. *OED*'s second citation, from the 1808 *Monthly Pantheon*, talks of a collector purchasing a work for its title-page autograph 'according to the modern fashionable literary nomenclature'.

16 Contemporary interest in authenticity and acknowledgement that poetic identity is a fictional (though not a false) construction go hand in hand. As Margaret Russett argues in *Fictions and Fakes: Forging Romantic Authenticity, 1760–1845* (Cambridge: Cambridge University Press, 2006), p. 5, 'the acknowledgement of subjectivity *as* fiction is an ethical condition of authenticity in its fully Romantic sense'.

17 COGIN, 'On Imitation', p. 52.

18 In Hazlitt's essay 'On Genius and Common Sense', *Table-Talk* (London: Warren, 1821), p. 95, he argues that, although Shakespeare had the Protean ability to transform himself into whatever he chose, most genius is 'just the reverse of the cameleon; for it does not borrow, but lends its colours to all about it'. Hood, like Hazlitt, situates the chameleon ambivalently as a symbol of imitation – sometimes the mark of the secondary writer, but equally the mark of the transcendent genius, who incorporates all he sees. Keats's famous remark about the 'camelion poet' occurs in a letter to Richard Woodhouse of 27 October 1818; it is quite possible, however, that Keats's response to Hazlitt's imagery filtered through to Hood through conversation with the Reynolds family.

19 James Najarian, 'Canonicity, Marginality, and the Celebration of the Minor', *Victorian Poetry*, 41 (2003), p. 572. Najarian's article draws on the work of, among others, Margaret Russett (see above) and John Guillory, *Cultural Capital: The Problem of Literary Canon Formation* (Chicago: University of Chicago Press, 1993).

20 Ibid.

21 Hood, *Whims and Oddities*, 1 (London: Lupton Relfe, 1826), pp. 33–4. Isaac Watts was the author of popular moral verses such as *Divine Songs for Children* (1715). Thomas Campbell's 'Hohenlinden' (1802) treats a battle of 1800 in which Napoleon vanquished the Austrians. Tom Tug was a character in Charles Dibdin's musical farce *The Waterman* (1774) and a nickname for watermen generally.

22 J. Fraser, 'Thomas Hood', p. 337.

23 See P. O'Leary, *Regency Editor: A Life of John Scott* (Aberdeen: Aberdeen University Press, 1983).

24 Mark Parker, *Literary Magazines and British Romanticism* (Cambridge: Cambridge University Press, 2000), pp. 35–6. Parker's study is groundbreaking in recognizing the ideological interplay of texts, editors, contributors and readers in early nineteenth-century magazine culture. I disagree, however, with his disappointed, conservative reading of Hood's and Reynolds's contributions to the *London Magazine*.

25 John Scott, 'The Signs of the Times', *London Magazine*, 3 (February 1821), p. 157.

26 Horatio Smith ('H'), 'Farewell in England, Written off the Land's End, December 1819', *London Magazine*, 1 (January 1820), p. 59.

27 Bryan Waller Procter, 'On May Day', *London Magazine*, 1 (May 1820), p. 490.

28 *Letters*, p. 369, H.F. Chorley had described Hood as a Liberal in the *Westminster Review*, April 1838, p. 125.

29 Ibid., p. 630. Hood's inherently moderate but far from detached stance is best studied through reading his letters.

30 Thomas Noon Talfourd, *Literary Sketches and Letters, Being the Final Memorials of Charles Lamb* (New York: Appleton, 1848), p. 156.

31 Parker, *Literary Magazines*, pp. 121, 135.

32 Thomas Griffiths Wainewright ('Janus Weathercock'), 'Janus's Jumble', *London Magazine*, 1 (June 1820), p. 627.

33 Charles Lamb ('ELIA'), *London Magazine*, 2 (August 1820), p. 146.

34 John Hamilton Reynolds, ('Edward Herbert'), 'Exmouth Wrestling' *London Magazine*, 2 (December 1820), p. 609.

35 Hood, 'The Lion's Head', *London Magazine*, 5 (January 1822), p. 2.

36 Hood, 'The Lion's Head', *London Magazine*, 6 (September 1822), p. 195.

37 Hood, 'The Lion's Head', *London Magazine*, 4 (October 1821), p. 352; 'The Lion's Head', *London Magazine*, 5 (March 1822), p. 201; 'The Lion's Head', *London Magazine*, 6 (July 1822), p. 3.

38 See 'Elia to his Correspondents' in 'The Lion's Head' for November 1821 and De Quincey's reply to James Montgomery's queries about whether the character in which the Opium Eater speaks is real or imaginary in 'The Lion's Head' for December 1821.

39 Hood, 'The Lion's Head', *London Magazine*, 6 (September 1822), p. 195.

40 Hood, 'The Lion's Head', *London Magazine*, 5 (March 1822), pp. 201–2.

41 Hood, 'The Lion's Head', *London Magazine*, 6 (November 1822), p. 388.

42 INCOG, 'Presentiment: A Fragment', *London Magazine*, 6 (December 1822), p. 518.

43 *Selected Poems of Hood, Praed and Beddoes*, ed. Susan Wolfson and Peter J. Manning (London: Penguin, 2000), p. 319.

44 'Ode: Autumn', *PW*, p. 180.

45 Ibid., p. 181.

46 'Sonnet: Silence', *PW*, p. 196.
47 'No!', *PW*, p. 364.
48 Cronin, *Romantic Victorians*, pp. 6–7.
49 Harold Bloom, *The Visionary Company* (London: Faber, 1962), p. 428.
50 'The Lion's Head', *London Magazine*, 7 (January 1823), pp. 3–4.
51 'The Sea of Death: A Fragment', *PW*, pp. 183–4.
52 'Faithless Sally Brown: An Old Ballad', *PW*, p. 44.
53 Hood, 'The Lion's Head', *London Magazine*, 5 (March 1822), p. 201. Cacoethes Rhymendi is 'rhyming mania'.
54 John Hamilton Reynolds, ('Edward Herbert'), 'The Literary Police Office, Bow Street', *London Magazine*, 7 (February 1823), pp. 157–9.
55 Hood, 'Fancy Portraits', *Whims and Oddities* 1 (London: Lupton Relfe, 1826), p. 143. In 1814 Reynolds published *Safie: An Eastern Tale*, an open homage that brought generous praise from Byron. By 1820 he had moved on to *The Fancy*, a series of poems purporting to be the work of the boxer Peter Corcoran. The collection includes 'The Fields of Tothill: A Fragment', a self-consciously Byronic poem in ottava rima that disclaims its own chances of publication since it isn't set in Turkey and the hero's mind and face aren't 'murky'. Its deliberately déclassé heroine is Bessy, whose father is a fight manager and professional badger-baiter.
56 'The Stag-Eyed Lady, a Moorish Tale', *London Magazine*, 5 (May 1822), p. 422. In a humorous footnote to the poem Hood observes of the line 'And makes a bad man – absolutely bad': 'this is better than "power that makes weak men wicked, makes wicked men mad." (*See Preface to the Expedition of Orsna, and the Crimes of Aguirre, by Mr Southey*)'.
57 'The Stag-Eyed Lady: A Moorish Tale', *PW*, p. 54.
58 Wallsend, on Tyneside in Northumberland, was a centre for coal mining and shipping until the mid nineteenth century, when the pits flooded.
59 Hood, 'The Lion's Head', *London Magazine*, 4 (September 1821), p. 236.
60 Charles Lamb ('ELIA'), 'Witches, and Other Night Fears', *London Magazine*, 4 (October 1821), p. 387.
61 See John Strachan, 'The St James's Street Mermaid and the Case for Thomas Hood's Authorship of "The Mermaid"', *The Charles Lamb Bulletin*, 106 (April 1999), pp. 78–82, and Joseph Riehl, 'The St James's Street Mermaid and the Case for Thomas Hood's Authorship of "The Mermaid": A Postscript', *The Charles Lamb Bulletin*, 106 (April 1999) p. 83. I believe that the puns, the attention to advertisement, and reference to 'Goodwin Sands' (the home of the Mermaid of Margate) point to Hood as the source.
62 Hood, 'The Mermaid', *London Magazine*, 6 (December 1822), p. 569. Joanna Southcott claimed to be a millenarian prophetess. In 1814, aged sixty-four, she was supposed to give birth to Shiloh, but disappointingly failed to do so.
63 John Hamilton Reynolds, *The Naiad: A Tale, With Other Poems* (London: Taylor and Hessey, 1816), p. 11.
64 'The Mermaid of Margate', *PW*, p. 45.

65 Henkle, 'Comedy as Commodity', p. 309. Henkle inaccurately claims than Fin follows the mermaid 'to his death at sea'.

66 Fiona J. Stafford, *The Last of the Race: The Growth of a Myth from Milton to Darwin* (Oxford: Clarendon, 1999).

67 'The Last Man', *PW*, p. 41.

68 Ibid., pp. 42–3.

69 Thomas Campbell, 'The Last Man', *The Complete Poetical Works of Thomas Campbell*, ed. J. Logie Robertson (Oxford: Oxford University Press, 1907), p. 234.

70 Stafford, *The Last of the Race*, p. 231, says Hood's 'The Last Man' is 'nothing but a sick joke'. A.J. Sanbrook, 'A Romantic Theme – The Last Man', *Forum for Modern Language Studies*, 2 (1966), pp. 32–3, calls Hood's 'The Last Man' 'a sick poem'. James Reeves, *Five Late Romantic Poets* (London: Heinemann, 1974), p. 149, accuses the poem of 'a harsh Hebraic outlook' and a 'loss of humour and humanity'.

71 Mary Shelley, *The Journals of Mary Shelley 1814–1844*, ed. Paula R. Feldman and Diana Scott-Kilvert, 2 vols (Oxford: Clarendon, 1987), vol. 2, pp. 476–7.

72 John Wilson, *Blackwood's Edinburgh Magazine*, 21 (January 1827), p. 57. Interestingly, *Blackwood's* delights in 'The Last Man' as a parody of Campbell and Shelley and does not register its language of equality and fraternity as politically challenging.

73 Sara Lodge, 'Romantic Reliquaries: Memory and Irony in the Literary Annuals', *Romanticism*, 10 (Spring 2004), pp. 23–40.

74 James Tassie (1735–99) was a prolific sculptor and merchant, who invented a new medium, vitreous glass paste, which he used for making small portrait medallions and reproductions of antique gems and cameos. These were immensely popular as keepsakes and as affordable studies of Classical subjects.

75 John Keats, 'On A Picture of Leander', *Gem* (London: Marshall, 1829), p. 108.

76 Hood, 'On a Picture of Hero and Leander', *PW*, p. 436.

77 'The Widow', *CW*, vol. 6, p. 150.

3

Performing the city: the audience as subject

Even is come; and from the dark Park, hark,
The signal of the setting sun – one gun!
And six is sounding from the chime, prime time
To go and see the Drury-Lane Dane slain, –
Or hear Othello's jealous doubt spout out, –
Or Macbeth raving at that shade-made blade,
Denying to his frantic clutch much touch; –
Or else to see Ducrow with wide stride ride
Four horses as no other man can span;
Or in the small Olympic Pit, sit split
Laughing at Liston, while you quiz his phiz.
(Hood, 'A Nocturnal Sketch', 1832)[1]

Thomas Hood is a performative writer. In the introduction to his only completed novel, *Tylney Hall*, he compares himself ('with all due modesty as to talents') to the actor David Garrick, in Reynolds's famous portrait, poised between Tragedy and Comedy.[2] Actors and actresses make frequent appearances in his poetry, as in 'A Nocturnal Sketch' above, which evokes both the charm of seeing Shakespeare at the patent theatre, Drury-Lane, and the alternative attractions of Andrew Ducrow's equestrian stunts at Astley's Amphitheatre and the face-pulling comedian John Liston at the Olympic Pavilion. When he describes seeing 'Ducrow with wide stride ride / Four horses as no other man can span' his own triple rhymes mimic poetically the feat of stretching over several mounts while continuing to circle the ring. When he conjures the reader amongst spectators who 'in the small Olympic Pit, sit split / Laughing at Liston, while you quiz his phiz', the caesuras make the line itself crack up at Liston's jokes. Hood, like John Hamilton Reynolds, wrote a number of stage entertainments for performers including Frederick Yates and Charles Mathews, whose theatrical 'At Homes' entranced London audiences by presenting a wild variety of comic personalities within the apparent intimacy of a drawing-room setting. He also worked as a theatrical reviewer and was the author of poems that, set to music, became popular songs on the contemporary stage.

This chapter considers Hood's poetry in relationship to the so-called 'minor' or 'illegitimate' theatre of the 1820s and 1830s. As Jane Moody demonstrates, in *Illegitimate Theatre in London 1770–1840*, to which this chapter is indebted, early nineteenth-century 'illegitimate' theatre – i.e. dramatic performance outside the two patent houses of Covent Garden and Drury Lane – is a testing-ground for the possibilities of cultural democracy. The patent theatres' post-1752 monopoly on spoken drama, designed to suppress theatrical forms of political opposition, created, as Moody argues, a distinct 'dramatic sphere of bodily perfor-mance'[3] involving music, dance, and spectacle. Unlicensed theatres, obliged creatively to step around their technical prohibition from staging spoken drama, developed forms of performance characterized by mixed genre (melodrama, burletta, pantomime), the combination of speech with music and spectacular effect, and thinly-veiled political commen-tary. The rise of 'illegitimate' theatrical culture in the late eighteenth and early nineteenth centuries, the ideological disputes played out in its dialogue with 'legitimate' genres, and its success in overturning the terms of cultural monopoly, constitute a narrative long veiled by read-ings of the period that claimed a decline in public theatre and a con-comitant poetic turn toward closet drama.

Hood's poetry is practically and ideologically allied with the forms, subjects, and modes of illegitimate theatre. Appreciating this fully can help us to comprehend its innovative and popular appeal, and the linkage between the kind of social variety it depicts, the audience it solicits, and the political sympathies it represents. Hood's verses, with their overt performativity, love of melodrama and burlesque, and em-phasis on physical spectacle, draw on the rich traditions of the unli-censed stage. Depicting washerwomen and body-snatchers, drapers and dustmen, they represent a new class of subject in poetry. Among the voices they imagine are that of a nosy neighbour watching a house fire from the street, a servant trying to compose an 'ode to peace' despite constant interruptions from his mistress's bell, and Toby the Learned Pig, reflecting sadly that he is fated to go from studying Bacon to becom-ing it. In producing art that presented the quotidian variety of London back to its inhabitants, Hood was part of a trend, shared by the con-temporary periodical press and popular theatre, that involved turning the mirror on the audience and the metropolitan street, eliding the boundaries between performer and spectator. Depicting ordinary social incident in theatrical terms, Hood draws attention to class itself as an effect of performance and to the ubiquity of social 'feinting'. He dramatizes the conflict between aspiration and reality, the fictive inner life we nurture and the outer life we negotiate, with serio-comic deftness. Indeed, Hood is also an early practitioner of the dramatic monologue. Tennyson and Browning were once credited as originators of the vogue for dramatic monologue in the 1830s. Recent scholarship has high-lighted the work of neglected women poets of the 1820s and 1830s, especially Felicia Hemans and Letititia Landon, in (re)inventing this most characteristic of Victorian poetic forms. Hood is another writer whose contribution to this genre has been ignored and, I shall argue, his comic monologues are a salutary reminder of the dramatic mono-logue's roots in popular theatre.

Green Room colleagues

The *London Magazine* inculcated a strikingly warm and broad approach to theatre, extolling drama as a medium that presents and solicits inter-action grounded in natural fellow-feeling. William Hazlitt, introducing his first commentary on 'The Drama' in the first number of the *London Magazine*, announced that 'we feel a sort of theoretical, as well as instinctive predilection for the faces of play-going people, as among the most sociable, gossiping, good-natured, and humane members of society. In this point of view as well as in others, the stage is a test and school of humanity. We do not much like any person or persons who do not like plays and for this reason, *viz.* that we imagine they cannot much like themselves or any one else.'[4] Hazlitt, in his regular features on 'The Drama', developed a vivid and intellectually vigorous language for dis-cussing theatre that raised the status of acting as an art; in describing his visits to the Surrey and the Coburg, and his delight in ballet, farce, and pantomime, he also challenged those readers who might have con-sidered the minor theatres inappropriate subjects for serious reflection. Hazlitt, however, was not alone in singing the delights of performance in the *London*'s pages. John Hamilton Reynolds and Thomas Noon Talfourd also reviewed plays. Reynolds took readers to a wrestling match and on an imaginary visit to a theatrical Green Room.[5] Charles Lamb in his Elia essays wrote fondly of his first theatre visits and dis-cussed the reasons why modern audiences no longer considered Restora-tion comedies acceptable viewing.[6] During Hood's time as an editor, the *Magazine* also began to publish excerpts from melodramas and come-dies by living dramatists, on the grounds that these otherwise often vanished without permanent record.[7] Hood's father had published the *Monthly Mirror*, of which theatrical criticism formed a major part. At the *London* he was surrounded by playgoing colleagues who were writing about theatre; many of them were also themselves writing drama. Among Lamb's plays is 'Mr H', a comedy about a silent gentleman, reputedly inspired by Hood's anecdotes of his dame school, kept by the Misses Hogsflesh in Tokenhouse Yard, whose brother never spoke. John Hamilton Reynolds adapted *Gil Blas* into a five-act comic opera, performed at the English Opera House in 1822, in which Hood likely had a hand, and which starred Fanny Kelly – an actress beloved of Lamb and celebrated in poetry by Hood and Reynolds.[8] The social worlds of 'illegitimate' theatre and journalism were closely intertwined. Among those working in both spheres from the 1820s to the 1840s, who knew Hood well, were Douglas Jerrold (whose son became Hood's first biographer), J.R. Planché, Alfred Henry Forrester, Mark Lemon, Horace and James Smith, and Charles Dickens. Publications such as *The London Magazine*, indeed, consisted of a company of writers not unlike a troupe of performers: when Hood apostrophized the *Magazine* fondly in his 'Literary Reminiscences', he lamented: 'Hadn't you an Opium-Eater, and a Dwarf, and a Giant, and a Learned Lamb, and a Green Man?'[9] The *Magazine* format, like that of the minor theatres, allowed performers to appear in different types of piece, as well as different characters, on a single occasion: the mixture of genres was analogous to the repertoire an actor might span in a busy evening.

Hood, like Lamb, Wainewright, and Reynolds, performs different characters in the *London*. In the May 1822 *Magazine*, he published 'Mr. Martin's Pictures, and the Bonassus, a Letter from Mrs. Winifred Lloyd to her friend Mrs Price, At the Parsonage House in – in Monmouthshire'. Mrs Lloyd's 'tourist's' account of a visit to London is comically faulty and ingenuous – 'My darter is quite inchanted with the metropalus and longs to be intraduced to it satiety, which please God she shall be as soon as things are ready to make her debutt in' – but also sharp and vivacious.[10] Comedy of this period is particularly fascinated by characters like Mrs Lloyd, who have achieved upwardly mobility without becoming fully culturally literate. Thomas Moore's *Fudge Family in Paris* (1818) was influential in establishing the genre, also evident in Dickens's sketches, such as 'The Tuggs's at Ramsgate' (1836), which depicts a family of greengrocers who inherit money and go on holiday. Hood is additionally drawing on memories of Sheridan's Mrs Malaprop and on the epistolary novels of Smollett: Winifred Lloyd is the married name of the maid from Smollett's *The Expedition of Humphrey Clinker*. The reader's pleasure in reading 'her' letter involves decoding meaning from words that have been misapplied or misspelled; we are also invited, from a position of greater cultural sophistication, to find her limited interpretation of Martin's pictures funny. The comedy, however, is not all on one side. Winifred innocently exposes the cultural pretensions of the exhibitions she attends. The sublime terrors and vast scale of Martin's pictures are cut right down to size: as Winifred comments on the 'Welsh Bard', 'there was so many mountings piled atop of one another . . . that it made my neck ake to look after them'. Her daughter, looking at 'The Storming of Babylon', sees only a bunch of flowers in a garden that 'would look bewtiful on a chaney teacup'. After Martin's exhibit, the Lloyds visit the 'Bonassus' – a bison – which also proves surprisingly tame: 'it is no ways veracious' and 'eats nothing but vegetables'. Implicitly the 'high' and 'low' show are compared and neither overwhelms. The 'letter', which appeared after an account of the 'Fine Arts in Edinburgh' and before Griffiths Wainewright's review of John Martin's exhibition, jostles the authoritative voice of 'the criketal gentleman' for, as Winifred asserts, 'there is no saying for people's tastes'. Being Winifred frees Hood not only to laugh from above, at her material readings, but to laugh from below, at Martin's determination to transcend such readings. Isobel Armstrong, in a very brief allusion to Hood in *Victorian Poetry: Poetry, Poetics, Politics*, characterizes him as 'to some extent a ventriloquist for the working class'.[11] The connotations are unflattering: pretending to speak 'for' a dummy class risks sounding forced, patronizing, even manipulative. Armstrong's aside, however, doesn't do full justice to the acknowledged theatricality of Hood's approach to voice and the way in which, as here, speaking in a personated character enables him to make game of the unlearned, unselfconscious speaker, but also the self-consciousness and self-importance of the cultural landscape against which they are positioned.[12] Hood brings what he learns from eighteenth-century comic prose and drama to bear on his work, which, from the first, uses stage convention to explore the flimsiness of the boundary between critical arbiter and consumer, writer and reader, performer and spectator.

Odes and Addresses to Great People

Hood's first book of poetry, *Odes and Addresses to Great People* (1825), written in collaboration with John Hamilton Reynolds, has an explicitly theatrical background. The title is an echo of *Rejected Addresses*, a comic volume produced by Hood's colleagues, James and Horace Smith, in 1812. The occasion for the Smiths' poems was the reopening of the Drury Lane Theatre after fire, which invited competitive submission of a poetic address to initiate the first performance. The Smiths produced a successful volume of bogus addresses purporting to be by famous authors such as Wordsworth and Byron, but in fact parodying the individual styles of these poets. Hood's and Reynolds's *Odes and Addresses to Great People* is a different kind of production but, like *Rejected Addresses*, inhabits a dramatic demesne. Their introductory address represents the anonymous authors coming forward 'totally overcome, like a flurried manager, in his every-day clothes, to solicit public indulgence'. Paying compliments to those Great People not included in the volume it notes that:

> Mr. Colman, the amiable King's Jester, and Oath-blaster of the modern Stage, merits a line . . . Mr Kean, the great Lustre of the Boxes – Sir Humphry Davy, the great Lamplighter of the Pits . . . yea, several others call for the Muse's approbation; – but our little Volume, like the Adelphi House, is easily filled, and those who are disappointed of places are requested to wait until the next performance.[13]

Odes and Addresses compares itself with a minor theatre, the Adelphi, in a simile that elides the stage and the house: its addressees are simultaneously actors and audience. Like *Rejected Addresses*, this innovative production succeeds by 'doing' different voices: both creating monologues that celebrate individuals prominent on London's public stage and (less obviously to a modern reader) incorporating parody of contemporary poetics.

In the first poem in the collection, 'Ode to Mr Graham, the Aeronaut', Hood conjures the voice of a fellow-traveller in a hot air balloon, sailing over London and marveling at how small its luminaries appear from the sky. Among those revealed as 'low' by his literally elevated perspective are Thomas Campbell, Southey, Byron, Rogers, Moore, Scott, and *Blackwood's Magazine*. The aerial view is a levelling one: Graham's co-flier ('poor, and much beset') observes that debt, credit, and reputation are alike meaningless in the sky. The 'Ode to Mr. Graham' cleverly balances a realistic and deflationary account of the celebrities and places passing below the balloon (St Paul's resembles a 'tea urn') with buoyant, unironized delight in the idea of flight, whose beauties (clouds like 'Birds of Paradise') figure the range of possibility open to 'the free creative mind'. Tellingly, Hood plays with an image of transcendence that is itself concrete: the descent of the balloon, though imbued with a gentle sense of loss, also invokes the magic of the mundane: 'The earth is close! / The City nears – / Like a burnt paper it appears, / Studded with tiny sparks! / Methinks I hear the distant rout / Of coaches rumbling all about – / We're close above the Parks!'[14]

The 'Ode to Mr. Graham' is, arguably, a dramatic monologue; as Coleridge immediately perceived, it is also a 'spirited parody on the introduction to Peter Bell'. Hood, by identifying his own flight 'in

Fancy's airy car' with the concrete situation of a flight over London, larks about with Wordsworth's poem through implicit contrasts. The tag which prefaces the 'Ode to Mr. Graham' in *Odes and Addresses*, '*Up with me! – up with me into the sky! –* Wordsworth *– on a Lark!*' paraphrases a line from Wordsworth's 1802 poem 'To a Skylark' ('Up with me! Up with me into the clouds!') but is also surely intended to remind readers of *Peter Bell*, where Wordsworth describes himself ascending into the sky in a little boat.[15] Wordsworth's *Peter Bell* was by 1825 an established comic object amongst Hood's circle. John Hamilton Reynolds had in 1819 published a spoof poem entitled *Peter Bell: A Lyrical Ballad*, which pre-empted the publication of the real *Peter Bell*, creating some confusion and much amusement at Wordsworth's expense. Keats had been a conspirator in this critical joke, writing a review of the spurious *Peter Bell* in the *Examiner*, which, however, emphasized that the writer of the parody was a profound admirer of Wordsworth who sought only to ridicule those aspects of his poetry that detracted from his genius. Hood does not parody Wordsworth's style, as Reynolds had done. Instead, his tour, dwelling on London's real landmarks – the London Docks, the Isle of Dogs, the City Road – implicitly contrasts itself with Wordsworth's mythic panorama, which embraces the Pacific Ocean, the Andes, Lybia and Siberia as well as the 'realms of Faery' and various planets, before returning to a rural home. Hood was a lifelong admirer of Wordsworth. But, as Keats and Reynolds had done before, here he lampoons Wordsworth's egotistical sublime, establishing his own work in a different territory and a different key. Cruikshank's cover for Dickens's *Sketches By Boz* (1836) would depict a man in a balloon ascending before a cheering crowd. In *Odes and Addresses*, Hood and Reynolds similarly eschew the model of the lone poet mounted on Pegasus, countering it with an image of the author as showman, urban topographer, saluting the metropolitan audience as subject.

'An Address to the Steam Washing Company' is, even more than 'Ode to Mr. Graham', a performance piece, as tags from *The Beaux' Stratagem* and *The Merry Wives of Windsor* suggest. It begins with an address to 'Mr. Scrub – Mr. Slop – or whoever you be! The Cock of Steam Laundries, – the head Patentee / Of Associate Cleansers, – Chief founder and prime / Of the firm for the wholesale distilling of grime'. In humorous couplets the Steam Laundry is berated for making the washerwoman redundant, supplanting the individual handworker with industrial machinery and depriving women of their livings. The poem then passes into the washerwoman's 'own' voice for a lengthy colloquial tirade, misspelled and peppered with malapropisms, but vigorous and appealing:

Poor Wommen as was born to Washing in their youth!
And now must go and Larn other Buisnesses Four Sooth!
But if so be They leave their Lines what are they to go at –
They won't do for Angell's – nor any Trade like That,
Nor we cant Sow Babby Work – for that's all Bespoke, –
For the Queakers in Bridle! and a vast of the confind Folk
Do their own of Themselves – even the bettermost of em – aye, and evn
　　them of middling degrees –
Why God help you Babby Linen ant Bread and Cheese!
Nor we can't go a hammering the roads into Dust,
But we must all go and be Bankers,
　　– and that's what we must!
God nose you oght to have more Concern for our Sects,
When you nose you have suck'd us and hanged round our Mutherly necks,
And remembers what you Owes to Wommen Besides washing –
You ant, curse you, like Men to go a slushing and sloshing
In mob caps, and pattins, adoing of Females Labers
And prettily jear'd At you great Horse God Meril things, ant you now by
　　you next door neighbours.[16]

Like Winifred Lloyd's letter, Bridget's 'remonstrance' is framed as a written document, but its rhythms convey the impression of a spoken monologue. Hood's exploration of vernacular, here and in later verse and prose, is not only a comic trope but an outlet into a free phonetic approach to language which is alive with puns (Lines, Sects), oaths (God help you, curse you), onomatopoeia (slushing, sloshing) and broken words that verge on nonsense (Four Sooth, Horse God Meril). The orderliness of couplet form is broken up by lines that exceed regular metrical limits, spilling over to convey the irrepressible flow of Bridget's complaint. Uneven capitalization and the idiosyncrasies of spelling and punctuation allow Hood to direct the emphasis of the sentences, and invite the reader imaginatively to voice the lines. Briefly, we become Bridget, laughing at the comic figure she cuts, yet also conscious of the pathos of her situation. The mutual act of performance narrows the gap between writer and reader.

This poem, like the 'Ode to Mr. Graham', also intervenes in contemporary debate about poetics. Leigh Hunt had in 1816 published a seminal essay 'On Washerwomen' in the *Examiner*, which was reprinted, alongside Hazlitt's work, in *The Round Table* (1819), where Hood almost certainly read it. In 'On Washerwomen' Hunt proposes that literary skill is often best deployed in small but concentrated sketches of characters and manners; he links a new interest in subjects not 'confined to the received elegances of society' to Wordsworth, but asserts that 'in one respect we go farther than Mr Wordsworth, for . . . we can manage to please ourselves in the very thick of cities'.[17] He then exemplifies his theory with a character sketch of the London washerwoman. Washerwomen – a feature of Hampstead, where the Hunts lived – thus became associated with the Cockney School. Caroline Anne Bowles, later Southey's wife, published in 1823 a 'Letter from a Washerwoman' in *Blackwood's Magazine*, which was in fact an attack on the Cockney poets.[18] In Bowles's faux-naïf, misspelled 'Letter', a washerwoman complains of the behaviour of her poet lodger, who has eloped with her daughter Nance, having first posed Nance as 'Hairy Toe', the muse of erotic poetry, and, in a procession with flambeaux, set light to the laundry, leaving her ruined and with only some poetic fragments in lieu of the rent. Bowles's impersonation critiques various aspects of Cockney poetry, connecting the love of 'low' subject matter with low behaviour, licentiousness, and an uneducated union between the classical and the metropolitan. By 1824 a further layer had been added to the washerwoman controversy. A Patent Steam-Washing Company was set up at Mitcham in Surrey, threatening the livelihoods of self-employed laundresses, who, like so many nineteenth-century workers, faced the prospect of joining the 150 women on the company's production line. *The Times* printed a 'letter' from Rachell Soapsudds, who entertains the idea of marching down to Mitcham to destroy the works 'ass the femal prize yards didd at the French revelation'.[19]

Hood, then, in presenting a washerwoman's poetic remonstrance was reviving both political and aesthetic sources of recent debate. It is interesting to speculate how Bridget Jones's complaint might have looked next to an Ode to Henry Hunt, the radical orator, which Hood proposed to Reynolds in his original plan for the volume. Washerwomen were Cockney subjects. By including one in *Odes and Addresses*, and apparently taking her part in an industrial dispute, Hood was potentially identifying himself with Cockney School poetics and politics; yet he was also engaging in comic impersonation not unlike Caroline Bowles's. The dramatic monologue is politically useful here: it devolves responsibility to the reader to determine precisely how it should be read.[20]

Odes and Addresses uses theatrical motifs and conventions to culturally levelling effect. It mingles admiring addresses to the clown Joseph Grimaldi, the actor-manager Robert Elliston, and the actress Maria Darlington with addresses to an MP, churchmen, a prison reformer, and a road engineer, giving these male and female figures equal billing and emphasizing the performativity of their various roles. In 'Ode to the Great Unknown' the author of the Waverley novels is hailed as a superlative vanishing act ('A vox and nothing more, – yet not Vauxhall; / A head in papers, yet without a curl! / Not the Invisible Girl!'). Reynolds, in his address to The Dean and Chapter of Westminster, calls them 'reverend showmen' and 'exhibitors of giant men', because they charge an entrance fee to see wax replicas of defunct celebrities; he suggests they keep a monkey near Poets' Corner to 'catch the gapers'. Since Westminster Abbey also sold plots in Poets' Corner at a high price, Reynolds's critique also touches on the commercial basis by which 'great' poets are publicly identified. Lamenting the adored clown's retirement in the 'Ode to Joseph Grimaldi, senior', Hood comments that the Poet Laureate is much more dispensable: 'high' and 'low' representative aesthetic actors are compared, to the former's disadvantage. In this alternative, genial *Spirit of the Age* it is Grimaldi whose extraordinary art unites a generation. The musicality and playfulness of the volume, which Coleridge so enjoyed, invoke London as a public stage and celebrate the pleasures of participating in its public show.

Reviews and polymonologues

During 1826 Hood worked as a theatre reviewer for the *Atlas*, a new journal whose envisaged global coverage was indicated in its format: it claimed to be printed on 'the largest sheet ever issued from the press'. Periodicals became at this time a literary analogue to the expanding nation, acting as map and panorama for the proliferating city, which increasingly looked to see itself represented in all its multitudinous variety. The minor theatres, too, responded to this desire, both in their performances and in their auditoria. The Coburg, famously, commissioned a mirror curtain, in use by 1821, consisting of sixty-three plates of glass in a gold frame. Lowered before the evening's performances, it reflected the spectators back to themselves in shining splendour, allowing them to see themselves 'on stage'.[21] Hood's reviews, in common with other contemporary critiques, take as active an interest in depicting the audience as the play:

> That stout lady's visage, in the left-hand box, might pass for Aurora's – intensely rosy – and a leash of pearls (are they not?) escaped perhaps from her tiara, are stealing down her brow. The whole front row, 'with dreadful faces throng'd and fiery arms,' according to the tremendous lines in MILTON, is all in a flutter of fans. There are but two cool persons in the house – that sugar-baker, in his great-coat, in the pit, and the anchorsmith up in the gallery. A momentary relief! The box-door opens . . . and lets enter a current of air that cools us all on one side, like a sole on a fishmonger's slab; but the comfortable zephyr is soon smothered by the entrance of two stout Lancashire agricultural gentlemen with the chill off.[22]

The different spectators are confidently attributed characters ('sugar-baker', 'anchorsmith') in such a way that, as prospective audience members, we are encouraged to perform similar acts of viewing and reading, identifying social types and regarding ourselves as prospective participants in the minor drama. Jon Klancher has argued that a primary purpose of the polite periodicals of the 1820s was to enable their audience to perform such acts of social reading, thereby demonstrating, through their capacity for self-abstraction, their bourgeois credentials.[23] This is partly true. Yet, since the socio-cultural identity of both the reading public and the periodical writer is in flux in this period, the acts of social reading practised and inculcated by the periodical, rather than confirming class identity, can also serve to emphasize the instability and subjective construction of class, its dependence on role play.[24]

When Hood began writing for the stage in the 1820s, it was for the comedian Frederick Yates and Charles Mathews, whose *At Homes* likewise broke down barriers between audience and actor and explored the shifting middle ground between the 'vulgar' and the 'genteel' in terms of subject and form. For his *At Homes* at the Lyceum, Mathews wore ordinary 'private dress' and appeared on a stage that was fitted out like a living room.[25] The playbills invited the audience as if to a private, domestic entertainment rather than a public performance. What they saw was Mathews, a remarkable mimic, imitating, with exciting rapidity, a remarkable range of different characters that one might encounter in a particular social space, from the 'high' to the 'low', the actual to the imaginary, slipping between modes that could include caricature, social satire, tragedy, and farce. Mathews's wife testifies in her *Memoirs* that Hood's script formed the basis for one of Mathews's most successful *At Homes*. The social scenes imagined in the *At Home* Hood wrote are a race meeting at Newmarket and a ship launch at Woolwich. Among the named characters are Dr Cullender, physican, optician, and musician (a version of Dr William Kitchiner); Mr Humanity Stubbs the animal rights activist (a version of Richard Martin MP); Mr Rattle, 'an auto-biographer in embryo – a re-collector of what will be; he is continually sowing seeds for reminiscence'; and Mr Moritz, a jilted German, who unsuccessfully attempts multiple forms of suicide, only to find that his guns go off harmlessly, the rope breaks, and the sea, rather than drowning him, makes him so sick that he vomits the overdose he has swallowed. Both Mr Rattle and Mr Moritz are characteristic of Hood's comic resistance to the cult of Werther and the kind of existential self-involvement it implied. The *At Homes*, by contrast, dramatize the performative nature of ordinary social interaction, particularly the richly awkward frissons associated with behaving appropriately in public environments peopled with diverse and unpredictable figures. Malapropism and class anxieties form a rich ground for alternating sympathy and satire. In 'Harlequin and Mr Jenkins – Or Pantomime in the Parlour', Hood's afterpiece to Mathews's *At Home*, Frederick Yates sprang through eight different costumed characters, male and female, master and servant, British and foreign. This 'poly-mono-logue', a stunt for which Mathews and Yates were renowned, is a high-speed tour of different voices, different 'selves'. Showcasing the versatility and reflexes of the actor, it marries an old *commedia dell'arte* tradition with a new emphasis on reproducing the spectacle of metropolitan mobility, where travel is ubiquitous and identity is increasingly fluid, constructed, assumed.

Hood's theatre work for Mathews and Yates relates directly to his poetry. The *Comic Annual* would contain character sketches (such as 'The Sorrows of an Undertaker'), poems notionally written by different social types ('Domestic Didactics by an Old Servant'; 'Poems, by a Poor Gentleman') and dramatic monologues ('The China-Mender'; 'Our Village: By A Villager') whose comic turns echo those of the theatrical poly-mono-logue. The format of the *Comic Annual* – short poems, prose sketches, ballads, caricatures, 'fancy portraits', topical squibs, punning woodcuts – resembled the generic mix of illegitimate theatre performance. (Recognition and imitation worked in both directions. By the 1830s Mathews and Yates had renamed their entertainments *Comic Annuals*, appropriating the title of Hood's by now famous annual miscellanies.) Like Mathews's *At Home*, Hood's *Comic Annual* also invited the public into a quasi-private, family space. Hood shared details of illnesses that had delayed production, teased his imitators, reported complaints from imaginary critics, treating the reader on one occasion as if s/he were the Annual's intended, who had 'asked it out' and must intend to marry it,[26] and at another time like 'an old friend of the family' who had known the Annual since its Child-Hood and should be treated 'with all the freedom and confidence that pertain to such ripe connexions'.[27] Hood's annual Christmas performance established him as an accessible, dramatic figure akin to a Mathews or a Liston. It is no wonder that many readers thought of Hood as 'an intimate friend, a member of our family'.[28] Hood deliberately played across the boundaries that conventionally separate public and private. In doing so he called attention to the theatre of the street, the shop, the drawing room, and the scullery – spaces often neglected by poetry – and invited a mixed audience, who took pleasure in seeing themselves among the crowd reflected there, as in the Coburg's mirror curtain. Tellingly, in his illustration to Reynolds's 'Sonnet to Vauxhall' in the first *Comic Annual*, Hood

ROCKET-TIME AT VAUXHALL—A PROMINENT FEATURE.

3.1 Hood's 'Rocket-Time at Vauxhall' (1830), like Reynolds's 'Sonnet to Vauxhall', which it accompanies, studies the crowd, while the crowd 'studies the Sublime'

observes not the show but the crowd: the prominent feature in 'Rocket-Time at Vauxhall – A Prominent Feature' (Fig. 3.1) is the massed noses of the spectators, up which we are invited to gaze.

Viewing the viewer

Hood's poems, like Dickens's and Thackeray's urban sketches of the 1830s and 1840s, make us highly aware of our position as viewers of a social drama that is constantly unfolding and of which we are part. In 'Going to See a Man Hanged', Thackeray places us amongst the spectators, observing a couple who look like a thief and his moll on the roof of a building. In Dickens's 'Horatio Sparkins', we follow a girl intrigued by a 'mysterious, philosophical, romantic, metaphysical' suitor whom she 'reads', in terms of her preferred fictional narrative, as a disguised nobleman, but who turns out to be a linen-draper, whose real name is Samuel Smith. Hood's poems explore similar micro-dramas. Unlike Tennyson's or Browning's dramatic speakers, frequently named and sometimes historical characters, Hood's voices are often anonymous. Since they could be anyone, they readily draw the reader into

their spectatorship: indeed, since their accounts depend on observing
everyday environment and event, they suggest the extent to which
dramatic monologue externalises the mind's normal process. In 'Don't
You Smell Fire?' (1827), for example, a conflagration at the local
pawnbroker's excites *Schadenfreude* as well as sympathy:

> The engines! – I hear them come rumbling;
>   There's the Phoenix! the Globe! and the Sun!
> What a row there will be, and a grumbling,
>   When the water don't start for a run!
> See! there they come racing and tearing,
>   All the street with loud voices is fill'd;
> Oh! it's only the firemen a-swearing
>   At a man they've run over and kill'd!
>
> . . . Oh dear! what a beautiful flash!
>   How it shone thro' the window and door;
> We shall soon hear a scream and a crash,
>   When the woman falls thro' with the floor!
> There! there! what a volley of flame,
>   And then suddenly all is obscur'd!
> Well – I'm glad in my heart that I came: –
>   But I hope the poor man is insur'd![29]

The fire, which likely involves the death of the pawnbroker's wife,
shouldn't be a pleasurable drama but, as readers, we are caught up in
the noise, bustle, and spectacle, piously hoping that the man is insured
but giggling at the sight of him in his nightshirt and the antics of the
incompetent firemen. Implicitly, since the pawnbroker profits from
others' misfortunes there is a certain poetic justice about the fact that
his misfortune is now the scene of others' guilty entertainment. 'Don't
You Smell Fire?' makes manifest, as later monologues do, the inner play
between social and anti-social impulses, the conventionally repressed
and expressed self.

In 'Over the Way' (1834) the speaking character is a man who has
become obsessed with the young lady who lives across the street. Staring
out of his window, he develops an intense relationship with the object
of his covetous viewing, yet it is evident that he has never spoken with
her and that she is completely unaware of him. The window through
which he looks might as well be the box of a theatre. Indeed, he com-
plains that he 'dodges her at the play' but that, alas, 'at private theatres
she never acts'. Private theatres enabled early nineteenth-century viewers,
for a fee, to become actors for the evening, performing their favourite
roles: they offer another example of the audience taking a new and
active role as the subject of illegitimate drama. The fanciful speaker of

'Over the Way' has imaginatively cast himself and his beloved in melo-
dramatic roles. He plays the flute, refuses food, loads a suicidal pistol,
dreams of fighting duels, plucking his heroine from 'the Clyde, the
Tweed and Tay', rowing her in a fairy shallop, and racing to Gretna to
elope. Unfortunately these theatrical scenarios come to naught when he
realizes, from the postilions and white favours he sees, that Mary has
married someone else. Like the daughter who discovers that the mysteri-
ous 'Horatio Sparkins' is just a draper, in Dickens's sketch, the viewer
of 'Over the Way' has been acting out a romance only to find that he
is in a burlesque.

One of Hood's great strengths as a writer is his sympathetic ability
to conjure the gap between the fictive existence we nurture and the
factual existence we negotiate. In 'Over the Way' that gap finds expres-
sion in the speaker's self-delusion, where failure to read the theatre of
the street according to the correct genre also implies a failure to recog-
nize his own class situation. Hood's monologues, with their emphasis
on the process of viewing and the theatre of the everyday, draw atten-
tion to social and class identity as itself an effect of performance.

Class acts

Like Lamb and Dickens, Hood came from a lower middle-class back-
ground and knew at first hand the bitter 'struggle to maintain caste'[30]
and the amphibious position of those who fall between social categories,
including authors. In his novel, *Tylney Hall*, Hood executes a brilliant
sketch of Twigg, a London tradesman who, having inherited wealth,
retires with his family to the country aiming to become a gentleman
farmer. To impress the neighbours, the Twiggs get up a 'fête champetre',
but disaster strikes as the animals break loose and upset the tables of
food and drink. The rustic festival over which the Twiggs aim to preside
collapses, as the rift between the class act they mean to perform and
their off-stage origins produces unintended farce.

Some of Hood's most winning poems similarly dramatize the perfor-
mance involved in ordinary social situations. In 'Domestic Asides; Or,
Truth in Parenthesis' (1831), we overhear a hostess responding cordially
to some unwelcome guests but become, in alternate lines, privy to her
real, uncharitable thoughts. The parentheses act syntactically like a
cupped hand; like a stage actress, the lady voices the expected public
lines then whispers to the audience her private sentiments.

'I really take it very kind,
This visit, Mrs. Skinner!

I have not seen you such an age –
(The wretch has come to dinner!)

... 'And Mr. S., I hope he's well,
Ah! though he lives so handy,
He never drops in now to sup, –
(The better for our brandy!)

'Come, take a seat – I long to hear
About Matilda's marriage;
You're come, of course, to spend the day! –
(Thank Heav'n, I hear the carriage!)'[31]

The structure of the poem's title is similar to that of a play and 'asides' invoke an explicitly theatrical technique. This is again a dramatic monologue – but a monologue that wears its double form on its sleeve. The monologue betrays the mind's door-keeping, allowing us to see those thoughts it chooses to repress and those it admits into the drawing-room of conversation. Here the physical situation of the monologue involves social door-keeping and the decision whether to be 'at home' to callers or not. The overt actions that form the context for the poem, then, cleverly echo the inner psychological process it exposes.

Hood's innovative method draws attention to the ubiquity of the social feint, the way in which the conflicting demands of outward form and inner feeling routinely lead to a dialogue between expressed and repressed ideas. Reading between the lines, as the poem directs us to do, we can piece together a class-conscious scenario: the Skinners are an unpolished family, with too many children and an unsteady father; they have come visiting, perhaps hoping to be asked to stay for dinner because their own resources are strained. We may well have some sympathy at first with the hostess, unexpectedly invaded by unwanted guests, but by the end, seeing her two-facedly invite them to dine another day, while informing her servant that she is 'not at home' to the Skinners in future, we are likely to side with the repressed family (excluded from the monologue as they will be from the house) against the self-serving individual.

Hood reused the fruitful idea of counterpointing expressed and repressed ideas, conveying the latter as unofficial 'asides' sandwiched between the official lines, in several other monologues. In the 'Ode to Peace: Written On the Night of My Mistress's Grand Rout' (1832) we are presented with a poem apparently written by a servant, where the conflicting demands of composing poetry and of admitting guests to his mistress's party result in verse that is humorously at odds with its own subject:

Oh Peace! oh come with me and dwell –
  But stop, for there's the bell.
Oh Peace! for thee I go and sit in churches,
  On Wednesday, when there's very few
  In loft or pew –
Another ring, the tarts are come from Birch's.
Oh Peace! for thee I have avoided marriage –
  Hush! there's a carriage.
Oh Peace! thou art the best of earthly goods –
  The five Miss Woods.
Oh Peace! thou art the Goddess I adore –
  There come some more.
Oh Peace! thou child of solitude and quiet –
That's Lord Drum's footman, for he loves a riot.[32]

In exposing the humorous incompatibility between what the monologue desires to express (pensive, silent solitude) and what it seeks to repress (noisy social demands) this poem also comments on the fraught relationship between the conventions of literary persona and subject and the realities of domestic experience. The Romantic lyric, evoked here in the servant's misquotation of Keats's 'Ode on a Grecian Urn' ('thou . . . bride of quietness . . . foster-child of silence'), depends on the assumption of an 'I' that can dwell on absence and tranquillity. The objects that it addresses occupy and project a vision of the thinking mind that depends upon temporary non-interference from worldly chores. Where the author is a domestic servant, Hood shows, the conditions of lyric authorship are unlikely ever to obtain. The traditional vocabulary and heaven-hailing stance of poetic address ('thou art the Goddess I adore') are at odds with the proper nouns of trade and the position of the man who must deal with the continual calls of superiors and colleagues ('the tarts are come from Birch's'). Here the monologue serves not only as an image of the mind as a site of competing versions of self but as a comment on genre. By interposing the claims of business with the conventions of poetic apostrophe, the monologue deliberately intrudes the social upon the solipsistic, drawing attention to what lyric represses and implicitly proposing itself as a more inclusive alternative form.

This is also true of 'A Parental Ode to my Son, aged three years and five months' (1837), one of Hood's funniest and most engaging pieces. Again, Hood implicitly counterpoises his theatrical mode of address to the Romantic lyric: specific lines respond comically to those in Wordsworth's 'Ode: Intimations of Immortality'.[33] In Wordsworth's vision of childhood the atmosphere is reflective, the author retains control of the subject's relation to himself. In Hood's poem the real infant subject constantly intrudes on the process of writing the poem, poking peas into his ear and threatening to break the mirror with his skipping-rope, literally undermining his own idealized portrayal:

> Thou darling of thy sire!
> (Why, Jane, he'll set his pinafore a-fire!)
>   Thou imp of mirth and joy!
> In love's dear chain so strong and bright a link,
> Thou idol of thy parents – (Drat the boy!
>   There goes my ink!)[34]

The dramatic technique of the 'aside' again enables this poem to conjure the busy physical space in which its action occurs. That territory, which cannot be preserved from unexpected incursions, becomes a model for the mind, whose process is similarly marked by competing demands and conceptions of self. The poem, performing simultaneously the voiced role of the writer and the silent role of the naughty child, encourages us to picture events just outside the frame of direct representation, pointing to the unsaid and even the unconscious, in a way that anticipates the work of later Victorian dramatic monologues.

Dramatic monologue and illegitimate theatre

'Dramatic monologue' was not in widespread use as a term until the late nineteenth century. It remains a contested category, but, as Herbert Tucker has observed, the practical usefulness of the term does not seem to be impaired by the failure of historians and taxonomists to agree a definition.[35] Where early critics focused on identifying a checklist that would describe the 'perfect' monologue, modern criticism tends toward a more inclusive stance that stresses the continuity between the dramatic monologue and other forms of 'double poem' such as the framed narrative or dream poem.[36] With a less rigid approach to demarcating the genre has come an expanded vision of its history. Recent studies have emphasized the role of women poets such as Letitia Landon and Felicia Hemans in (re)inventing the dramatic monologue, stressing its usefulness to women as a form that could combine self-protection and self-assertion, allowing women to explore the performativity of gender and class and to voice subjects conventionally excluded from poetry.[37] Where once the foundational dramatic monologues were taken to be Tennyson's 'St Simeon Stylites' and Robert Browning's 'Porphyria's Lover', both published in 1842, earlier nineteenth-century prototypes are now routinely cited.

Hood's name, however, has been largely absent from discussion of the dramatic monologue; it deserves inclusion. Alongside poem such as

'St Simeon Stylites' and 'Porphyria's Lover' we might then consider poems such as 'The China-Mender' (1833). In this poem we hear the voice of a servant who has gone to the china-mender after many of her mistress's favourite knick-knacks have been accidentally broken by a suitor, Mr Lambert. This poem displays many of the features once identified as hallmarks of dramatic monologue: a first-person speaker who is identifiably not the poet, aspects of whose character are unwittingly revealed; an internal auditor; action in the present in a specific place; colloquial language; some sympathetic involvement with the speaker; and a degree of ironic discrepancy between the speaker's view of herself and the broader picture of circumstances that the reader is encouraged to develop. Here the servant's preoccupation with the possible marriage between Mr Lambert and her mistress, and the fact that she happens to mention the property she herself will inherit, may incline us to consider that her twice daily visits to the china-mender represent an offer to join that, consciously or unconsciously, goes well beyond crockery:

> But you'll join 'em all of course, and stand poor Mr. Lambert's friend;
> I'll look in twice a day, just to see, like, how they mend.
> To be sure it is a sight that might draw tears from dogs and cats;
> Here's this pretty little pagoda, now, has lost four of its cocked hats;
> Be particular with the pagoda: and then here's this pretty bowl –
> The Chinese prince is making love to nothing because of this hole;
> And here's another Chinese man, with a face just like a doll –
> Do stick his pigtail on again, and just mend his parasol.
> But I needn't tell you what to do; only do it out of hand,
> And charge whatever you like to charge – my Lady won't make a stand.[38]

Why have monologues like this escaped notice? Partly because the drama they articulate is self-consciously minor. We are not dealing here with an ascetic or a psychopath: the imagined events are, literally, not a matter of life and death. There are also issues of quality: 'The China-Mender' is self-evidently a less sophisticated poem than 'St Simeon Stylites'. But its artful, artless gossiping reflects the class of the protagonist and the genre of performance it is recalling: the servant role in which actresses like Fanny Kelly excelled and which was a staple of comic theatre.[39]

In the effort to read the dramatic monologue as a response to new conditions of selfhood and of poetic self-expression there is some danger of overlooking the relationship between dramatic monologue and 'minor' theatre. Commentary on the dramatic monologue has, rightly, stressed its emergence as a historically particular response to changing ways of conceiving the self – socially, psychologically, epistemologically

– and to the voice of Romantic lyric, which frequently presented itself as 'autonomous, self-conscious, atemporal, and male'.[40] But by preferring 'serious' over 'comic' examples and emphasizing the function of the dramatic monologue as a site of debate between expressive and phenomenological modes of reading that draws attention to the struggle to relate the experience of consciousness to awareness of its culturally constructed nature, we may privilege those monologues in which such struggle is most apparent and those that most reward analysis, rather than oration. Alan Sinfield's broad definition of the dramatic monologue as 'a poem in the first person spoken by, or almost entirely by, someone who is indicated not to be the poet'[41] is often now regarded as too loose to capture the historical specificity of the genre. Sinfield's inclusive approach, however, is helpful in foregrounding the diverse antecedents from which Victorian monologues evolve and the multiple forms they can take. Hood's monologues are indebted to the vernacular play of Swift, Smollett, and a tradition of 'complaint'[42] and 'epistle' that underlies the form of the 'Remonstratory Ode'; but they also reflect his love of popular theatre, spectacle and song.

Commentators who reject Sinfield's broad definition would likely exclude a poem such as 'Over the Way' from the category of dramatic monologue despite the fact that it features a first-person speaker who is identifiably not the poet, aspects of whose character are unwittingly revealed; action in the present in a specific place; colloquial language; some sympathetic involvement with the speaker; and a degree of ironic discrepancy between the speaker's view of himself and that of the world. It lacks an internal auditor, but, more significantly, it is presented on the page in triplets with a burden ('Over the Way!') suggestive of a comic song. Its performed qualities are so overt, its feint so transparent, that its pleasure derives more from humour and domestic detail than from psychological acuity. Purists might, similarly, find 'The China-Mender' wanting in the subtlety, scope, and depth of characterization that they regard as essential to 'true' dramatic monologue. But to say that the loquacious servant of 'The China-Mender' is a stock character and lacks complexity is merely to say that her dramatic monologue relates more closely to the conventions of 'low' comedy and burlesque than those of high drama. Excluding such poems from analysis as or alongside dramatic monologue tends to deny a shared theatrical context. By choosing to keep *Maud: A Monodrama* distinct from the social comedy of 'Over the Way', we may be reproducing a literary-historical narrative which, as Jane Moody asserts,[43] long regarded closet drama as the representative type of early nineteenth-century production, overlooking the cultural centrality of illegitimate theatre.

Just as the dramatic monologue was enabling for women authors, allowing them to play with gendered assumptions about the relation between body and poetic voice, self-disclosure and professional identity, so, for lower middle-class authors such as Hood, the monologue offered an opportunity to assume a variety of mantles, exploring the performativity of class. Hood can use monologue to expose the delusions of fictive self-dramatists, who have misinterpreted their social role ('Over the Way') and to elicit sympathy for them. 'Interrupted' monologues such as 'Ode to Peace' and 'A Parental Ode', by impinging the assaults of domestic reality on poetic apostrophe, question the exclusiveness of Romantic lyric and the assumptions it entails about the poetic self. Glennis Byron notes that women poets were especially drawn to 'fictionalised speakers placed within contemporary society rather than figures from literature, myth or history'.[44] Hood is similarly drawn to speakers who belong to the present and whose voices might not conventionally be heard in poetry; his subjects (such as Toby, the Learned Pig) are others' objects: attending to them as subjects involves acknowledging a London landscape peopled with potential protagonists.

The burgeoning world of illegitimate performance allowed early nineteenth-century audiences to see, as never before, their own varied complexion represented on the stage; the stage, in turn highlighted the performativity of even the least apparently theatrical of lives. Readers inhabited the multiplicity of characters evoked in Hood's *Comic Annual*s as they did the multiple characters in Charles Mathews's *Comic Annual* performances. Hood's poems, with protagonists who were dustmen, body-snatchers, hangmen, drapers, washerwomen, housemaids, firework-makers and seamstresses feature the same diversity of characters as popular songs and shows of the period. Indeed, many of Hood's poems became professional as well as amateur performance pieces. Monologues such as 'Number One' and 'I'm Going to Bombay' were written with performance in mind and transferred readily to the playlists of actors and singers. Their availability to an extremely wide public in a variety of media makes Hood's poems a part of the emergent, hotly contested, trend toward cultural democracy produced and reproduced in illegitimate theatre of this era.

Speech and social protest

Hood's comic monologues, his social protest monologues, and his songs overlap in ways that challenge strict differentiation between different kinds of performative verse. Bridget Jones's 'Letter of Remonstrance' to the Steam-Washing Company (1825) is humorous, but the subject – the effect of industrialization on handworkers – is serious and topical. 'The Sweep's Complaint' (1835) voices a kind of social protest, against legislation forbidding sweeps to cry their trade in public, but it is also replete with jokes and puns. 'Our Village: By a Villager' (1833) is a monologue that gently parodies the content of Mary Russell Mitford's *Our Village*, a nostalgic series of prose sketches of village life that portrayed episodes in the life of the community. Hood's imaginary yokel paints a much less glowing picture of the framework of life in his village, Bullock Smithy, which boasts thirteen pubs but very few other sources of income or entertainment. The rectory is empty, for the rector 'don't live on his living like other Christian sort of folks' and six empty houses are well-papered outside by notices of sales and election placards, but not inside: a touch that, with a quotation from Goldsmith's *The Deserted Village*, just hints at rural depopulation and discontent. 'Our Village: By a Villager' isn't a poem of social protest, but it does sketch a picture of the limitations of village life that deliberately opposes itself to the myth of the rural idyll: 'As for hollyoaks at the cottage doors, and honeysuckles and jasmines, you may go and whistle; / But the Tailor's front garden grows two cabbages, a dock, a ha'porth of penny royal, two dandelions, and a thistle.'[45] The villager's monologue ends with the Poor House: 'But I haven't come to that – and I hope I never shall.' The spectre of want always hovers around Hood's comedy; in *York and Lancaster*, a stage comedy Hood wrote in 1828, prefiguring Dickens's *Nicholas Nickleby*, knockabout farce with incompetent masters and a disobedient pupil only partially masks a troubling and topical issue: Yorkshire schools, recently the subject of newspaper reports, where unwanted children endured systematic abuse at the hands of unscrupulous adults.

Hood's earlier dramatic monologues prepared the ground for explicit protest works such as 'The Lay of the Labourer' and 'The Song of the Shirt', where he directly assumes the voices of the individuals about whose hardships he is complaining. The audience for these poems was already familiar with Hood's range of dramatic voices: the habit of reading Hood's *Comic Annual* as a form of family entertainment made it easy for these works to be 'owned' by their readers. The structure of the dramatic monologue's feint means that, as Sinfield describes, 'we experience the "I" of the poem as a character in his own right but at the same time sense the author's voice through him'.[46] In 'The Lay of the Labourer' and 'The Song of the Shirt' this middle ground between first-person and third-person speaker is significant: it enables the poem to articulate directly the misery of the exploited worker, yet simultaneously mediates that expression through the compassionate observer who solicits the reader to listen to their song. The poem effects theatrically the kind of social, cross-class understanding it aims to build.

'The Song of the Shirt' appeared in the Christmas number of *Punch*, 1843. It was instantly popular, set to music, hawked by ballad-mongers, sewn into handkerchiefs by campaigners against sweated labour in the textile industry. By May 1844 it was the climactic number in *The Sempstress: A Drama*, by Mark Lemon (*Punch*'s editor), taking the stage at the Theatre Royal, Haymarket. *The Sempstress* is a melodrama. It takes familiar elements: a dutiful daughter, a miserly father, a faithful lover, and a cruel villain, and shows the audience a trajectory that passes from rustic happiness to desolation before uniting its hero and heroine in matrimonial felicity. Lemon's *The Sempstress*, however, turns this familiar story, via Hood's poem, into a modern tale of urban exploitation: Draper, the heroine's employer, turns out to be the villain who stole her father's savings, and thus directly rather than indirectly responsible for her ruin. The well-established parameters of the popular form enable it to say something that would have been much more threatening under other circumstances: that the excesses of capitalism are responsible for the miseries of labour. Hood's monologue is the centrepiece of the performance, sung in the second act by the heroine to 'the music of the "Song of the Shirt" ', which has been played each time the curtain has risen.[47] *The Sempstress* takes Hood's poetry back to the realm of 'minor' theatre, whence so much of its power derives, making political claims that are implicit in the forms, subjects and modes he shares with the illegitimate stage throughout his career.

Notes

1 'A Nocturnal Sketch', *PW*, p. 221.

2 Hood, *Tylney Hall*, 3 vols (London: Baily, 1834), vol. 1, p. viii.

3 Jane Moody, *Illegitimate Theatre in London, 1770–1840* (Cambridge: Cambridge University Press, 2000), p. 18.

4 William Hazlitt, 'The Drama No. 1', *London Magazine*, 1 (January 1820), pp. 64–5.

5 John Hamilton Reynolds, 'The Green Room' (Letters of Edward Herbert), *London Magazine*, 5 (March 1822), pp. 236–43.

6 Charles Lamb, 'My First Play', *London Magazine*, 4 (December 1821), pp. 603–5 and 'The Old Actors', *London Magazine*, 5 (April 1822), pp. 305–11.

7 See the series entitled 'Beauties of the Living Dramatists', begun in the *London Magazine*, 5 (January 1822).

8 Alvin Whitley, 'Thomas Hood as a Dramatist', *University of Texas Studies in English*, 30 (1951), p. 187, argues that Hood could not have worked on

Gil Blas, as family tradition suggested, because Hood's first meeting with Richard Brinsley Peake, its producer, postdated the opera. As Hood's *Letters* (to which Whitley lacked access) show, however, Peake's account of his first meeting with Hood is unreliable – Hood certainly knew Peake earlier than Peake's faulty memory would suggest. Whitley's article otherwise remains a valuable account of Hood's theatrical involvements.

9 'Literary Reminiscences', *CW*, vol. 2, p. 366.

10 'Mr Martin's Pictures and the Bonassus', *CW*, vol. 4, p. 421.

11 Isobel Armstrong, *Victorian Poetry: Poetry, Poetics and Politics* (London: Routledge, 1993), p. 239.

12 Hood would reuse the device of the misspelled letter, authored by a cultural ingénue, in his *Comic Annual* (1830–9) and in *Up the Rhine* (1839).

13 *Odes and Addresses to Great People* (1825), address to the first edition, reprinted in *CW*, vol. 5, p. 21.

14 'Ode to Mr. Graham', *PW*, p. 4.

15 Wordsworth himself suggests the connection between this little boat and a balloon in the first stanza of the prologue to *Peter Bell*. The position of the 'Ode to Mr. Graham' at the beginning of *Odes and Addresses* mirrors the position of Wordsworth's flight as a prologue.

16 'An Address to the Steam Washing Company', *PW*, p. 23. 'Angells' probably means 'anglers' (Hood is, as usual, playing with the literal and figurative possibilities of 'lines'). 'Horse God Meril' perhaps approximates 'horsegod-mother', defined by *OED* as 'a coarse-looking old woman'.

17 Leigh Hunt, 'The Round Table', *The Examiner*, 15 September 1816, pp. 587–9. The essay on washerwomen was reprinted in Hazlitt and Hunt's collection *The Round Table* (Edinburgh: Constable, 1817), where Hood likely read it.

18 Caroline Anne Bowles, 'Letter from a Washerwoman and Poetical Fragments', *Blackwood's Edinburgh Magazine*, 13 (February 1823), pp. 232–8.

19 'Washing By Steam: Letter from a Laundress', *Times*, 15 October 1824, p. 3. See also the article on the 'Patent Steam-Washing Company', *Times*, 17 November 1824, p. 2, which took the side of the company, and Progress, against the washerwomen.

20 By 1828, in Charles Somerset's farce *A Day After the Fair*, the character of the washerwoman displaced by the Steam-Washing Company had become a theatrical 'type'. Polly, the wily maidservant who is trying to get rid of her tiresome new master, impersonates 'Sukey Scrub', who claims to have seventeen children to support. The farce, like Hood's poem, makes the figure of the washerwoman comic, but its sharpest jabs are reserved for the Company. Polly's master tells her not to use 'disrespectful language' against 'the Steam-Washing Company, or any other – how do you know but I might have been one of the directors myself?' Polly replies: 'If you vas, then I should say you're no better than an old vashervoman, too.' The similarities between Hood's monologue and Somerset's farce are telling: both use 'type'

and ostentatious impersonation to represent a topical subject within a framework of established conventions.

21 Moody, *Illegitimate Theatre*, pp. 152–3.

22 Hood, *Atlas*, 6 August 1826, p. 185.

23 Jon Klancher, *The Making of English Reading Audiences 1790–1832* (Madison, Wisconsin: University of Wisconsin Press, 1987), pp. 47–75.

24 My argument here is indebted to Greg Dart, 'Romantic Cockneyism: Hazlitt and the Periodical Press', *Romanticism*, 6 (Autumn 2000), pp. 143–62.

25 Moody, *Illegitimate Theatre*, pp. 193–7.

26 *Comic Annual* (London: Tilt, 1832), p. vii.

27 Preface to *Hood's Own* (1839), reprinted in *CW*, vol. 1, p. viii.

28 J. Fraser, 'Thomas Hood', p. 337. Hood's second, uncompleted, novel, serialized in *Hood's Magazine*, was suggestively entitled *Our Family*.

29 'Don't You Smell Fire?', *PW*, p. 103.

30 *Letters*, p. 225.

31 Hood, 'Domestic Asides; Or, Truth in Parenthesis', *PW*, p. 222.

32 'Ode to Peace', *PW*, p. 296.

33 Hood's line 'Thou human humming-bee, extracting honey / From every blossom in the world that blows' recalls Wordsworth's assertion that 'the meanest flower that blows' can tap the most profound feelings, while Wordsworth's invocation of 'young Lambs bounding' is mirrored in Hood's 'lamb-like frisk', and Wordsworth's encomia ('Thou Child of Joy') are parodied in Hood's repeated ejaculations: 'Thou imp of mirth and joy'.

34 'A Parental Ode', *PW*, p. 483.

35 H.F. Tucker, 'From Monomania to Monologue: "St Simeon Stylites" and the Rise of the Victorian Dramatic Monologue', *Victorian Poetry*, 22 (1984), pp. 121–2.

36 See Armstrong, *Victorian Poetry: Poetry, Poetics and Politics*, p. 13.

37 See Glennis Byron, *Dramatic Monologue* (London: Routledge, 2003), pp. 56–82; Kate Flint, ' "As a Rule, I Does Not Mean I": Personal Identity and the Victorian Woman Poet', in R. Porter (ed.), *ReWriting the Self: Histories from the Renaissance to the Present* (London: Routledge, 1996), pp. 165–6.

38 'The China-Mender', *PW*, p. 452.

39 Of course Tennyson and Browning, too, experimented with comic voice in poems such as 'Northern Farmer: New Style' and 'Mr Sludge, "the Medium" ', but the bias of their conception of dramatic poetry is earnest.

40 E. Warwick Slinn, 'Dramatic Monologue', in Herbert F. Tucker (ed.), *A Companion to Victorian Literature and Culture* (Oxford: Blackwell, 1999), p. 309.

41 Alan Sinfield, *Dramatic Monologue* (London: Methuen, 1977), p. 8.

42 The relationship between complaint and the dramatic monologue is foregrounded by poems like Hood's 'Fragment: Evidently Supposed to be Spoken by Mrs. Reynolds', *PW*, p. 661, an impression of his mother-in-law that, voicing her many public grievances, privately complains about her.

43 Moody, *Illegitimate Theatre*, p. 2.
44 Byron, *Dramatic Monologue*, p. 58.
45 'Our Village: By a Villager', *PW*, pp. 263–4.
46 Sinfield, *Dramatic Monologue*, p. 25.
47 Mark Lemon, *The Sempstress: A Drama* (London: Dick's, 1886).

4

A common centaur: Hood and the grotesque

Tim Turpin he was gravel blind,
  And ne'er had seen the skies:
For Nature, when his head was made,
  Forgot to dot his eyes

So, like a Christmas pedagogue,
  Poor Tim was forc'd to do –
Look out for pupils, for he had
  A vacancy for two . . .

Now Tim he woo'd a servant maid,
  And took her to his arms;
For he, like Pyramus, had cast
  A wall-eye on her charms . . .

But just when Tim had liv'd a month
  In honey with his wife,
A surgeon ope'd his Milton eyes,
  Like oysters, with a knife.

But when his eyes were open'd thus,
  He wish'd them dark again:
For when he look'd upon his wife,
  He saw her very plain.

Her face was bad, her figure worse,
  He couldn't bear to eat:
For she was any thing but like
  A Grace before his meat.

Now Tim he was a feeling man:
  For when his sight was thick,
It made him feel for everything, –
  But that was with a stick.

So with a cudgel in his hand –
  It was not light or slim –

He knocked at his wife's head until
  It open'd unto him.

And when the corpse was stiff and cold,
  He took his slaughter'd spouse,
And laid her in a heap with all
  The ashes of her house.

But like a wicked murderer,
  He liv'd in constant fear
From day to day, and so he cut
  His throat from ear to ear.

The neighbours fetch'd a doctor in:
  Said he, this wound I dread
Can hardly be sew'd up – his life
  Is hanging on a thread.

But when another week was gone,
  He gave him stronger hope –
Instead of hanging on a thread,
  Of hanging on a rope.

Ah! When he hid his bloody work
  In ashes round about,
How little he supposed the truth
  Would soon be sifted out . . .

So he was tried, and he was hung
  (Fit punishment for such)
On Horsham-drop, and none can say
  It was a drop too much.[1]

                    (Hood, 'Tim Turpin: A Pathetic Ballad', 1827)

'Tim Turpin: A Pathetic Ballad', from Hood's first collection of *Whims and Oddities* (1826), is a mordantly funny poem in what became known as his signature style. 'Pathetic Ballad' is a typically ironic subtitle. When Hood announces that Tim was a 'feeling man' – 'but that was with a stick' – the pun captures the ambivalence about 'feeling' that this poem relishes. We know that, humanely, we ought to feel sympathy for the sightless, horror for the homicidal, but the poem allows us, like its protagonist, to be temporarily blind to that mode of 'feeling' and, instead, to relish the violently tactile 'feel' of language: its capacity to knock, to slice, and to drop. The reader, laughing at the smart metrical cut and thrust of the verses and the pay-off of each closing punch-rhyme, is both complicit with the homicidal Tim and with the poem's wry complacency about Tim's final fate. Central to 'Tim Turpin' is a vision of the body that recurs throughout Hood's work: it is grotesque. Lacking pupils, Tim Turpin is but one of numerous characters in Hood's poetry to suffer some kind of physical deformity, from the hapless amputee Ben Battle and the armless warriors in his illustration 'Foot Soldiers' to the one-legged Miss Kilmansegg and the sailor, John Jones, who is bitten in half by a shark. In 'Poem, – From the Polish', a polar explorer writes to his fiancée to warn her: 'I've said that you should have my hand, / Some happy day to come; / But, Kate, you only now can wed / A finger and a thumb.' The unfortunate Mary in 'Mary's Ghost' is likewise obliged to tell her lover that he can't possess her, as her body has been snatched for anatomization: 'I can't tell where my head is gone, / But Doctor Carpue can: / As for my trunk, it's all packed up / To go by Pickford's van.'[2] The body is, like the body of language in Hood's work, forever subject to reconstruction; it also perpetually threatens to become confused with legitimate objects of consumption. Thus, Tim Turpin's 'eyes' (with a hint of a Cockney pun) are opened like 'oysters' with a knife. His wife's body parts become mingled with the ashes of her house, until the dustman complains that there is more 'dust' in the heap than he had been contracted for. Apparently legitimate assaults on the body (surgery, capital punishment) and illegitimate assaults (murder and attempted suicide) succeed and echo each other: the poem's zest derives largely from the breezy equanimity of its treatment of these different kinds of violence and the social and anti-social dimensions of the reader's participation in the poem's own physical breaks and reconstitutions. Grotesque physical combinations (eyes without pupils; body parts amongst household rubbish) and verbal combinations (eyes/oysters) are mirrored in the grotesque mixture of reactions (attraction/revulsion) 'Tim Turpin' solicits.

This chapter will argue that Hood is a primary exponent of the grotesque in the early nineteenth century, and that a closer investigation of Hood's use of the grotesque can help us to understand not only his own work in different genres but also the typicality and topicality of the grotesque idiom in this period. Hood's grotesquerie, which continues to discomfit and confuse commentators, has been a key factor in his critical neglect. Readers have frequently projected the 'whims and oddities' of Hood's verse on to his own figure as an author, choosing to view his grotesquerie as the peculiar vision of a sick man, whose mind had a peculiarly morbid warp. This projection of the grotesque work on to the figure of its author is, as I shall discuss below, a characteristic consequence of the way that grotesque renders boundaries between author, artwork, and reader dangerously fluid: readers' projection of grotesque responds to projection in the idiom. To regard Hood simply as himself a grotesque 'eccentric' figure is, however, to ignore the centrality of nineteenth-century grotesque and the continuity between Hood's work in the grotesque and that of his contemporaries, from Keats to Dickens to Browning. It is, moreover, to ignore the sources, the meanings, and the effects of the grotesque in nineteenth-century aesthetics, particularly the political implications of grotesque play at this time. A contextualized analysis of his grotesque has hitherto been lamentably missing from accounts of Hood; and Hood has been substantively missing from our, still inadequate, accounts of nineteenth-century grotesque. I aim to help to fill these critical lacunae, and also to suggest why they exist – why our trouble with Victorian grotesque and the unresolved matters it represents in its own time are still intricately intertwined.

The word 'grotesque' famously originated in the fifteenth century with the excavation in Italy of rooms of an earlier period, now below street level (hence their description as 'grottoes') decorated with friezes that combined human, animal, and vegetable elements in fantastical hybridized figures. Used in the Renaissance to describe what became a fashion in visual art for fantastic ornamentalism, 'grotesque' came only gradually in the eighteenth and nineteenth centuries to be applied to literary work, and then often as a mode of critique rather than a positive stylistic attribution, a tension that remains in the modern use of 'grotesque' as an adjective. 'The grotesque' eludes definition: the instability of the term recapitulates the instabilities it can identify yet cannot capture. Despite its significant resistance to analysis, however, there is a groundswell of critical agreement about the various attributes that are characteristic of grotesque art. A central characteristic is heterogeneity of elements that resist harmonisation. As Michael Hollington suggests in *Dickens and the Grotesque*: 'grotesque art may be said to be an essentially mixed or hybrid form, like tragicomedy, its elements, in themselves heterogeneous (human forms, animal forms, the natural, the supernatural, the comic, the monstrous and misshapen), combining in unstable, conflicting, paradoxical relationships'.[3] Colin Trodd, Paul Barlow, and David Amigoni, in their introduction to the essay collection *Victorian Culture and the Idea of the Grotesque*, describe the grotesque as an 'aesthetic of the *irreconcilable*'.[4] It bodies forth the disconcerting, the unresolved, the contradictory – frequently muddling the categorical constituents of human, animal, and vegetable; subject and object; man and machine; live and dead; concrete and abstract; male and female; sane and mad; funny and terrifying, the grotesque disregards the classificatory boundaries, rules, and proportionalities of 'normative' human appearance and behaviour.

A second fundamental characteristic of grotesque art is its preoccupation with the body. It is typically somatic and graphic, evoking a pre-rational, visceral reaction in its viewers that makes them conscious of their own existence as physical entities. According to Mikhail Bakhtin, the great celebrant of medieval and Renaissance grotesque, this rude emphasis on the primal is levelling and liberating. Bound up with the carnivalesque revelry of feast days and subversive reassertion of pagan motifs within a Christian society, the grotesque, in Bakhtin's view, with its excessive, endlessly fecund images of ingestion, digestion, and excretion, re-establishes human connection with natural cycles of birth, death, and regeneration, bringing the human literally back 'down to earth' and joyfully reclaiming a sense of communal life denied by the rigidity of hierarchical social forms.[5] The grotesque is frequently, however, also associated with disquiet and self-alienation. Wolfgang Kayser's much darker view of grotesque, coloured by the atrocities of the Second World War, identifies in it a primitive horror of demonic powers within and beyond man that cannot be controlled, but merely invoked in the quasi-magical attempt temporarily to disarm them.[6] Bernard McElroy is among those modern commentators who relate the grotesque to the Freudian 'uncanny'.[7] Often populated by doubles, whose relationship to the 'self' is porous, the wild and violent energies of the grotesque, in this reading, become symptomatic of personal and cultural repressions. The idea of the grotesque as a form of displaced energy originates in the nineteenth century: it is central to Ruskin's famous dictum in *The Stones of Venice* (1851) that in the grotesque 'the mind, under certain phases of excitement, *plays* with *terror*', a process characteristic of the nineteenth-century mechanical labourer, whose alienation from dehumanizing work finds release in a mode of play that mimics its compulsively generative activity.[8]

All of these readings of grotesque – as an aesthetic of irreducible heterogeneity, as play that temporarily subverts hierarchical order, as paralysing anxiety displaced into creative hyperactivity – are potentially illuminating for an understanding of Hood's work. Verbally, generically, and formally his work is crowded and fascinated with unstable mixtures, from the camelopard to the centaur, the learned pig to the talking ghost, the comic 'pathetic' to the multiple pun. Mobility and uncertainty, with all of their middle-class ramifications, are a stock in trade of his performative work. Much in Hood's work answers to a Bakhtinian conception of carnivalesque subversion, pointedly popular, and indebted to ancient traditions of levelling play. Yet a darker seam is also present: the evident and latent violence in much of Hood's grotesquerie suggests energies inscribed in play, in the plasticity and proliferation of thoughts, forms, words, whose recurrent and immoderate shape-shifting resembles the symptoms of terror and anger. In some of Hood's best poems ('The Dream of Eugene Aram', 'The Dead Robbery',

'Miss Kilmansegg and Her Precious Leg') repressed violence returns via obsessive grotesque recurrence.

Perversely but significantly, both Bakhtin and Kayser regarded the Victorian era as a period of decline in grotesque art.[9] Their equal determination to define grotesque vitality as eroded by Victorian values suggests the extent to which the grotesque presented by the Victorian per se was a repressed force in early twentieth-century criticism. Some excellent work has been done in the last twenty years on the Victorian grotesque, but much remains to be said. Michael Hollington's *Dickens and the Grotesque* is extremely valuable and I draw on it here. Isobel Armstrong's chapters on William Morris and Gerard Manley Hopkins in *Victorian Poetry: Poetry, Poetics, Politics* set a new standard for reading the politics of grotesque poetry. Chris Snodgrass and Linda Gertner Zetlin have produced excellent recent studies of Aubrey Beardsley's, and Virgina Swain of Baudelaire's, grotesquerie. Most existing studies of nineteenth-century grotesque, however, concentrate on individual authors and on work after 1840. Trodd, Barlow, and Amigoni's rich and rewarding collection of essays, *Victorian Culture and the Idea of the Grotesque* (1999), which has informed my work on Hood, fruitfully examines grotesque within an interdisciplinary cultural context: but its coverage is deliberately eclectic. As the introduction states: 'we have tried . . . to do justice to our subject by resisting some of its most obvious manifestations: [such as] Hood's use of the grotesque "comic-vernacular" in the popular literature of the 1830s.'[10]

Since it is such an 'obvious manifestation' of nineteenth-century grotesque – Michael Hollington rightly notes that 'if one figure can be said to create and disseminate the taste for the grotesque in the 1830s it is Thomas Hood'[11] – it is all the more remarkable that Hood's work has never been formally examined by a modern critic in terms of the grotesque tradition. Hood himself described his 'Good Genius' as a 'Pantagruelian familiar', which conjured up diverting 'Grotesques, and Arabesques and droll Picturesques'.[12] Edgar Allan Poe, whose 1840 *Tales of the Grotesque and Arabesque* helped to popularize the concept of the grotesque, argued that it was in his 'species of brilliant *grotesquerie*, uttered with a rushing *abandon* which wonderfully aided its effect, that Hood's marked originality of manner consisted; and . . . which fairly entitles him, at times, to the epithet "great" '.[13] Henry Chorley, in a review of 1838, named the grotesque as the particular medium in which Hood's 'fancy expatiates' and, citing Victor Hugo's celebrated comments on the grotesque in his preface to *Cromwell*, compared Hood with Hugo himself.[14] John Ruskin cited Hood's work, with that of George Cruikshank and Alfred Rethel, as an example of the 'bitter, or pathetic spirit of grotesque to which mankind at the present day owe more thorough moral teaching than to any branch of art whatever'.[15] Yet we have been slow to acknowledge and contextualize Hood's grotesque art, projecting instead uneasiness about the content of his poetry and illustration on to the figure of the artist, who is often denigrated as morbid, vulgar, and even 'sick'. John Heath-Stubbs expresses ill-concealed disgust at the unnerving effect of Hood's treatment of 'painful' subjects in humorous terms:

> I doubt if any sensitive person can now read Hood's humorous [poems] with much pleasure . . . Their subjects are, in fact, often painful. Frustrated spinsters, deserted maidens, ghosts, cannibalism . . . And this sort of thing, I believe, came in with the frayed nerves of Tom Hood. The little illustrations, rather horridly grotesque, which embellish the original Annuals, go with the verses all too well.[16]

Heath-Stubbs's visceral distaste extends even to the bindings of Hood's volumes, which he recalls as 'peculiarly hideous'.[17] Ian Jack, like Heath-Stubbs, reacts negatively to the combination of comic treatment and potentially tragic matter in Hood's work, ascribing this to something aberrant in Hood's personality:

> Hood was a splendid human being, but we must not let our admiration for his courage blind us to the curious and unpleasant qualities that often appear in his verse. There is something sinister about his sense of humour: his pages are thronged with comic mourners and undertakers, and a corpse is always good for a horse-laugh. The nightmares of his imagination often burst out, like a skeleton falling from a cupboard.[18]

Readings of individual poems have likewise been marked by aversion, a critique that recoils from ambivalent treatment of horrible subjects as itself 'horrid'. Fiona Stafford follows A.J. Sanbrook in characterizing Hood's brilliantly grotesque poem 'The Last Man' as 'nothing but a sick joke'.[19]

Projection of the grotesque, by commentators, on to the figure of its author is not confined to Hood. John Carey's otherwise brilliant account of Dickens in *The Violent Effigy* is marred only by the book's treatment of Dickens's grotesquerie as if it were chiefly a matter of personality: Dickens becomes, in Carey's study, himself a *lusus naturae*, buzzing with uncontrollable, conflicted energies; the cultural ambience of grotesque in which Dickens was working is largely ignored.[20] Such projection is not coincidental. Projection is fundamental to the activity entailed in the grotesque text. The collapse of secure distinctions between subject and object, between that which acts and that which is acted upon, gives the grotesque its peculiar power. In the case of the grotesque artwork itself, its displaced energies forever threaten to spill outward: unable to be resolved or contained on the page, the aesthetic of the irreconcilable conveys its contradictions to the reader, who mirrors, in his or her disconcerted response, the unsettled expression before them and becomes likely, in turn, to project grotesque ambivalence back on to the text and its author. The permeable screen between subject and object in grotesque art is also necessarily a permeable screen between author, artwork, and reader. The grotesque text thus threatens to effect the magical logic about which it so often speaks: it threatens to reveal the reader as himself or herself grotesque. A reader of *The Old Curiosity Shop*, viewing, with pleasure yet apprehension, the picture of Nell asleep surrounded by antique curiosities, may wax *curious*, akin to the overwrought suits of armour in the picture. If you leer at Mr Lear, you yourself become leary, and others may leer at you. The two-way mirror implied by grotesque is crucial to its demotic force: the reader of the grotesque is always implicated in the work; the form countenances no boundaries as absolute, no body as safe. This potentially violent threat inherent in the idiom, as much as in its specific content, helps explain why Hood's work has troubled readers from Henry Crabb Robinson to William Rossetti, Edmund Blunden to J.C. Reid. Blunden, reviewing Hood's drawings and engravings remarked that 'this gentle spirit, viewed through these spectacles, is a monster'.[21] It is tempting, punningly, to look through the monstrous 'spectacles' of grotesque art and view the author as a monster, but to do so is to refract rather than to interrogate the grotesque. The sections that follow seek to trace sources, analogues, and contexts for Hood's grotesque writing and illustration and to consider their implications.

The grotesque tradition in the early nineteenth century

Hood's grotesquerie, like that of many of his contemporaries, bears strong traces of a long inheritance of visual and verbal work in the grotesque tradition. Two rich and related sources of grotesque imagery in Hood's writing are the realm of cheap traditional literature, including ballad and fairy tale, woodcut and emblem book, and the realm of fairground, pageant, and pantomime: the carnivalesque as manifested in nineteenth-century popular culture.

As we have seen, Hood was born and spent his first years in the Poultry, in the heart of the City of London. Smithfield, the site of the rowdy Bartholomew Fair, was within easy walking distance. Contemporary fairground exhibits included the 'Sicilian' dwarf, Caroline Cachrami; Patrick O'Byrne the Irish Giant; the Invisible Girl; Toby, the

Learned Pig; and the St James's Street Mermaid. Guildhall, the starting-point each year of the Lord Mayor's Show, a pageant dating from 1215, was only a stone's throw away. Each May Day saw a parade of chimney-sweeps, dressed in their traditional costume; among them would be a dancing character whose body was wholly concealed by a wicker frame covered in branches and green leaves: the 'Jack-in-the-Green'. All of these carnivalesque events and characters feature in Hood's writing. When, in September 1831, Hood's sister-in-law, Marianne Reynolds, married Henry Green, Hood commemorated the event with a mischievous drawing, in which Henry is represented as a Jack-in-the-Green, while his new wife is literally turning Green as the ceremony proceeds (Fig. 4.1).[22] Hood's unmarried sister-in-law Charlotte, meanwhile, is depicted with a hook instead of a hand, probably for catching herself a husband. Her shadow is that of a devil with a pitchfork. Hood himself, identified by his initials, stands behind the altar, apparently sipping the communion wine. Like the mock-priest of a medieval parody mass, Hood, in the picture, transforms the participants in the wedding into

SKETCH BY HOOD TO CELEBRATE THE MARRIAGE OF
MARIANE REYNOLDS

4.1 Hood, sketch of the wedding of Marianne Reynolds to
H.G. Green (1831)

irreverent visual emblems. The presence of the Jack-in-the-Green and other grotesque elements in this private sketch suggests the extent to which such motifs in Hood's writing and illustration draw on traditional imagery still visible in the street life of nineteenth-century London.

Both Hood and Dickens were fervent admirers of the famous clown Joseph Grimaldi, whose retirement from the stage in 1823, in Hood's words, 'seem'd to beat / A muffled drum for Fun's retreat'. Dickens wrote a biography of Grimaldi; wherever he went, Hood kept a picture of the clown on his study wall.[23] Grimaldi's routines, deriving from *commedia dell'arte*, were grotesque in a manner that Bakhtin would surely recognize as consistent with the Rabelaisian tradition.[24] Hood's 'Ode to Joseph Grimaldi' gives a detailed picture of aspects of the act that involved physical contortion and extraordinary consumption:

Ah, where is now thy rolling head!
Thy winking, reeling, *drunken* eyes . . .
Thy oven-mouth, that swallow'd pies –
Enormous hunger – monstrous drowth!
Thy pockets greedy as thy mouth![25]

Hood's style, not only in his poetic tribute to Grimaldi but in general, is indebted to the mode of performance in which Grimaldi was working: active, exuberant, excessive, relishing contortion, surprise, peculiarity. The *London Magazine*, reviewing Hood's second volume of *Whims and Oddities*, recognized the similarity: 'We are glad to see Mr Hood once more at the door of his show, for we love to see him play his word-catching antics . . . He is the Grimaldi of literature – makes faces, walks upon his head, and paints black and white.'[26]

Hood had written his own pantomime, *Harlequin and Mr Jenkins*, and knew intimately the conventions associated with Harlequin's amorality, his adult childishness, his visual tricks with a wide variety of props. One of Grimaldi's famous tricks involved constructing a human figure from vegetables. Hood, for this feat of animating the inanimate, humorously compares Joe Grimaldi to 'Joe Frankenstein', an analogy that creatively links different kinds of grotesque composition.[27] Between the 1820s and the 1830s, at the same time as he was producing comic verse, Hood supplied captions for a couple of sets of etchings entitled *Comic Composites for the Scrap Book*. Each of the drawings in these sets illustrates a different profession: the gardener, the carpenter, the grocer, and so on. In each case the physiognomy of the figure is a collage of articles of trade associated with that profession.[28] The face of the grocer is produced from a mortar and pestle (the latter acting as the nose), a screw of tea (the eye), candles and other comestibles (Fig. 4.2).

4.2 'The Grocer' (1834), with a caption by Hood

Hood's caption reads 'Frankenstein wanted to make man, and so, Sir, / He tried his first attempt upon a Grocer!' The face of the artist is formed of brushes, paints, palette, and sketchbooks. Hood's caption reads 'On mind and matter there has been great schism / And here's the doctrine of MATERIALism'. Neatly, Hood's play on the idea of matter's primacy is expressed through a medium where objects have 'become' subjects. The *Comic Composites* incarnate the energetic commerce of the town, where things, like the old clothes in Dickens's literary sketch 'Meditations in Monmouth Street' (1836) take on the life and identity of persons. They also, however, resemble the grotesque portraits of Giuseppe Arcimboldo, which were painted in the 1590s. Arcimboldo, who had worked as a designer of elaborate pageants for the Habsburgs, drew on that culture of emblem and visual pun to produce composite faces including a gardener made of vegetables and a cook made of kitchen utensils. *Comic Composites for the Scrap Book* is recognizably a nineteenth-century production, but visually it quotes a Renaissance tradition in grotesque art. It provides a helpful context in which to read Hood's own 'Fancy Portraits' in the *Comic Annual*, where, for example, the author George Crabbe is portrayed as a crustacean, and 'Captain Head' becomes a monstrous limbless cranium on horseback. 'Fancy Portraits' of this kind, involving grotesque visual punning, were a common feature of early nineteenth-century comic magazines.

As a trained engraver, who favoured woodcut, Hood was highly conscious of the language of visual symbol and metaphor present in many forms of popular, traditional publication: folk tales, cheap prints, political cartoons, chapbooks, emblem books. Quarles's *Emblems*, with their frequently grotesque illustrations were first published in 1635, but emblem books remained popular devotional texts throughout the eighteenth and early nineteenth centuries. Quarles's *Emblems* was one of the 'pet books' of Robert Browning's childhood. Hood twice refers – once in an early theatre review for the *Atlas* and again in *Tylney Hall* (1834) – to one of Francis Quarles's emblems, which clearly had a significant impact upon him.[29] The emblem is the illustration to the text 'Oh wretched man that I am! Who shall deliver me from the body of this death?', which literalizes the Biblical lines by depicting, in Hood's words, 'a little figure of a man enclosed within the ribs of a gigantic skeleton, like a bird in a cage' (Fig. 4.3).

The grinning skeleton, which props its head on its hand, resembles many of the skeleton figures of Death in Hood's woodcuts.[30] Again, Hood's vivid recollection of this image from Quarles suggests the roots of his own grotesque iconography in much earlier literature. He was not alone in reworking such early sources. Interest in Hans Holbein's famous series of admonitory woodcuts the *Dance of Death* revived strongly in the early nineteenth century. As Michael Hollington has shown, Dickens aged eleven borrowed the *Dance of Death* from a Soho booksellers; he returned to consult it in the early 1830s at the British Museum, and in 1841 purchased a dissertation on the *Dance of Death* written by the antiquarian and republican Francis Douce in 1833; vignettes from the Dance of Death appear in *Nicholas Nickleby*, *Dombey and Son*, and *The Old Curiosity Shop*. Thomas Rowlandson produced an English *Dance of Death* (1814–16) stylistically influenced by Hogarth, in which Death appeared in modern contexts such as an anatomy lesson. The engraver Richard Dagley's compilation of verse interleaved with illustration, *Death's Doings* (1826), dedicated to Douce, contained the

ROM. VII. 24.

*O wretched man that I am ! who shall deliver me
from the body of this death ?*

4.3 Francis Quarles, 'O wretched man that I am! who shall deliver me from
the body of this death'. Quarles's *Emblems, Divine and Moral* are a
prominent influence on Hood's grotesque

skeleton figure of Death appearing in a variety of modern settings
including a life assurance office, a boxing ring, and a cricket match.
The second edition of *Death's Doings* (1827) included Hood's 'The
Volunteer'. Seeing his poetry in this context underlines the extent to
which the skeletons, which Ian Jack imagines tumbling from the closet
of Hood's 'sinister' imagination, are part of a shared language of gro-
tesque with deep roots in popular culture (Fig. 4.4).

Tom Hood's biography of his father notes that, when Hood experi-
mented with oil painting in the 1830s, he produced a sketch of 'Death
and the Little Girl' – the traditional figure of Death in a churchyard
with a child resting on his knee, which he intended to be the subject of
a future poem.[31] Given his personal interest in 'Death and the Maiden',
it is unsurprising that, when Hood reviewed Dickens's *Master
Humphrey's Clock*, he acutely divined that the key to the work lay in

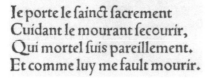

Ie porte le fainct facrement
Cuidant le mourant fecourir,
Qui mortel fuis pareillement.
Et comme luy me fault mourir.

4.4 Hans Holbein, 'The Pastor' from *The Dance of Death* (1538), and Hood, ' "Dust O!" ' (1827)

its iconography, remarking that the image of Little Nell 'surrounded, or rather mobbed, by ancient armour and arms, antique furniture and relics sacred and profane, hideous or grotesque' was like an Allegory of the purity of childhood beset by Violence, Superstition, and Passion.[32] Dickens echoes this analysis in his own account of Nell, beset by fantastical wares existing 'in a kind of allegory', in his preface to *The Old Curiosity Shop*, a fact that suggests that Hood's perceptive interpretation affected Dickens's reworking and understanding of the project.[33] Hood's emblematic and allegorical grotesque is often so similar to Dickens's (compare, for example, Hood's 'Bianca's Dream' and 'The Lady's Dream' with Dickens's *A Christmas Carol*) because both are drawing on a shared inheritance of traditional work in the grotesque idiom, often with a memento mori theme.

Various factors may be held responsible for reawakening interest in grotesque forms of popular satire and moralitas between the 1820s and the 1840s. This period of intense postwar urban expansion made the city, especially, appear an inchoate, unresolved space: itself a model of grotesque vitality battening on the bodies of its inhabitants. Death appears in Hood's poetry as a soldier, firing coffins out of a cannon, but also as a dust merchant, collecting citizens' remains for resale. Overcrowded graveyards and the trade in body parts (hair for wigs, teeth for dentures, bones for fertilizer) and in whole corpses for anatomization all served to highlight the extent to which a modern economy involved living off others' loss. The *London Magazine*'s diary for May 1827 reported the 'shocking case' of an apothecary who, by the subterfuge of complaining about the smell of a corpse he had attended, secured permission to seal it up, which afforded him the opportunity to pursue his real aim of stealing one of its eyes, substituting that of a sheep. The widow, however, detected the imposition when, kissing her husband's face one last time, the false eye rolled out. The widow was seized with convulsions and the apothecary was forced to return the eye, producing one, however, of a different colour.[34] Whether this particular story is true or not, the *London Magazine*'s inclusion of it in its diary of recent events highlights the type of grotesquerie that was part not only of the imaginative literature of these years but of quotidian city life. G.A. Walker in *Gatherings from Grave Yards* (1839), which addressed the sanitary crisis of overflowing inner-city cemeteries, told of a girl who had recognized her mother's finger in a pile of rubbish.[35] Meanwhile, an expanding funeral industry, like other industries in this era, developed its own department stores: Jay's Mourning Warehouse, which opened in 1841, followed by competitors, likely inspired Hood's 1844 prose dialogue 'The House of Mourning: A Farce', in which a curious visitor discovers the delights of the Intermediate Sorrow Department and considers fabrics entitled 'The Inconsolable' and 'The Luxury of Woe'.[36]

Political factors also influence the prominence of the grotesque in this period. Victor Hugo's 1827 preface to his play *Cromwell*, which Henry Chorley would cite, in 1838, as an analogue to Hood's work, declares that grotesque is the 'new type', comedy the 'new form', that characterize modern art. Where ancient art was preoccupied with ideals of beauty and following formal models, Hugo asserts, modern art is free and frank in its capacity to explore the hundreds of shapes, the thousands of peculiar combinations, in which human and aesthetic form are manifest. *Cromwell*, himself an arch-grotesque, is rehabilitated in Hugo's reading as 'a complex, many-sided being, a combination of contrary elements, of many evils combined with many good qualities'.[37] The grotesque is connected by association with political revolution, and with democratic freedom to disestablish governing regimes, in life and art, that restrict representation. Thomas Wright's *A History of Caricature and Grotesque in Literature and Art* would also positively link the growth of grotesque to that of effective political criticism and hence political reform: 'the popular reformers have always been the first to appreciate the value of pictorial satire as an offensive weapon. Such was the case with the German reformers in the age of Luther; as it was again with the English reformers in the days of Charles I'.[38] Hood, too, made this connection, asserting that Rabelais was a more effective critic of papist abuses than contemporary churchmen.[39] Monstrosity, as Chris Baldick has shown,[40] was a common figure in this period for the threat of revolution: multitudinous, uncontainable, fascinating, and frightening; in Radical hands the awakening giant or dancing skeleton became warnings to the rich of the levelling power of mortality and the dormant, but still live, threat of popular violence. Although Hood's poems eschew overt political threat, the violence that occurs within them is an exercise of power, in which the reader is permitted to participate, that continually conveys the possibility of change and overthrow.

Outside Guildhall, in the nineteenth century, stood the fourteen-foot-high figures of two giants, known as Gog and Magog. These giant figures had in the Renaissance been carried aloft in great civic processions such as the Lord Mayor's Show. Amongst the songs that Hood wrote in the late 1820s for the comedian Charles Mathews', theatrical performances, is 'Gog and Magog: A Guildhall Duet' in which the two Guildhall Giants complain that they have never been invited inside to dine with the Mayor and aldermen:

> MAGOG
> They said, a Hundred Years ago,
>   That we should dine at One;
> Why, Gog I say, our meat by this
>   Is rather over-done.
>
> GOG
> I do not want it done at all,
>   So hungry is my maw,
> Give me an Alderman in chains,
>   And I will eat him raw![41]

Hood here uses the traditional figures of the giants to voice a mildly provocative complaint. The City of London and its functionaries were widely accused of overconsumption and protectionism: from lavish dinners to lavish taxes upon the goods destined for Greater London, whose distribution they controlled. The giant's traditional cannibalistic desire allows the expression of violent threat within a context of humour and fantasy, a pattern common in Hood's grotesque writing.

Frederick Fairholt in his 1859 history of the Giants in Guildhall, lamented that few people now knew their origins or what they represented. The Giants were, Fairholt explained, a reminder to the monarch of the limits of his power. Fairholt, like Hood born into the book trade, was helped in preparing his history of the Guildhall Giants by the radical publisher William Hone, who had conducted his own research on the subject and had in 1823 employed George Cruikshank to draw the Giants. These connections illustrate the extent to which Hood's interest in grotesque figures, such as Gog and Magog, was based on local encounter with a visual tradition dating from the Renaissance (the Guildhall is a stone's throw from Hood's birthplace), but also the political context for antiquarian interest in reviving knowledge of these emblems of popular power. The giants, like the people of the City of London, deign to abide by the authority of the law and the Crown: their grotesque size, strength, and wildness, however, are held in check only by tacit compromise.

Fairholt's book is nostalgic. The pageants of many medieval cities were in decline. He reported that, whereas in Salisbury, in 1814, he had seen a giant exhibited in the street 'attended by two men grotesquely habited bearing his sword and club', by the 1840s the Salisbury giant, a structure of lath and hoop that allowed a man to walk inside, was 'mouldering to decay' in a warehouse.[42] Literary interest in the grotesque carnivalesque in the early nineteenth century is also attributable to perception of its gradual decline as a feature of street life. An Act of 1834 forbade chimney-sweeps to call or hawk in the streets, an ordinance bewailed by Hood, who foresaw an end to the May Day processions. In 1843 Bartholomew Fair was relocated from Smithfield to a suburban site where it dwindled and died. The 'rushing abandon' of Hood's and Dickens's grotesquerie arises in an era of increasing state control of public spaces used for popular entertainment: their work can be viewed as a translation from the public stage to the public page of many of the carnivalesque qualities traditionally belonging to pantomime, pageant, street-ballad, and other forms of public performance.[43]

Thackeray, reflecting in 1840 'On the Genius of George Cruikshank', noted that Cruikshank's genius lay in the grotesque, and compared him with Harlequin. Such a vision however, he lamented was no longer fashionable. Children and adults, Thackeray reminisces, used to gather around the booksellers' shops, such as Hone's and Knight's: 'there used to be a crowd round the window in those days of grinning, good-natured mechanics, who spelt the songs, and spoke them for the benefit of the company, and who received the points of humour with a general sympathizing roar. Where are these people now? You never hear any laughing at H.B. [Hablot Browne]; his pictures are a great deal too genteel for that.'[44] Thackeray identifies the grotesque in the 1820s and 1830s with a popular oral/visual culture that he regarded, by 1840, as already on the wane. An important aspect of grotesque aesthetics in Hood as in Dickens and Cruikshank is that they consciously hark back to cultural products from earlier eras less alarmed by the commonality implied by 'low' comedy. Alongside the popular forms discussed above, the works of Rabelais, Swift, Sterne, and Hogarth are among those products.

Hood and Dickens, with Thackeray and George Cruikshank, were present at a dinner of the Antiquarian Society in 1842 where Cruikshank gave a celebrated after-dinner rendition of 'The Loving Ballad of Lord Bateman' in the earthy style of a street-ballad singer, which led to Cruikshank publishing an illustrated version of this ancient song. Hood, like Dickens, was brought up in a cultural economy where ballads were a staple of the literary diet; by the 1840s, the ubiquity of the ballad stall and ballad singer were perceived to be in decline, fit subjects for revival at a dinner of nostalgic 'antiquarians'. Many of the grotesque images in Hood's blackly comic ballads have their origins in traditional broadside narratives. 'Mary's Ghost', who announces that her body has been anatomized by body-snatchers, is a contemporary version of 'William and Mary', a ballad about a dead lover who returns to haunt his erstwhile partner; 'Sally Simpkin's Lament', where the unfortunate John Jones is bitten in half by a shark, is a comic treatment of the ballad of 'Bryan and Pereene'. Both 'William and Mary' and 'Bryan and Pereene' appear in Percy's *Reliques*. Another of Hood's grotesque poems about body-snatching, 'Jack Hall', also has roots in traditional street-ballad that have not previously been recognized. 'Jack Hall' is clearly a pun on 'jackal' – body-snatchers are the flesh-eaters of the urban jungle – yet it also seems significant that the real Jack Hall was a thief who, after several celebrated escapes from the gallows, was hanged at Tyburn in 1707. Famously, he 'died game', and the combative spirit toward authority that he maintained to the end made him the subject of various eighteenth-century popular representations: memoirs, a puppet show, and an anti-authoritarian ballad, which survived, under various guises, in the oral tradition until the 1840s.[45] Hood, in making 'Jack Hall' his body-snatching protagonist of 1827, was drawing on a very old broadside legend and giving it a new urban twist. Certain elements of the robber hero survive in Hood's Jack Hall, who, like his folk ancestor, proves evasive when the time comes for reckoning with his life. Tempted by the prospect of double and triple mortgages on his mortal frame, he sells his own body to science several times and dies leaving twelve doctors wrangling over his corpse, which mysteriously disappears during their altercations. Grotesque elements in 'Jack Hall', then, as in so many of Hood's other poems and illustrations, can be traced to popular motifs over two centuries old. This is not to say that Hood's grotesque is identical with that of earlier periods – the uses to which Hood and Dickens put traditional grotesque imagery point up the particular commercial and social proliferations and anxieties of their own time. But the fact that grotesque imagery involves a return to older iconography is significant. As McElroy among others has argued,[46] psychologically the grotesque implies 'the return of the repressed'; Hood's grotesque draws power from the fact that its iconography is itself often a form of return, to popular sources in street theatre and street literature increasingly marginalized and repressed by the industrialization and gentrification of the metropolis.

'In the Husk of a Brute Eternally Inhumed': Hood and the boundaries of the human

Hood's preoccupation with the grotesque is a feature of his work from his earliest contributions to the *London Magazine* to late poems such as 'The Elm Tree: A Dream in the Woods', and 'Miss Kilmansegg and Her Precious Leg'. Although German influences – notably works by Goethe, Schiller, and the illustrator Moritz Retzsch – do permeate Hood's grotesque vision, particularly after his residence in Germany, the tenor of his interest in the continuity and interchangeability of organic forms was set early. 'The Apparition' (*Comic Annual*, 1831), a Tayside tale almost certainly gleaned from Hood's childhood visits to Dundee, describes a wake held for a dead ferryman. Mourners watch, transfixed with horror, as the corpse begins to move: when the grave clothes are thrown aside, the source of the movement is revealed to be a crab, which has presumably been feeding on the dead body. In the end the crab itself is killed, dressed, and eaten. A joke played by Hood on his friends, the Dilkes, in 1833 featured a letter written as if from 'LP', a poor female committing her child to the Dilkes' care, lamenting that she had eleven offspring with only straw to lie on and no prospects.[47] The letter was followed by a sucking pig. Hood's edible infant falls somewhere on the grotesque continuum between Swift's 'Modest Proposal' and Carroll's pig-baby. Both these narratives delight in temporary uncertainty regarding the boundary between human and brute, subject and object. This debatable land is vital to the territory of Hood's writing and can enable us to draw illuminating connections between examples of his work in different periods, diverse forms, and apparently disparate genres.

In Hood's work the line between 'man' and 'beast' is permeable. From an early period Hood was intrigued by the concept of metempsychosis:

the doctrine that souls transmigrate from one body to another, regardless of whether that body is human or animal. The corollary of human participation in a cycle of consumption is that humans, too, are liable in one way or another to be translated into something other than 'themselves'. Hood's poetry returns again and again to the frightening yet fascinating possibilities of such metamorphosis. Thomas Griffiths Wainewright, fellow contributor to the *London Magazine*, described Hood in the early 1820s as 'our new Ovid'.[48] Many of Hood's early poems involve quasi-Ovidian metamorphoses. In 'The Two Peacocks of Bedfont' (1822) a pair of haughty sisters find themselves transformed into a pair of peacock-shaped yew trees. In 'The Two Swans: A Fairy Tale' (1824) a princely youth is rescued from a tower, which is wrapped in the folds of an enormous serpent, by his lover, who has taken the form of a swan. The two escape as swans, only to be changed, once they reach safety, into 'a gentle girl and boy'. In Hood's version of 'Hero and Leander' (1827) it is the sea-nymph Scylla, a character whose namesake in Ovid suffers the grotesque transformation of her lower body into a whirlpool of barking dogs, who lures Leander down to his death. And in 'Lycus the Centaur' (1822), the finest of Hood's early narrative poems, another Ovidian metamorphosis dooms the human Lycus to live a monstrous half-life as a centaur in a nightmare world where animals and even trees seem to contain trapped human flesh. Still earlier in his poetic career Hood had attempted a dramatization of Keats's *Lamia*, in Hood's description 'an Enchantress, by nature a serpent, but now under the disguise of a beautiful woman'.[49] Hood's reworking, though uneven in quality and apparently unfinished, is interesting for its departures from Keats, not least its translation of Keats's narrative poem into a drama, a development that demands literal interpretation of hybrid forms and metamorphoses, which Keats allows to remain purely figurative. Whereas in Keats's version of *Lamia* the climactic scene involves Lamia translating back into her loathly serpentine state under the searching gaze of the philosopher Apollonius, in Hood's version the violent climactic scene involves Lamia stabbing her lover's friend, Mercutius, who has come to expose and, it appears, to rape her. As he threatens Lamia, Mercutius tells her that she can blame herself for invoking the beast in him, which is a reflection of that in her:

> As it works 'twas wrought on – look – say what I am,
> For I have no recognisance of myself.
> Am I wild beast or man – civil or savage –
> Reasoning or brutal – or gone utter mad –
> So am I as thou turned me . . .
> I know not what I am – nor how I am,

But by thy own enforcement – come to force thee,
Being passion-mad.[50]

Both Keats's and Hood's *Lamia*s conjure up the grotesque sexual threat and promise of 'losing oneself'. But where Keats's poem explores the relationship between illusion and desire, art and life, poetry and philosophy, Hood's is more concerned with the relationship between man and animal. The inverted sexual climax, where Lamia 'stings' and causes Mercutius's death, is energized by the force field she creates whereby others cannot distinguish their own agency and desire from hers: customary distinctions between subject and object, and between human and animal dissolve. One phrase appears almost identically in both 'Lycus the Centaur' and 'The Two Swans': 'imprison me quite in the husk of a brute' / 'in gross husks of brutes eternally inhumed'. The narrative in all these poems concerns the human beguiled and captured by a passion that results in its transformation into the non-human. The metamorphoses, indeed, literalize the possibility that human and animal are separated only by self-perception:

There were woes of all shapes, wretched forms, when I came,
That hung down their heads with a human-like shame;
The elephant hid in the boughs, and the bear
Shed over his eyes the dark veil of his hair;
And the womanly soul turning sick with disgust,
Tried to vomit herself from her serpentine crust . . .

Then rose a wild sound of the human voice choking
Through vile brutal organs – low tremulous croaking;
Cries swallow'd abruptly – deep animal tones
Attun'd to strange passion, and full-utter'd groans
All shuddering weaker, till hush'd in a pause
Of tongues in mute motion and wide-yearning jaws.[51]

The human voice in 'Lycus the Centaur', here groaning in a parody of orgasm, is 'wild' in a double sense: it is both agonized by alienation from society and naturally savage. The poem adds a grotesque dimension to Circe's realm which is not in Ovid and which Hood seems to have borrowed from Dante's *Inferno*, Canto XIII: when Lycus tries to eat an apple, he finds that the fruit is in fact 'flesh at the core' and that by daylight his fingers are 'crimson'd with gore'; his attempts to feed himself are thus revealed as violent and cannibalistic. The terrible suspicion that underlies this guilty horror is that there are no secure hierarchies between organic forms, which suffer equally. Lycus is a 'monster', alien to animals and to humans, occupying the perpetual grotesque twilight of irreconcileable yet connected states. His misery at the fear and loathing he inspires even in a child recalls the similarly pathetic isolation of Frankenstein's monster and raises similar questions about what 'makes man'. Circe's kingdom realizes a truth that Hood's urban poetry also explores: all bodies are equally fissile, corruptible, consumable, merging at some stage into other bodies via a process they cannot control; the human organism has no immunity from the life that surrounds it.

'Lycus the Centaur', like 'The Two Peacocks of Bedfont' and 'Hero and Leander', was reprinted in Hood's volume of 'serious' verse *The Plea of the Midsummer Fairies* (1827) in the same year that he published his second solo volume of 'comic' verse, *Whims and Oddities*. At first glance these books of poetry may seem to have little in common with each other. Yet, considered as excursions into the grotesque, they exhibit striking similarities. *Whims and Oddities* contains 'Pythagorean Fancies', a prose piece in which the narrator confesses:

> Of all creeds – after the Christian – I incline most to the Pythagorean. I like the notion of inhabiting the body of a bird . . . For a beast-body I have less relish – and yet how many men are there who seem predestined to such an occupancy, being in this life even more than semibrutal! How many human faces that at least countenance, if they do not confirm, this part of the Brahminical Doctrine. What apes, foxes, pigs, curs, and cats, walk our metropolis – to say nothing of him shambling along Carnaby or Whitechapel –

A BUTCHER!
Whoe'er has gone thro' London Street,
Has seen a Butcher gazing at his meat,
  And how he keeps
  Gloating upon a sheep's
Or bullock's personals, as if his own;
  How he admires his halves,
  And quarters – and his calves,
As if in truth upon his own legs grown; –
  His fat! *His* suet!
His kidneys peeping elegantly thro' it!
  His thick flank!
  And *his* thin!
    His shank!
    His shin!
Skin of his skin, and bone too of his bone![52]

Like Lycus the Centaur, Hood's butcher becomes a composite creature, a semi-brutal biped-quadruped. The ambiguous construction of 'his' allows the calves and shins he displays to signify both the butcher's

4.5 Hood's doodles and 'Unconscious Imitation' (1827)

body and the animal bodies he sells. Hood goes on, in 'Pythagorean Fancies', to present the figures of a camel-driver who has come, through 'retributive metamorphosis' to resemble his camel, with a hump and a long, drooping visage, and a man staring up at a giraffe, whose form and posture symmetrically mirror those of the animal (Fig. 4.5).

Hood's letters and notes are full of similar doodles, in which the profile of an old woman is morphing into that of a parrot or a man is becoming a goose.[53] Hood meditates on the fact that not only do people resemble animals but there are brutes, such as the orang-utan, that 'by peculiar human manners and resemblance, seem to hint at a former and better condition'. He reimagines the colonization of America as a meeting between penguins (Quakers) and kangaroos (native Americans) and muses that, as a mariner, he would not have been able to eat a penguin without 'strong Pythagorean misgivings'. The difficulty of distinguishing between animal flesh, which may be consumed, and human flesh, which should not, recurs in many of Hood's poems, including 'A Legend of Navarre', 'The Supper Superstition', and 'The Sausage-Maker's Ghost', while poems such as 'The Lament of Toby, the Learned Pig' give such a human face to animal characters that eating them appears akin to cannibalism. In 'A Recipe – for Civilization', in *Whims and Oddities* (1826), Hood, indeed, raises the possibility that the only definite characteristic separating man and beast is the former's preference for cooked over raw food; no physiological index is reliable:

Surely, those sages err who teach
That man is known from brutes by speech . . .
Neither can man be known by feature
Or form, because so like a creature,
That some grave men could never shape
Which is the aped and which the apeo.[54]

There is a long tradition in grotesque art of composite creatures that conjoin characteristics of man and beast, often in order to caricature the bestial qualities of men. Hood's vision clearly draws on the Classical tradition (Ovid, Pythagoras), and on a range of later sources from Rabelais through to Swift. However, the nineteenth century provided new contexts for reading the relationship between human and animal that are significant for Hood's deployment of this traditional grotesque motif. One of these contexts is new social and legal concern about the appropriate treatment of animals. In his first book, *Odes and Addresses to Great People* (1825), Hood addressed one of his odes to Richard Martin, MP for Galway, who was responsible for the first modern Act of Parliament for protecting the rights of animals. Hood teases but praises Martin as 'the Wilberforce of hacks' and suggests – again invoking metempsychosis – that when Martin's spirit shifts from flesh to feather, the 'martin' he becomes ought to be karmically protected. If he achieves his aims, Hood predicts, when Martin dies:

The biped woe the quadruped shall enter,
    And Man and Horse go half and half,
As if their griefs met in a common *Centaur!*[55]

The double-figure of the centaur is, here, appropriately expressed in the double-figure of the pun: a typical example of Hood's comic grotesquerie that demonstrates the extent to which the concerns of his 'comic' and 'serious' work are thematically linked. In both, the indeterminate and morphologically plastic construct of the body suggests relationships between apparently separate entities that are in fact not fixed and discrete but open to renegotiation, and, consequently, social relationships of identity and power that are also tellingly liable to change.

A second and related context for new readings of the relationship between animal and human in the nineteenth century was zoological and geological study that identified similarities between human and animal physiognomy and postulated sequences of development that supported the possibility that humans had evolved from other mammals. Hood and his family were avid visitors to the London Zoological Gardens, which opened in 1828 and were, reputedly, the first in the world to operate on a scientific basis of study and to provide each creature with a purpose-built habitat. The transformation of the 'zoo' in this period from a menagerie designed purely for human entertainment to a comprehensive scientific institution, concerned with learning about species relationships and animals' natural behaviour and requirements, shadows contemporary advances in thinking about animals' capacity to feel. Hood's playful writing and illustration on the subject of the 'animal' consistently explores the similarities between different kinds of organism. His poem 'Ode to N.A. Vigors Esq. On the Publication of "The Gardens and Menagerie of the Zoological Society"' (1831), for example, teases the zoo's secretary about the letters he might have to write on behalf of the various animals to their relatives in foreign parts. Exploring, with customarily creative literalism, the idea of a 'Zoological Garden', Hood also imagines the instructions that a gardener, such as Mr Vigors, might give to anyone who planned to 'cultivate brutes':

> Earth up your Beavers; train your Bears to climb;
> Thin out your Elephants about this time;
> And set some early Kangaroos in pots.[56]

Such confusion between the categories of animal and vegetable borders on the comic grotesquerie of nonsense verse. This is most commonly associated with the poetry and illustration of Edward Lear, who trained as an artist depicting zoological specimens. But Hood is an earlier exponent of verse and illustration that play with the possibility of contiguity between human, animal, and vegetable life forms. Variations on this theme can be seen in 'A Strange Bird' (*Comic Annual* 1831), 'Cock of the Walk', and 'From the Zoological Garden' (*Comic Annual* 1833) which represents curiously humanoid plants (Fig. 4.6). There is a striking similarity between these drawings and Edward Lear's later, more famous, sketches of bird-men and surreal botany. But they also resemble George Cruikshank's 'Zoological Sketches' of 1834, which show 'Fellows of the Zoological Society' as a sequence of pairs: a giraffe and a man with the face of a giraffe, a chimp and a dwarf, a stork and a man-stork etc. Such similarities between work by Hood and Cruikshank in the 1830s and Lear in the 1840s, which does not merely meld organic forms but explores physiological analogy and the language of zoological and botanical classification, highlight the shared ambience of curiosity at this time surrounding possible relationships between the development of human and non-human bodies, and the way that this curiosity informs nineteenth-century grotesque art (Fig. 4.7).

A humorous prose sketch by Hood makes a surprising appearance in Gideon Mantell's *The Medals of Creation or First Lessons in Geology and in the Study of Organic Remains* (1844). This is a serious primer,

4.6 Hood, 'Miss Tree' (1826), 'A Strange Bird' (1831), and 'From the Zoological Gardens' (1831)

dedicated to Charles Lyell, for the student or collector who wants to familiarize himself or herself with trilobites, fossil ferns, and 'dinosaurians'. But it concludes with Hood's 'A Geological Excursion to Tilgate Forest 2000 AD', which describes a dinosaur being unearthed and the discovery that the monster was a vegetarian. Hood's 'Geological Excursion' shows his interest in the geological excavations of the day and their implications for a new understanding of the origins and development of life. Mantell is struck by the absence of man and man's cre-

4.7 George Cruikshank, 'Fellows of the Zoological Society' (1834)

ations from the fossil record and imagines a time when man's remains will be among the bones discovered by future geologists. Hood, too, enjoys imagining millenarian scenarios in which man's supremacy is undermined: this is the backdrop to his poem, 'The Last Man' (1826), which shows the manner in which grotesque art may simultaneously upset various different norms concerning 'natural order'. In this poem, typically, man's vulnerability to being consumed – and potentially superseded – by other animals is concomitant with the toppling of social class. Evolutionary and revolutionary scenarios coalesce.

Several of the poems in *Whims and Oddities* contain grotesque material where the susceptibility of the body adumbrates wider instability regarding the body politic. 'A Legend of Navarre' tells a story from the reign of 'Lewis the Great' in which a Baron dies and is laid out by his widow and household. When the King and his retinue stop at the Baron's house, the widow, in the market for a new husband, stages a banquet and is so pressed to accommodate all the visitors that her husband's corpse is stored upright in a closet:

Oh what a hubbub in the house of woe!
All, resolute to one irresolution,
Kept tearing, swearing, plunging to and fro,
Just like another French mob-revolution.
There lay the corpse that could not stir a muscle,
But all the rest seem'd Chaos in a bustle.[57]

The outcome of this chaos is that one of the visiting royal retinue, a Forest Ranger, feeling hungry in the middle of the night, puts his hand into the corner cupboard, feels 'a something cold, in fact, the carcase', and assuming it is venison, sticks his hunting-knife into the body. The 'dead' Baron is roused from his coma by this blow and comes charging down the stairs to reclaim his former position. Hood's comparison between the baronial household, caught between funeral and junket, and the French mob-revolution, is suggestive. The revolution, in Hood's metaphor, is the type of a grotesque state, 'resolute to one irresolution', a potentially cannibalistic banquet in the midst of death. The fact that the baron who seemed dead is unexpectedly restored hints at a retributive end to this kind of chaos; yet the poem clearly relishes the grotesque energy generated by ambivalence – live, dead; man, beast; funny, horrible. The unstable relationship between human and animal is mirrored in the overthrow of caste: the poem briefly entertains anarchy in both these realms, before deciding to restore order.

A similar effect occurs in 'The Monkey-Martyr: A Fable', also in *Whims and Oddities* (1827), in which a monkey, fired with the conviction that his race, like slaves or weavers, is oppressed, sets out to liberate a 'brute bastille', a menagerie. The monkey has, however, only half-unbolted the lion's cage when Nero, the lion, *bolts* him. Again, grotesque instability concerning human and animal is mirrored in class overthrow, and again the narrative outcome expresses ambivalence. As a fable the moral of this story is clearly that the revolutionary is deluded and that the nature of revolution is to consume its instigators. However, the poem's translation of the revolutionary narrative to the animal sphere is equivocal: all caged animals are, after all, in a state that is far from natural or free. Hood's grotesquerie blends elements of both revolutionary desire and its retributive countercheck.

Hood's preoccupation with the boundaries of the human, then, and the interest his visual and verbal work consistently displays throughout his career in metamorphosis, metempsychosis, cannibalism, and hybridity, reflects a long tradition in grotesque art. It should also, however, be seen in the context of intense nineteenth-century debate about the relationship between human and animal – a debate with legal, scientific, and social dimensions of which Hood's work shows constant awareness. Moreover, the plasticity of the body in Hood's work is a type for other kinds of potential disorder and revision. His poems of dismemberment, transformation, and accidental consumption often also suggest the collapse of class boundaries. Violence within these texts is typically both relished and punished. The grotesque becomes a way of entertaining revolution without condoning it. Its very lack of locus, its ability simultaneously to signify more than one thing, makes the grotesque the perfect medium through which to express the ambivalence of a writer who desires political change but deplores mob violence. Should we be laughing? Hood uses the grotesque to play with fear – but it is often others' fear of a British Terror with which he plays, a fear which, in his writing, repeatedly proves groundless, and even ludicrous. On the other hand, our own ambivalence, our sense of cognizant delinquency in being amused by the terrible, allies us with Hood and his grotesque subjects, making us conscious of our own potential brutality, and the violent energies we routinely repress.

The revenge of the reified: Hood and the grotesque market

Endlessly proliferating, fascinating, and unsafe, the early nineteenth-century city still appears to modern eyes a grotesque space, inevitably mediated by the representations of authors working in the grotesque idiom in this period, predominantly writing from and about an urban situation. Hood's grotesquerie is strongly coloured by his imbrication in an expanding market in which change is omnipresent and omnipotent, and subjects and objects can be exchanged with shocking ease. Like his contemporaries Hood uses the grotesque to critique the human consequences of runaway capitalism: in this section I shall be comparing grotesque work by Hood with poems by Robert Browning and Christina Rossetti in which exploitative transactions are examined through grotesque imagery where person and thing are fatally confused. Yet the nineteenth-century grotesque is also capitalism's child. If ambivalence about violence is one of the axes on which it turns, the other is ambivalence about trade. Many characteristics of grotesque – accumulation, embellishment, combination, exchange, mobility, mutability – are also features of the marketplace. The poems I shall be discussing gain their energy from the fusion of pleasure and disgust in the grotesque exchanges they invoke.

Hood's poetry and prose of the 1830s and 1840s shares many of the grotesque characteristics of his earlier work, but, as he grows more confident as a writer and more disaffected regarding the gulf between rich and poor and the various social punishments meted out to those already staggering under the burden of poverty, so his work in the grotesque mode becomes more trenchant and more openly politically engaged. The early nineteenth century saw more hangings than any other period in British history.[58] Poaching, petty theft, forging, and passing false coin were all capital offences and, as the protection of property was increasingly strictly enforced and the exchange of currency for all goods became ubiquitous, more bodies paid with their lives for petty crimes to which poverty had tempted or driven them. The ethics of hanging for passing false currency were the subject of contemporary debate: Hood and Cruikshank were both opposed to capital punishment for such venial crimes. 'The Rope Dancer: An Extravaganza, – After Rabelais', a prose piece from the 1834 *Comic Annual*, shows Hood using elements of the Rabelaisian grotesque to explore the penalty that is due to befall a prisoner (Tonio) for passing a counterfeit coin:

> Oh, ye City Croesuses, what think ye of a man having his quantum suffocate of twisted hemp for making money! For my own part, if I was to swing for saying so, I'd cry out like a Stentor, that one of God's images ought not to be made worm's meat of for only washing the King's face. 'Twould be a very hard-boiled case, and yet, 'fore Gog and Magog, so it was. For gilding a brass farthing he was to change twelve stone of good human flesh to a clod of clay; to change a jolly, laughing, smiling, grinning, crying, wondering, staring, face-making face for a mere caput mortuum; to change prime tripe, delicate cow-heel, succulent trotters, for a mouthful of dust; to change a garret for a grave; to change a neckcloth for a halter. Zounds! what a deal of change for a bad half sovereign![59]

Hood, via pun and parallelism, compares the grotesque exchanges involved in the process of capital punishment to those changes involved in the capital transaction. The language of grotesque, with its incongruous admixtures and metamorphoses, serves to highlight the absurdly incommensurate nature of the crime and the punishment. Unsurprisingly, then, 'The Rope Dancer' ends with the prisoner escaping the scaffold. He has in his pocket a 'whim', which turns out to be a tarantula. Released into the crowd, this creature provokes a riotous dance in which all order is dissolved:

> as grotesque a burlesque as ever was flung, and floundered, and flounced, and bounced, and shuffled, and scuffled, and draggled, and wiggle-waggled, shambled, gamboled, scrambled and skimble-skambled by Grimaldi in Mother Goose.

This comic 'Dance of Death', as Hood describes it, is an embodiment of what Bakhtin would term the carnivalesque spirit, an anarchic movement of the crowd which revokes condemnation to the stasis of death represented by the gallows. The impression of mob energy is created through word-play, the onomatopoeic and rhyming verbs of motion falling helter-skelter upon one another, culminating in a final pun (tarantula/tarantella), which Hood illustrates as a dancing insect. The body of language, in all its visual and aural profusion, is central to the Rabelaisian 'extravaganza', which involves multiple elements of energetic disruption, duality, proliferation, and performativity centred upon the physical body, the fearful possibility of its dissolution and the boisterous pleasure of its release. Tonio has been due to make a grotesque exchange – a life for a false coin. He is saved by another kind of grotesque transformation, as the bite of his tarantula invests the bodies of his persecutors with a relentless and unstoppable energy: he had been due to 'dance' for their entertainment; instead they dance for his.

A similar retributive movement occurs in 'The Dead Robbery' (1837). Hood was well aware of the mechanics of body-snatching, which makes an early appearance as the theme of 'Mary's Ghost' and 'Jack Hall' (1827). The Burke and Hare scandal of 1828, however, made everyone aware that body-snatchers might go a step beyond looting corpses from graveyards and commit murder to supply fresh cadavers to anatomists. A significant element of the scandal was public realization that, as Sir Walter Scott put it, vagrants were worth ten pounds dead who had not been worth so many pence when alive: as objects they were infinitely more valuable than as subjects.[60] Hood's final body-snatching poem explores via black comedy the perverse values implicit in this economic reality. In 'The Dead Robbery', Peter Bunce, a man whom the desperation of poverty has driven to attempt suicide with an overdose of laudanum, awakens in a graveyard just in time to recognize that he has been presumed dead, buried, and is now the intended prey of body-snatchers. Peter speaks to the body-snatcher and his astonished discovery that, destitute as a man, as an anatomical 'subject' he is worth ten pounds, leads him quickly to kill the snatcher with his own spade, stick him in his own sack, and – in a perfect role reversal – turn the trader into the very commodity in which he previously dealt. Initiated into the joys of capitalism, indeed, Peter is not satisfied with this first transaction. He proceeds to visit the various surgeons who pay for bodies, take their money, and then kill each of them in turn. The original supplier, then the buyers, become the wares.

'Here', said the purchaser, with smile quite pleasant
Taking a glimpse at his departed brother,
'Here's half a guinea in the way of present –
Subjects are scarce, and when you get another,
Let *me* be first.' – Bunce took him at his word,
And suddenly his old atrocious trick did,
   Sacking M.D. the third,
Ere he could furnish 'Hints to the Afflicted.'[61]

Peter's margins keep growing as the night progresses, but his entrepreneurial killing spree comes to an end when, asking directions to yet another doctor, he is directed to a doctor of law. Like Tonio, Peter does not, however, swing on the gallows: Hood lets him escape and live 'securely till four score, / From never troubling Doctors any more!' In this grotesque poem, 'live' and 'dead' are unstable categories; subject becomes object and vice versa. Peter Bunce's revenge is the revenge of the reified. He exacts upon his social 'superiors' the logic of their own values. He is like Holbein's skeletal Death, abruptly felling those who least expect it, but Peter also executes the ruthless objectivity of the market: if people can be viewed as commodities without any regard for their human worth, it follows that every body is up for grabs.

William Rossetti found 'The Dead Robbery' disturbing: his uneasy critique tells us a great deal about the impression made by Hood's grotesque and the way in which the very success of the grotesque in generating discomfort may lead to critical failure and editorial exclusion. Rossetti's vivid description, 'the horse-laugh passes into a nightmare laugh: a ghoul sets it going, and laughing hyaenas chorus it',[62] projects images surrounding consumption of flesh on to the text and the audience (the origin of the laughter is suggestively unclear). Alfred Ainger excludes 'The Dead Robbery' completely from his two-volume set of Hood's 'serious' and 'comic' poems (1897). Neither John Clubbe nor Susan Wolfson includes it in their respective *Selected Poems*. Yet this is a strong poem and a salient one for understanding the way in which the grotesquerie present in Hood's early verse, whether 'Lycus the Centaur' or 'Mary's Ghost', permeates and galvanizes his later protest verse. In 'The Dead Robbery' the instability inherent in grotesque exchange generates the energy that propels the narrative's reckless recurrence. This is also true of Hood's late masterpiece 'Miss Kilmansegg and Her Precious Leg' (1844), in which subjects and objects are also grotesquely confused, with fatal consequences.

Miss Kilmansegg is born and raised in an environment of extraordinary wealth. Her ancestors traded in golden pigs and golden bulls, translating a Hesiodic agrarian 'golden age' into one of insistent materialism and capitalization. Her birth produces a grotesque orgy of consumption which Hood compares with the extreme feasting at the birth of Rabelais's Gargantua; hundreds of men are 'turn'd into beasts, / Like the guests at Circe's magical feats / By the magic of ale and cider'. As she grows up, everything that surrounds Miss Kilmansegg is gold, from her dolls to her pets to the substance that is given to her for pain relief: Dantzic Water (which contains leaf gold); the organic and animate are consistently confused with the artificial and inanimate. This grotesque (con)fusion leaches into the girl's mind and body such that gold runs 'in her thoughts and fill'd her brain, / She was golden-headed as Peter's cane / With which he walked behind her'. It is inevitable, then, that, when she is thrown in a riding accident and loses her right leg, she will demand a golden prosthesis, a literal golden calf, to supply the deficit.

The protagonist's serio-comically dismembered body recalls that of Ben Battle in 'Faithless Nelly Gray' and John Jones in 'Sally Simpkin's Lament': her composite figure, when she is supplied with the golden leg, recalls Hood's 'Fancy Portraits' and 'Comic Composites' in which various items of trade 'stand for' parts of the body. In this poem of social criticism, however, the grotesque semi-translation of subject into object is explicitly glossed as a consequence of runaway capitalism. Miss Kilmansegg's horse is called 'Banker'. He is a hunter, whose breeding compels him to bolt with 'a girl worth her weight in guineas'. The wild ride he takes her on runs suggestively through Piccadilly, the Cellar, and Bond Street, ditching her finally outside the premises of a goldsmith. Like the anarchic movements of 'The Rope Dancer' and 'The Dead Robbery', Miss Kilmansegg's uncontrollable flight and fatal crash both resemble the ruthless energy of the market, which threatens life and limb, and exercise a form of *revenge* on the market, by forcing its inhumane values to their logical conclusion. Miss Kilmansegg, indeed, feels, as she is whirled away by Banker, that she is doomed 'to be torn by powers of horses and wheels, / like a spinner by steam machinery'. And the cobblestones 'seem uttering cries', that invoke the idea that her 'accident' is, for those not born into affluence, a form of moral pay-off:

> 'Batter her! shatter her!
>   Throw and scatter her!'
> Shouts each stony-hearted chatterer!
>   'Dash at the heavy Dover!
> Spill her! kill her! tear and tatter her!
> Smash her! crash her!' (the stones didn't flatter her!)
> 'Kick her brains out! let her blood spatter her!
> Roll on her over and over!'[63]

'Stony-hearted chatterers' is carefully ambiguous. The cobbles are grotesquely personified: the cries they seem to utter may be Miss Kilmansegg's fearful interpretation of the staccato ring of her horse's hooves on the road's surface; they also, however, conjure up the resentful feelings that may be harboured by the 'dense dark mob' that surrounds her as she falls. The next voices we hear in the poem belong to this crowd. The grotesque conceit of stones demanding the body's dismemberment allows Hood to express, without condoning, the idea of retributive violence by the poor against the exploitative rich. As in many of Hood's earlier poems, anarchic qualities of grotesquerie indulge the desire for overthrow, which is, however, also disassociated through projection and contained within a metrical framework of order.

Miss Kilmansegg's golden leg, which provokes universal wonder and admiration, neatly captures the perverse eroticism and idolatry that capital inspires in the poem. It is a grotesque object-cum-subject, made more grotesque by the concentration of wealth that it represents, which should be figuratively supporting hundreds of people, rather than literally supporting one. When Miss Kilmansegg marries, it is evident that it is her leg, rather than her person, that has attracted her husband, a ruthless bounty-hunter. Having exhausted her liquid assets, he kills his wife to get the golden leg, using the leg itself as the murder weapon. The twist in the tale is that the inquest declares her death to be 'felo de se' (suicide) because she was struck by a part of her own body. The self-as-object revolts against the self-as-subject; distorted values work themselves out in a total sum that, within their own grotesque accounting, is wholly reasonable. As in 'The Rope Dancer' and 'The Dead Robbery', the outcome of this moral 'golden leg-end' is a form of revenge. Indeed, it is as if the anger of the many subjects whose work has gone into the making and upkeep of the symbolic golden leg is released in its vindictive act of violence. 'Miss Kilmansegg and Her Precious Leg' may well recall to the modern reader Marx's account in *Capital* of 'The Fetishism of the Commodity and its Secret' where he asserts that the modern conditions of production, where producers do not come into social contact until they exchange commodities, means that commodities themselves have a mystical character reflecting the social characteristics of the labour that has gone into them as if they were characteristics of the product itself:

> as soon as [the table] emerges as a commodity, it changes into a thing which transcends sensuousness. It not only stands with its feet on the ground, but, in relation to all other commodities, it stands on its head, and evolves out of its brain grotesque ideas, far more wonderful than if it were to begin dancing of its own free will.[64]

The grotesque fable of the early nineteenth century frequently actualizes the sensuous and quasi-independent life of objects that Marx describes as arising from the social labour that has privately gone into them and which, like the genie of Aladdin's lamp, will discover itself only through the act of exchange.

The topicality and typicality of the grotesque marketplace in 'Miss Kilmansegg and Her Precious Leg' (1844) is perhaps most evident when we compare it with two other, better-known, poems: Robert Browning's 'The Pied Piper of Hamelin' (1842) and Christina Rossetti's 'Goblin

Market' (1859). Browning knew Hood and Hood's work well. Among the poems by Hood that Browning particularly enjoyed were 'The Last Man' and 'The Haunted House': he confided in Alfred Domett that he relished the 'merry grim spirit'[65] of 'The Last Man'; Hood, meanwhile, published early grotesque outings of Browning's, such as 'The Laboratory', where a courtier of the 'Ancien Regime' delights in watching poisons being prepared that will deface and kill his former mistress and her new lover. Similarly, Hood's work was an important presence in the Rossetti household and William Rossetti would become Hood's editor. Comparison between Hood's work in the grotesque idiom and that of the Brownings and Rossettis thus offers rich and largely unexplored ground for comparison.

In 'The Pied Piper of Hamelin', as in 'Miss Kilmansegg', subject and object are transvalued with devastating consequences. Hamelin is infested with rats, which bite babies as well as cheeses, and infiltrate every nook and cranny. Rats are, indeed, the equivalent of gold in 'Miss Kilmansegg' and their proliferation is suggestive of money, which permeates the town and threatens it with the relentless force of insatiable consumption. The incompetent Mayor ('little though wondrous fat; Nor brighter was his eye, nor moister / Than a too-long-opened oyster') and Corporation face popular revolt until they are visited by 'the strangest figure! / His queer long coat from heel to head / Was half of yellow and half of red'.[66] This magical and peculiar composite man offers to rid the town of rats for 1000 guilders, a bargain to which the Mayor gratefully accedes. When, however, the piper succeeds in luring the rats to their death, the Mayor refuses to honour his contract. At which the piper charms away all of the town's children. Their prioritization of money is visited upon the Corporation as the piper forces an exchange upon them that literalizes their preference for object over person. Rats, children, and guilders form a series of groups that become convertible via the grotesque marketplace. Greed and exploitation are symbolically punished: the plague of consumption (rats) and the loss of innocence (children) that are visited upon Hamelin precisely correspond to the Corporation's mercantile sins.

In Christina Rossetti's 'Goblin Market' subject and object also become dangerously confused within a market whose propensities are wholly grotesque. Laura pays for luscious goblin fruits, temptingly arrayed before her by figures who are part rat, cat, or wombat, with the 'gold' of her hair. Her transgressive subject/object exchange resonates with suggestions of prostitution. The fruits she purchases are the epitome of Marx's 'sensuous' commodity: her fall is ambiguously into the erotics of capitalism and into sexual sin. The grotesquerie of the goblin men,

part animal/part human, is emblematic of the duplicity of their product
and of their market. They cajole the prospective buyer, scratch and bite
those who refuse their wares; the fruit, meanwhile, while promising to
satisfy desire and quench thirst, merely provokes insatiable drought and
wasting passion. Laura's purchase turns her into a grotesque figure,
young yet seeming old, gluttonous yet shrivelled and nauseated by her
diseased appetite. Famously, her sister, Lizzie, saves her from death by
allowing herself to be attacked by the goblins and pelted with their fruit,
whose juices Laura must lick from Lizzie's bruised flesh. According to
the poem's logic of exchange, Lizzie's terrible barter of self for thing
can be redeemed only by her sister's freely got and freely given goods.
Rossetti's wonderful poem offers many possible readings – as religious
parable, as lesbian romance, as feminist assertion that women who 'fall'
into prostitution can subsequently lead happy lives as wives and mothers.
But the poem's transactional economy, the centrality of the 'market' to
its narrative, is inescapable. The grotesque clusters around the market
as we do; the grotesque, attractive yet repellent, properties of the vendors
and of the fruits make manifest an ambivalence about the dangers of
insistent commerce and its transformative powers that is also crucial to
'The Pied Piper' and 'Miss Kilmansegg'.

   All of these poems allegorize the dangers of obsessive capitalism and
the subordination of human to economic value that it entails. Yet each
of them is, in its own way, enthralled by transaction, upon which the
moral of the story turns. The energy of these poems derives from lan-
guage that insistently chimes and replicates, spilling helter-skelter
through the verses like Browning's rats, Hood's gold, and Rossetti's
goblins:

> Chuckling, clapping, crowing,
> Clucking and gobbling,
> Mopping and mowing,
> Full of airs and graces,
> Pulling wry faces,
> Demure grimaces,
> Cat-like and rat-like,
> Ratel- and wombat-like.[67]

Although the grotesque market is the source of ruin, grotesque lan-
guage and imagery is also the source of wonder and delight. Words and
phrases themselves take odd composite forms ('demure grimaces';
'wombat-like', 'parrot-voiced') and seem to exchange and upend each
other's vocables ('clucking' is almost an anagram of 'chuckling'; 'clap-
ping' is a pararhyme of 'leaping'). As we voice the verse, our tongues
move pleasurably around the grotesque, enjoying the physical anomalies

it conjures and the physical difficulty of uttering them. The Mayor of Hamelin's oyster/eye (this Cockney pun also appears in Hood's 'Tim Turpin') is just one example of the way that words themselves envisage consumer and consumable changing for one another. I shall be discussing Hood's punning as a form of grotesque art in the following chapter, but it bears brief mention here that the obsessive coining of puns in 'Miss Kilmansegg' is a deliberate linguistic analogue to the Kilmanseggs' material obsession ('puns' is itself a pun on 'pounds'). Verbal accretion, decoration, and 'forced' doubling become part of Hood's critique of grotesque acquisitiveness, but are also part of poem's own acquisitive pleasure. All of the poems have an audience in mind that is at least partly composed of children and the fabulous nature of the narratives and the imagery hark back to the free play, the breathless excess and magical morphology, of fairy tale. In all of these poems, then, aspects of the market – ruthless acquisitiveness, uncontrollable proliferation, transgressive exchanges – are critiqued through grotesque forms, whose replicating, unstable, composite nature echoes the threat posed by commerce to the distinction between human and non-human, subject and object. Yet the grotesque in these poems works also to celebrate the commerce it distrusts: the poems derive energy from their fusion of pleasure and distaste. This pattern is common in nineteenth-century grotesque literature: it pervades, for example, Dickens's *A Christmas Carol* (1843) and *The Old Curiosity Shop* (1841); Thackeray's *Vanity Fair* (1848); and Browning's *The Ring and the Book* (1868–9). The doubleness at the heart of grotesque makes it a natural vehicle for the mingled anxiety and delight of Victorian capitalism. Our continued mixed feelings about the Victorian grotesque reflect, inter alia, our inheritance of that troubled legacy.

Conclusion

Of the imagery of George Darley, Thomas Beddoes, and Thomas Hood, John Heath-Stubbs wrote that, 'compared with that of their Romantic predecessors there is a morbidity, a love of the strange and grotesque, above all a harshness in their imagery and conceptions, which is repellent to normal minds'.[68] Even a sympathetic critic, Lloyd Jeffrey, felt obliged to find excuse for the 'rollicking ghastliness' of some of Hood's grotesquerie in the concealed bitterness of poverty and sickness: 'Is this the sadism of a near-invalid resentful of all healthy people, or does Hood sport with suffering to make his own easier to bear?'[69] V.S. Pritchett dubbed it a 'strange fact', in his 1946 essay on Hood, 'Our Half-Hogarth', that the social evils of the nineteenth century produced a response carved in the shape of the 'gargoyles of German gothic' rather than 'revolutionary realism'.[70] It is necessary to reconsider Hood as a grotesque writer partly because his grotesquerie has come between modern readers and an appreciation of his work. The apparent 'strangeness' of his imagery has estranged him; twentieth-century conceptions of the 'normal mind' and of realism as the appropriate medium for serious and politically engaged literature made Hood appear an odd, isolated, and even macabre figure. Lamb's affectionate phrase 'our half-Hogarth' takes on in Pritchett's essay a more doubtful colouring: Hood is himself grotesque, neither one thing nor another.

This chapter has endeavoured to place Hood's grotesque within frameworks and contexts that illuminate it as operating in an idiom in itself neither anomalous nor perverse, but rich in both traditional and contemporary analogues that reveal much about how Hood situates himself as a writer and illustrator. Hood's grotesquerie draws on visual, oral, and literary traditions of grotesque with ancient popular roots. Carnivalesque pageantry, street performance, and pantomime were vital features of the milieu in which Hood was raised, as was the world of ballad, moralitas, and emblem book. Like Dickens, Cruikshank, Thackeray, and others, Hood draws on the grotesquerie of this tradition for its *popular* qualities: its insistence on the public and physical body, its frequent violence, its emphasis on mutability, both oppose an increasingly gentrified conception of private entertainment and suggest the disruptive potential of the body politic: a common body from which the privileged distance themselves at their peril.

Hood's grotesque dwells particularly on the boundary between human and animal, subject and object. His preoccupation with metempsychosis, metamorphosis, cannibalism, and hybridity unites his work in different genres. It reflects contemporary debate (scientific, legal, religious) of which Hood was well aware, about the relative position of man and animal and the possible consequences of questioning traditional hierarchies and distinctions between them. Like Lear's, Hood's playful composite zoological forms foreshadow the evolution debate of mid-century. But the instability of the body in Hood's work also suggests the possible collapse of class boundaries and the lingering threat of revolutionary violence: a threat that, within a tight and regular framework of metrical and narrative pay-offs, is both allowed and denied.

The body is the primary site that connotes the convertible nature of all matter, the exchangeability of all goods. Hood's urban poetry uses the grotesque to explore the threat to human value posed by the insistent objectification and capitalization of the nineteenth-century marketplace. Early parodic ballads ('Mary's Ghost') and later, more explicitly critical, 'protest' verse ('Miss Kilmansegg and Her Precious Leg') deploy similar grotesque motifs and linguistic habits, mirroring in their verbal dis-memberments, reconfigurations, replications, and mutations the opera-tions of grotesque trade. Yet the grotesque, which as an idiom is always doubled, is also a medium whereby Hood, with authors includ-ing Browning and Rossetti, celebrates the anarchic energy of the market he fears. The work of that market is countered by play that simultane-ously undermines and underwrites its transformative power.

Notes

1 'Tim Turpin: A Pathetic Ballad', *PW*, pp. 87–8.
2 'Poem, – From the Polish', *PW*, pp. 234–5; 'Mary's Ghost: A Pathetic Ballad', *PW*, p. 77.
3 Michael Hollington, *Dickens and the Grotesque* (London and Sydney: Croom Helm, 1984), p. 1.
4 Trodd, Barlow and Amigoni, *Victorian Culture*, p. 2 (original emphasis).
5 Mikhail Bakhtin, *Rabelais and His World*, trans. Helene Iswolsky (Bloomington, Indiana: Indiana University Press, 1984), pp. 19–21.
6 Wolfgang Kayser, *The Grotesque in Art and Literature*, trans. Ulrich Weisstein (Gloucester, Massachusetts: Smith, 1968), pp. 184–5. Kayser's analysis was first published in 1957.
7 Bernard McElroy, *Fiction of the Modern Grotesque* (New York: St Martin's Press, 1989), p. 4.
8 Ruskin, *Stones of Venice*, vol. 3, p. 138 (original emphasis).
9 Bakhtin, *Rabelais*, p. 45. Kayser, *The Grotesque*, p. 100.
10 Trodd, Barlow, and Amigoni, *Victorian Culture*, p. 2.
11 Hollington, *Dickens and the Grotesque*, p. 35.
12 Hood, preface to *Hood's Own* (1839) reprinted in *CW*, vol. 1, p. ix.
13 Edgar Allan Poe, 'Thomas Hood', p. 276 (original emphasis).
14 H.F. Chorley, *London and Westminster Review*, 29 (April 1838), p. 124.
15 John Ruskin, appendix to *Modern Painters* vol. 4, reprinted in *Works of John Ruskin*, vol. 6, p. 471.
16 John Heath-Stubbs, *The Darkling Plain* (London: Eyre and Spottiswoode, 1950), p. 50.
17 Ibid., p. 49. A similar kind of projection was practised by early readers of William Morris. As Jerome McGann has noted, reviewers described Morris's *The Defence of Guenevere and Other Poems* as 'hard to decipher as if it were written in black letter' – in fact the typeface and layout of the poems was clean and modern; the grotesque is all in Morris's imagery. See Jerome McGann, ' "A Thing to Mind" The Materialist Aesthetic of William Morris', *Huntington Library Quarterly*, 55 (Winter 1992), pp. 55–74.
18 Ian Jack, *English Literature 1815–1832* (Oxford: Oxford University Press, 1963), p. 152.
19 Stafford, *The Last of the Race*, p. 231; Sanbrook, 'A Romantic Theme', pp. 32–3.

20 John Carey, *The Violent Effigy: A Study of Dickens' Imagination* (London: Faber, 1973). See, for example, pp. 101–2, where Carey claims that 'stilled life, and the still enlivened are the hallmarks of [Dickens's] imagination'.

21 Edmund Blunden, 'The Poet Hood', *Review of English Literature*, 1 (January 1960), p. 29.

22 The illustration, passed down through Marianne Green's son, is reproduced in Henry C. Shelley, *Literary By-Paths in Old England* (London: Grant Richards, 1909), p. 349.

23 See *CW*, vol. 5, p. 317 fn: 'In all his wanderings and changes there were two pictures which went with my father everywhere . . . the one of Charles Lamb . . . the other of Joe Grimaldi.'

24 See Bakhtin, *Rabelais*, pp. 278–9, on the links between images of abundant consumption and the universal aspirations of popular-festive forms.

25 'Ode to Joseph Grimaldi, Senior', *PW*, pp. 17–19.

26 Review, *London Magazine*, 16 (December 1827), p. 537.

27 A letter of 8 August 1823 from Hood to his sister shows that he enjoyed Richard Brinsley Peake's production of *Presumption; or, The Fate of Frankenstein* which played at the English Opera House that summer. See *Letters*, p. 41.

28 I have seen two copies of the first set of *Comic Composites for the Scrapbook* (London: Fores, 1827) but have had to rely on Walter Jerrold's account (and reproduction) of the 1834 set, which he owned, in *Thomas Hood: His Life and Times*, facing p. 252.

29 Hood, *Tylney Hall*, vol. 3, p. 29. See also Hood's review of 'The Death Fetch' in the *Atlas*, 30 July 1826, p. 170.

30 The skeleton figure of Death visiting the living appears in Hood's poems 'Death's Ramble' and 'Jack Hall' and stalks woodcuts including 'Dust O', 'Undertaker and Overtaker', and 'Firing Shells'.

31 *Memorials*, p. 277.

32 'Review: Master Humphrey's Clock', *CW*, vol. 8, p. 96.

33 As John Bowen has noticed, Dickens's preface to *The Old Curiosity Shop* links the death of Hood, who in 1845 had finally succumbed to a long illness, with that of Little Nell herself; Hood's spirit, in various ways, haunts this most grotesque of Dickens's novels. John Bowen, *Other Dickens: From Pickwick to Chuzzlewit* (Oxford: Oxford University Press, 2000), p. 146.

34 'Diary for the Month of May', *London Magazine*, 15 (June 1827), pp. 165–7.

35 G.A. Walker, *Gatherings from Grave Yards* (London: Longman, 1839), p. 202.

36 Hood's 'merry grim spirit' here departs little from reality: Jay's did indeed offer mourning dresses entitled 'the aesthetic' and 'the houri'. See John Morley, *Death, Heaven and the Victorians* (London: Studio Vista, 1971), plate 97.

37 Victor Hugo, preface to *Cromwell* in *The Dramas of Victor Hugo*, trans. I.G. Burnham, 4 vols (London: Nichols, 1896), vol. 4, p. 34.

38 Thomas Wright, *A History of Caricature and Grotesque in Literature and Art* (London: Virtue, 1865), p. 360.

39 Hood, 'My Tract', reprinted in *Memorials*, p. 351.

40 Chris Baldick, *In Frankenstein's Shadow: Myth, Monstrosity and Nineteenth-century Writing* (Oxford: Oxford University Press, 1987), pp. 17–23.

41 'Gog and Magog: A Guildhall Duet', *PW*, pp. 205–6.

42 Frederick W. Fairholt, *The Giants in Guildhall – their real and legendary history* (London: Hotten, 1859), pp. 62–3.

43 For a much more thorough account of this argument with respect to Dickens see Paul Schlicke, *Dickens and Popular Entertainment* (London: Allen and Unwin, 1985), pp. 6–7.

44 William Thackeray, 'On the Genius of George Cruikshank', *Westminster Review*, 34 (1840), pp. 6–7.

45 See V.A.C. Gatrell, *The Hanging Tree: Execution and the English People 1770–1868* (Oxford: Oxford University Press, 1994), pp. 140–3. 'Samuel Hall's Family Tree' is fully discussed as a chapter in Bertrand Harris Bronson, *The Ballad as Song* (Berkeley and Los Angeles: University of California Press, 1969). Roy Palmer, *The Sound of History: Songs and Social Comment* (Oxford and New York: Oxford University Press, 1988), p. 4, reprints the 1820s broadside of 'Jack Hall'.

46 Bernard McElroy, *Fiction of the Modern Grotesque* (New York: St Martin's Press, 1989), p. 4. McElroy tempers Ruskin with Freud's view of the uncanny: that it is produced by (often inseparable) 'repressed infantile anxieties, and surmounted modes of primitive thought'.

47 *Letters*, pp. 148–9.

48 Thomas Griffiths Wainewright, 'Janus Weatherbound; or The Weathercock Steadfast for Lack of Oil', *London Magazine*, 7 (January 1823), p. 50. Hood's 'The Two Peacocks of Bedfont' appeared in the *London Magazine*, 6 (October 1822), p. 304, under the pseudonym 'Ovid'.

49 'Lamia', *PW*, p. 674. Hood's 'Lamia' is unfinished and was not published until after his death: it was likely among his earliest experiments as a writer and he withheld it, recognizing its immaturity.

50 Ibid., p. 698.

51 'Lycus the Centaur', *PW*, p. 162.

52 Hood, 'Pythagorean Fancies', *CW*, vol. 4, pp. 236–7. The illustrations in *CW* do not correspond precisely to those in *Whims and Oddities,* to which I allude.

53 *Memorials*, p. 241, p. 270.

54 Hood, 'A Recipe - for Civilization', *PW*, p. 38.

55 Hood, 'Ode to Richard Martin, Esq.', *PW*, p. 10.

56 Hood, 'Ode to N.A. Vigors, Esq.', *PW*, p. 441.

57 Hood, 'A Legend of Navarre', *PW*, p. 80.

58 See Gatrell, *The Hanging Tree*, pp. 616–18. Figures are for England and Wales. In 1832 capital punishment was abolished for stock-theft, larceny

up to £5 from a dwelling-house, coining and forgery (except for wills). Further changes to the law meant in practice that, by 1837, only murder was a capital crime.

59 Hood, 'The Rope Dancer – An Extravaganza After Rabelais', *CW*, vol. 1, pp. 397–8.

60 Walter Scott, letter to Major Walter Scott, 11 January 1829, reprinted in *The Letters of Walter Scott*, ed. Herbert Grierson, 12 vols (London: Constable, 1936), vol. 11, p. 93.

61 Hood, 'The Dead Robbery', *PW*, p. 497.

62 William Rossetti, preface to *The Poetical Works of Thomas Hood*, 2 vols (London: Moxon, 1875), vol. 2, p. xvii.

63 Hood, 'Miss Kilmansegg and Her Precious Leg', *PW*, p. 574.

64 Karl Marx, *Capital: Volume 1*, trans. Ben Fowkes (London: Penguin: 1990), pp. 163–4.

65 Browning, *The Brownings' Correspondence*, vol. 11, p. 193. For Browning's admiration for 'The Haunted House' and 'The Bridge of Sighs' see vol. 10, p. 89.

66 Robert Browning, 'The Pied Piper of Hamelin', *The Poems of Browning*, ed. John Woolford and Daniel Karlin, 2 vols (London: Longman, 1992) vol. 2, p. 135.

67 Christina Rossetti, 'Goblin Market', *The Complete Poems* (London: Penguin, 2001), p. 14.

68 Heath-Stubbs, *Darkling Plain*, p. 23.

69 Lloyd Jeffrey, *Thomas Hood* (New York: Twayne, 1972), p. 70.

70 Pritchett, *Living Novel*, pp. 60–1.

5

Pun and pleasure: Hood's tied trope

Hood mercy on us has he not grown into a jiant with his puns . . . I some-
times think he has suffered a metamorphosis & become altogether a pun
is his I's & his no's & his air's & his here's about his head as formerly or
are they gone into the waggerys of his pen . . .

(John Clare, letter to Allan Cunningham, circa 1830)[1]

Admitting, however, the viciousness, the felonious sinfulness of punning,
it is to be apprehended that the liberty of the pun is like the liberty of the
press, which, says the patriot, is like the air, and if we have it not we
cannot breathe.

(Theodore Hook 'Punning', 1828)[2]

Thomas Hood and the pun are inextricably linked in literature's collec-
tive memory. Ian Jack regretted that Hood 'began to pun as soon as he
began to speak, and he died as he had lived'.[3] V.S. Pritchett in 1946
penned a memorable description of Hood 'forty-six, bankrupt and dying
of heart disease . . . and unable to stop making puns. They beset him
like a St Vitus' Dance. They come off his lips in an obsessional patter
as if his tongue had become a cuckoo clock and his mind a lunatic
asylum of double meanings.'[4] Pritchett claimed to source this tale of
Hood punning on his deathbed from Alfred Ainger's *Memoir* of Hood.
Strangely, however, Ainger's *Memoir* turns out to contain no such story:
it follows closely the accounts of Hood's children, who emphasized the
piety and tranquillity of their father's end.[5] Others who visited Hood
in his dying days make no mention of obsessive punning. Subsequent
biographers depict a quiet deathbed. But the legend of Hood's deathbed
pun persists. Ruskin's biographer, Alexander Wedderburn, claimed that
he told Ruskin of Hood's reputed last line: 'My dear, I fear you'll lose
your lively Hood' and that Ruskin admired it as an example of compo-
sure in the face of death.[6] The essence of this famous quip, however,
can be traced as far back as 1827, when Alfred Crowquill commented
in *Absurdities: in Prose and Verse* that no other author could 'urn a

lively Hood'.[7] While it is quite possible that Hood repeated this joke as he lay dying, it seems equally likely that Hood's 'deathbed pun' is a piece of cultural false memory that expresses a fascinating truth. Readers have wanted the last word on and of Hood to be a pun because he and the trope are so intimately identified with one another. Problematically, as in Clare's playful letter to Allan Cunningham, Hood himself has become a pun: a figure that might be doubled up with laughter, or with pain, an ambivalent object of sympathy and unease. Mixed feelings about the pun have coloured reactions to Hood and to his legacy; few critics have felt able to appreciate Hood's puns unreservedly, or to dismiss the suspicion that puns get in the way of something else they would like to see in him. Edgar Allan Poe, an admirer, none the less regretted that Hood's claim to 'greatness' was undermined by the 'little-ness' of his punning, the stock in trade of a 'literary merchant'.

> 'Frequently since his recent death,' says the American editor, 'he has been called a great author, a phrase not used inconsiderately or in vain.' Yet, if we adopt the conventional idea of 'a great author,' there has lived, perhaps, no writer of the last half century who, with equal notoriety, was *less* entitled than Hood to the term . . . for during the larger portion of his life he seemed to breathe only for the purpose of perpetuating puns – things of such despicable platitude, that the man who is capable of habitually committing them, is very seldom capable of anything else.[8]

Walter Redfern, an ardent enthusiast of punning, still worries that for Hood puns 'were a defence mechanism . . . that helped him shy away from the darker aspects of his vision'.[9] Less sympathetic critics have been simply repelled by the 'fevered', 'hideous', even 'pathological' qualities they attribute to Hood's recurrent punning.[10]

This chapter is devoted to puns and punning. It argues that Hood's puns should be viewed not as a curious tic or an embarrassing antic but as intrinsic to his perception and deployment of language. One cannot appreciate Hood's art without appreciating the richness and significance of his punning and the patterns of tension and release generated by the conflicting forces that his puns bring into play. Hood's writing, like Joyce's in the twentieth century, is continuously open to the multi-valency of words, their protean shapes, their continuous capacity for rearrangement and wayward interpretation; in both writers, punning recognizes an essential truth about language and consciousness, that the tendencies of both are always polysemous, and what is conventionally expressed is only a small fraction of the associations thought continu-ously generates. The energy with which visual and verbal signs flout any expectation of monogamous meaning, class, or register is essential to the vivacity of the page, and to the text's resistance to control. This chapter also aims to restore a lost background that can materially enhance our understanding of Hood's puns: the early nineteenth-century context of punning as an intimate form of social play, and especially the significance of punning in the 'Cockney' circle that included Hunt, Reynolds, Keats, Lamb, and Hood. Puns in this era are particularly associated with the lower middle classes. They are, I shall be arguing, a form of grotesque art and their radical instability shares many of the qualities and implications of the grotesque discussed in Chapter 4. Acknowledged to break a tacit socio-linguistic taboo, the pun – especially the deliberate, multiple, and 'forced' pun – increasingly signifies in this period what I call 'cognizant deliquency', a kind of self-conscious disinhibition that knowingly plays on the boundaries between social and anti-social behaviour. As such, the pun is a loaded trope, well-suited to highlighting other areas of social ambivalence and attempted repression. Hood's puns are not always political, but his commitment to punning is. Hood's love of punning and his attachment to other kinds of pluralism are inseparable. I hope, by looking at puns in Hood's work, to demonstrate their integral relationship to his tolerance toward religious pluralism, his distaste for restrictions on literal and figurative recreation, and his support for reform. Moreover, Hood's puns are symptomatic of his refusal to recognize given distinctions between different kinds of verbal output: the advertisement, the poem, the invoice, the letter, the article. Creatively conjoining the vocabulary of 'high' and 'low', literary and literal, Hood's puns, and refusal to deny or silence his perpetual perception of puns, assert a levelling literary agenda. Where all words are kissing cousins there can be no single, privileged, 'pure' discourse from which proscribed tropes are excluded.

Opposition to punning: a cultural history

Objections to puns in general, and to Hood's puns in particular, have been many and various. It is worth pausing briefly to consider this history of 'groaning' when someone ostentatiously 'lets' (like a fart), 'discharges' (like a firearm) or 'commits' (like a felony) a pun, because it conveys much about what is represented by the act of punning and about Hood's conscious determination to pun in the face of polite prejudice. At the roots of opposition to punning, as Jonathan Culler posits, may lie concern that the pun exposes the essential instability and provisionality of all communication systems:

> Speakers of English tend to think of the single, self-identical sound sequence correlated with a distinct idea – the word – as the norm or essence of

language, from which all else derives, and thus of homonyms, ambiguities, and so on as exceptions. This is, of course, an illusion . . . Puns present us with a model of language as phonemes or letters combining in various ways to evoke prior meaning and to produce effects of meaning – with a looseness, unpredictability, excessiveness, shall we say, that cannot but disrupt the model of language as nomenclature.[11]

The term 'pun' embraces various figures depending on similarity of form and disparity of meaning.[12] Much scholarly engagement with the pun has involved attempts to classify puns by type and to separate them from other forms of wordplay. Such attempts at definition, however, betray their own anxiety surrounding the loss of definition that the pun exposes.

From a neurological point of view it appears that punning associations are repressed, probably during the period of language acquisition when children are taught to prioritize 'meaningful' associations of words based on ideational content rather than visual or aural similarity. Tellingly, when frontal lobe activity, which plays a key role in editing verbal output, is damaged, then puns frequently spill out:

Some restraint, some caution, some inhibition, is destroyed, and patients with such [orbitalfrontal] syndromes tend to react immediately and incontinently to everything around them and everything within them . . . There is an overwhelming tendency, in such states, to word-play and puns.[13]

Incontinent punning, like swearing, can also be a feature of Tourette's syndrome and of manic states. Punning is thus, crucially, associated with social *disinhibition*. It carries both positive cultural memories of infant play, the pleasures of orality prior to communicative responsibility, and negative adult connotations of unstable, potentially anti-social verbal excess. The fact that, in extreme form, such disinhibition may indicate precarious mental health, helps to explain why repeated punning is often subject to negative readings as 'mad' or 'diseased' and associated with mental and physical dissolution. The pun, indeed, with its capacity to hover between different states, has often been used symbolically to explore the transitions undergone by the human body. Swift's 'The Dying Speech of Thomas Ashe', which 'was written several years before his death, to illustrate how an eternal punster might express himself on his death-bed', represents the transformation of live body into consumable body-as-object through puns:

Every fit of *coughing* hath put me in mind of my *coffin*; though *dissolute* men seldomest think of *dissolution* . . . He will soon be at the *Diet of Worms*, and from thence go to *Rat-is-bone* . . . Little did I think I would so soon see poor *Tom stown* under a *tomb stone* . . . And let punners consider how hard it is to *die jesting*, when death is so hard in *digesting*.[14]

The actor Macready remarked in his diary for 9 January 1834, 'I noted one odd saying of Lamb's, that the last breath he drew in he wished might be through a pipe and exhaled in a pun'.[15] Keats, dying in Italy, noted that he had never made more puns than he did in these last days.[16] The deathbed punster, it seems, is not merely part of Ruskin's admiring and Pritchett's horrified mythology of Hood, it is part of the mythology of the pun itself. Appreciation of this history should inform our reading of Hood's supposed 'deathbed pun', but also of his often traditional puns on the dead and dying body (compare the 'short fit of coffin' in 'Jack Hall' to the above extract from Swift). It should, moreover, make us wary of readings of Hood's puns that insist on their invalid/*invalid* origins. It is possible that Hood's childhood rheumatic fever gave him heightened access to the world as pun; partial deafness in one ear may have increased his perception of homonyms. But it would be wrong to attribute Hood's deliberate, career-long choice of the pun as a signature trope to the 'derangement' of which involuntary punning is occasionally a symptom.

The pun is perhaps to some degree always repressed and becomes in common with other jokes, as Freud believed, a compact unit that can economically enfold other kinds of psychically repressed material. But some societies and periods choose to indulge puns, and the disinhibition they represent, more than others. As Simon Alderson persuasively argues, we need to be alive to punning as a historical phenomenon. Word-play, including play with homonyms, is a salient feature of Classical, medieval, and Renaissance literature. But 'punning' as a discrete activity was identified as such in England only in the latter half of the seventeenth century. By the beginning of the eighteenth century, free play of puns in public life was already associated with a vanished era, particularly with the Stuart monarchy: reactions to puns entailed responses to the rhetoric and perceived ethos of that earlier time. It has often been assumed that Augustan critics were universally hostile to puns, but, as Alderson shows, the truth is more complex. In fact distinct pro-pun and anti-pun camps emerged, whose conflict was not merely semantic but involved social, historical, and political vested interests. Addison's negative view of the pun is grounded in a quasi-empirical theory of universal language: true wit can bear translation into a different language, wit that fails the translation test is false and 'you may conclude it to have been a Punn'.[17] Such theories, however, as Olivia Smith argues in the *Politics of Language 1791–1819*, were 'centrally and explicitly concerned with class division', based on an assumed dichotomy between 'refined' language, capable of abstraction, taken to reflect superior reason, and 'vulgar' language, characterized by concrete and local effects, which was taken to reflect more primitive mental capacity.[18] Punning falls foul of this emergent theoretical divide between 'refined' and 'vulgar' language habits. Reinforcing that divide mattered partly because linguistic class barriers were in actuality being eroded. As Alderson notes:

> Punning had long formed a significant part of the wit practiced in taverns, clubs, and especially coffeehouses . . . Perhaps the first thing that can be said about coffeehouse and tavern culture is its democratization of wit . . . the rhetoric of the antipunsters is clearly concerned about the risks attending this democratization . . . the distinction between social groups was threatened by punning; and in the coffeehouse context where punning primarily operated, and where distinctions of class had already been leveled, this meant that normal social and intellectual hierarchies could be uncomfortably reversed.[19]

The liberal unions that puns can effect between words of different kinds are echoed in the accessibility of the pun to all comers. Both threaten class boundaries. Trifling yet ostentatious, unbearably self-conscious, literally impertinent: accusations levelled at the pun look uncannily like those levelled at the parvenu. Alderson, moreover, suggests that 'the Augustan attack on the pun is in part an example of the rise of a Whiggish mercantile culture with a certain labor ethic being worked out in the public arena of wit'.[20] Puns are not obviously useful: they represent wasted labour. In the progressive rhetoric of the anti-pun movement, punning is a feature of the 'barbarous' customs of older times, which have now been superseded by a more rational, scientific, and industrious culture. In the rhetoric of the pro-pun movement, the same history of sixteenth- and seventeenth-century play is viewed in a positive and nostalgic light.

It is helpful to be aware of the nature of the contest over the pun in the eighteenth century, and of what is at stake in the pro-pun and anti-pun positions, to be fully alive to the sympathies that Hood and his fellow punsters of the *London Magazine* circle are expressing when they choose the pun as a characteristic mode of expression. Hood makes a conscious decision early in his career to flout the polite prejudice that deems puns unacceptable. In doing so he is siding with Swift and against Johnson in a linguistic debate whose ramifications are far-reaching. His love of puns is of a piece with his antipathy to the proscription of other supposedly 'vulgar' popular literary and theatrical forms (penny ballads, penny theatres), with his love of Rabelaisian comedy, Elizabethan word-games, and, all-importantly, the freedom of play as set against the restrictive demands of industry and utility.

Hood's two comic collections of *Whims and Oddities* are prefaced with quotations from Swift's collaborative comic work, *Memoirs of the Extraordinary Life, Works, and Discoveries of Martinus Scriblerus.*[21] The episode from which Hood quotes is noteworthy. The chapter is entitled 'Anatomy'. Crambe, Martin's servant, has fetched a dead body for anatomical experiments, which unexpectedly expels some air, leading him to suspect that it is alive and to drop it on the stairs, whereby an alarm of 'murder' is raised. Taken before the magistrate, Crambe is seized with a fit of punning on the body: 'as touching the body of this man, I can answer each head that my accusers alledge against me, to a hair'.[22] The puns, then, are associated with an episode of (comic) defensiveness and anxiety surrounding the 'matter' of the body, which literally and linguistically occupies an ambivalent status between subject and object. The transgressive anatomising of the body upon which the characters are about to embark is mirrored by a transgressive anatomizing of language, which may be both literal and metaphorical: 'touching', 'head', 'hair'. It seems that puns are particularly suited to the exploration of such unsafe, unstable subjects.

Crambe's self-exculpation: 'O Cicero! Cicero! if to pun be crime, 'tis a crime I have learned of thee: O Bias! Bias! if to pun be a crime, by thy example I was biassed' becomes the tag-line for *Whims and Oddities*. Hood, through quotation, while appearing to acknowledge the social 'crime' of using puns, subtly invokes a formidable host of literary authorities to defend them.[23] The Scriblerians number Swift, whose 'A Modest Defence of Punning' Hood also knew, Pope; Gay; Arbuthnot; Parnell and Harley. Their classical authorities for punning, cited by Crambe, are Cicero and the Greek sage Bias.[24] Hood's earlier comic collaboration with John Hamilton Reynolds, *Odes and Addresses to Great People*, had also played with anti-pun prejudices, declaring ingenuously in the advertisement for the second edition that: 'To the universal objection, – that the Book is over-run with puns, – the author can only say, he has searched every page without being able to detect a thing of the kind. He can only promise therefore, that if any respectable reviewer will point the *vermin* out, they shall be carefully trapped and thankfully destroyed.' The puns in *Odes and Addresses* are as boisterous and as plentiful as everywhere else in Hood's work – indeed, the deprecatory advertisement itself contains an overt pun – but Hood cleverly pretends innocence. The pun depends on recognition for effect; if readers spot puns, he insinuates, it must be because they are 'low' enough to see them. Referring to puns as 'vermin' pushes distaste for them into the realms of ridicule, while suggesting also puns' active ability to get everywhere and cause discomfiture disproportionate to their size.

Hood knew and spurned the objections of John Dennis (1657–1734) to puns, he also knew Samuel Johnson's famous complaints about Shakespeare's puns. A spurious letter in Hood's 1834 *Comic Annual*, 'Johnsoniana', by a verbose 'correspondent' styled Septimus Reardon, comically deflates anti-pun rhetoric. Again the tag is from Swift: 'None despise puns but those who cannot make them.' Mr Reardon hotly denies that Samuel Johnson was in fact an enemy to word-play. As evidence he cites table-talk where Johnson is exhibited punning vigorously ('You really believe then, Doctor, in ghosts?' – 'Madam,' said Johnson, 'I think *appearances* are in their favour').[25] Moreover, Reardon points out that the popularly received notion of Johnson's antipathy to puns is countered by 'the irrefragable fact, that in that colossal monument of etymological erudition erected by the stupendous Doctor himself (of course implying his inestimable Dictionary), the paramount gist, scope, and tendency of his laborious researches was obviously to give as many meanings as possible to one word'.[26] 'Johnsoniana' anticipates Hood's 1842 review of Knight's edition of Shakespeare, in which he argues that Johnson's censoriousness dulls his ear to flexibility of language and breadth of sympathy: tolerances that invite one another. Hood also, by comparing the way that puns and dictionaries multiply meaning, cleverly demonstrates the alliance between the businesses of lexicography and word-play, legitimately connecting Johnson's most famous achievement with the activity he affects to despise. Hood, then, took up an informed and knowing position on puns that favoured Shakespeare and the Scriblerians against Johnson. This alignment which, like that of the Augustan pro-punsters involved looking back nostalgically to the Old Poets and resisting modern proscriptions on the 'barbarousness' of their linguistic habits, embodied significant critical values broadly shared within the *London Magazine* circle. Hazlitt in his reminiscences 'On the Conversation of Authors' noted that at Lamb's Thursday evening parties 'the author of the Rambler was only tolerated in Boswell's Life of him'. He also commented that Lamb 'always made the best pun and the best remark in the course of the evening'.[27] Hood would assert that some of Lamb's puns 'contained the germs of whole essays',[28] a claim that shines reflexive light on the seriousness of his own engagement with the pun as a seminal and germane trope, embodying the essential fertility of language and the inefficacy of attempts to repress its social sports.

Punning and the 'Cockneys'

Leigh Hunt in his anthology of *Wit and Humour, Selected from the English Poets* (1846) lamented that:

> Puns are banished from good company at present, though kings once encouraged and Caesar and Bacon recorded them, and Cicero and Shakespeare seem to have thought them part of the common property of good spirits. They are tiresome when engrossing, and execrable, if bad; at least, if not very and elaborately bad, and of malice prepense. But a pun may contain wit of the first water. Those of Hood are astonishing for their cleverness, abundance, and extravagance.[29]

Hunt's description of the pun as once deemed 'the common property of good spirits' by Bacon and Shakespeare, but now 'banished from good company' is telling. As Nicholas Roe, Jeffrey Cox and others have shown, sociability and 'good spirits' were key values for Hunt and the 'Cockney' circle he established around communitarian ideas of liberty and mutual creativity.[30] Puns, like couplets, always reaching outward to verbal partners, belong to this vision of language as 'common property', the inclusive realm of 'good spirits' rather than the exclusive one of 'good company'. The enclosure of what were once 'commons' and the exile of extravagant, clever, yet potentially tiresome figures echoes Hunt's own political experience. The pun and the 'Cockney' often found themselves at the wrong end of very similar class-based attacks, and Cockney punning should be viewed in the context of a wider contemporary debate about 'vulgar' language that has recently recaptured critical attention. Hunt himself was a notorious punster; his puns are consonant with the neologisms, 'compounding of epithets', and 'juxtapositions of the cosmic and homely' that some contemporary critics found jarring and many modern critics have found an invigorating force in his writing.[31] Among the regulars at Hunt's Hampstead table were several other writers who were known as virtuosic punsters: Charles Lamb, John Hamilton Reynolds, and John Keats. Because what remains to us of these figures is their writing, we have tended to underestimate the possibilities of punning as a form of live, shared social play. We know from various witnesses that punning of this kind was a feature of the *London Magazine* circle, which intersected with Hunt's. To understand the full meaning of Hood's punmanship it is necessary to recapture this context for punning, as one of many manifestations of intimacy and freedom through verbal liberalism within that group.

Punning as a form of social play can take various forms. There is the punning riddle where one party has to guess the answer. We can see

Hood participating in this game with the Reynolds family through his affectionate early letters to his future wife, Jane Reynolds, where he includes a number of such riddles and their answers:

> Why are horses like Sentimentalists – Because they like to indulge in *wo* . . . What is the rudest kind of diction. Contradiction . . . Why is a hatter the most respectable of tradesmen. Because he serves the heads of the nation . . . Why are rabbits like Electors – Because they live in *burrows*.[32]

Keats also 'bandies' puns affectionately in his letters to his friends and family, especially George and Georgiana Keats.[33] Lamb regarded puns as an essential ingredient of letters, 'the twinkling corpuscula which should irradiate a right friendly epistle'.[34] The 'bandying' implies the mutuality of activity involved in swapping, conceiving and 'getting' puns. Keats looks out for 'a Pun or an Acrostic, a Riddle or a Ballad' to entertain his addressees: a list that suggests the value of the pun as a self-standing form, comparable to other, longer and more intricate items of amusement.[35] As a form of dinner-table and after-dinner entertainment, especially but not exclusively amongst men, punning could also become a form of light-hearted sparring: one pun explicitly or implicitly answering another. In John Hamilton Reynolds's *The Fancy*, the poetical boxer, Peter Corcoran, is also a punster, who threatens to '*plant a tickler* upon your *ribs* that shall *shake your sides*'.[36] John Clare noted that Reynolds 'would punch you with his puns very keenly without ever hurting your feelings'.[37] One can imagine that, in this situation, punning held some of the disinhibited charm of boozing and bawdy talk. Dinners amongst the *London Magazine* contributors sometimes involved chain punning on an agreed theme. Apparently once, where the agreed subject was 'spices', George Cary disconcerted everyone by seeming to hesitate. When they asked him what was keeping him, 'it's cumin' he triumphantly replied.[38] For Lamb, the pun's chief delight lies in its spontaneity: the best puns 'are those which will least bear an analysis', the vigour of puns 'is in the instant of their birth . . . A pun hath a hearty kind of present ear-kissing smack with it; you can no more transmit it in its pristine flavour, than you can send a kiss.'[39] Perfect as a sonnet, intimate and ephemeral as a kiss, the great pun in Lamb's reading is a social mystery, as impossible to reproduce as the occasion that gave rise to it. In an oeuvre where nostalgia is a key value, the pun for Lamb is a nostalgic trope, bursting like a bubble of laughter and conviviality, an embrace intense because unexpected and fleeting.

This sensibility meant that, although he enjoyed punning in their company, Lamb disliked it when Thomas Hood and John Hamilton

Reynolds chose in *Odes and Addresses to Great People* to make puns such an obvious (italicized) and prevalent feature of the text. Coleridge wrongly identified the anonymous *Odes and Addresses* as Lamb's work, praising the puns: 'The puns are nine in ten good – many excellent – the Newgatory transcendent.'[40] (Coleridge himself was interested in puns and meditated writing a Defence of Paronomasia.[41]) But Lamb, perhaps partly piqued not to be able to claim authorship, insisted that *Odes and Addresses* would be better without the puns: 'A Pun is a thing of too much consequence to be thrown in as a makeweight. You shall read one of the addresses over, and miss the puns, and it shall be quite as good and better than when you discover 'em. A Pun is a Noble Thing per se; O never lug it in as an accessory.'[42] This episode illustrates that there could be nuanced differences of opinion within the *London Magazine* circle about the proper place for puns. Keats, despite the pivotal role played by linguistic morphology in his writing, became tired of Hunt's dinner-party punning. Punning was a potent social marker and Hood in adopting the pun as the key trope of his comic poetry was making a signal choice: to extend toward an unknown readership the 'bandying' that for many of his literary peers would remain a private game. Hood is not unusual amongst his contemporaries in punning, but in taking the pun public and making it central to his oeuvre; he would go farther down this road than any author of his period. But the fact that Coleridge could mistake the work of Reynolds and Hood for Lamb's highlights punning as a common and collaborative pursuit among the *London Magazine*'s contributors. Hood's habit of punning is cultivated in a climate of linguistic experimentalism, within a circle that valued the pun and the creative and social frissons it produced.

Civil war: negotiating social and anti-social impulses

Much of the intimate pleasure of social punning in this period derives from awareness that it is publicly frowned upon. By the early nineteenth century Addison and Johnson had largely won the taste war to have the pun officially labelled 'the lowest form of wit'. But this very prohibition made the pun piquant. As a trope it signalled cognisant delinquency. This would continue to be true throughout the nineteenth century. Eleanor E. Christian provides us with a remarkable literary snapshot of Mr and Mrs Charles Dickens on holiday in 1840:

A great deal of amusement was excited by Mrs. Charles Dickens perpetrating the most absurd puns, which she did with a charming expression of innocence and deprecation of her husband's wrath; while he tore his hair and writhed as if convulsed with agony. He used to pretend to be utterly disgusted, although he could neither resist laughter at the puns nor at the pretty comic *moue* she made (with eyes turned up till little of the whites were visible).[43]

Here Catherine Dickens plays the incorrigible id, while Charles takes the role of the wrathful superego in a pantomime that tells us much about the internal process that puns were understood to provoke. The pleasure of sin, but awareness of the need for contrition, mingled delight and disgust, were key to the pleasure that thousands of readers experienced when reading Hood's punning poetry. Often, like Tennyson, they read Hood's poems aloud, dwelling on the word play and 'laughing till the tears came'.

The coupling of pleasure with acknowledgement of social disapproval of that pleasure are integral to the function of punning in the nineteenth century. Indeed Hood's advertisement for *Odes and Addresses*, claiming to wish to eradicate the '*vermin*', while evidently revelling in their possibilities, is entirely characteristic of a kind of play, common at this time, that involved appearing to deplore punning, while simultaneously perpetrating it. Theodore Hook's 'Cautionary Verses to Youth of Both Sexes' (1828) piously instruct the youthful reader:

'My little dears, who learn to read, pray early learn to shun
That very silly thing indeed which people call a pun:
Read Entick's rules, and 'twill be found how simple an offence
It is, to make the self-same sound afford a double sense.

'Most wealthy men good *manors* have, however vulgar they;
And actors still the harder slave, the oftener they *play*:
So poets can't the *baize* obtain, unless their tailors choose;
While grooms and coachmen, not in vain, each evening seek the *Mews*.

'. . . In mirth and play no harm you'll know, when duty's task is done;
But parents ne'er should let you go un*pun*ish'd for a *pun*!'[44]

Hook comments that 'puns are an acknowledged ingredient of the English language amongst the middling classes, and are, in their societies, the very plums in the pudding of conversation . . . amongst dapper clerks in public offices, hangers-on of the theatres; amongst very young persons at the universities; in military messes amongst the subalterns; in the City amongst apprentices; and . . . with old wits *razee*'.[45] Under the guise of negatively labelling the pun a disreputable lower-middle-class trope, however, Hook nonchalantly suggests the ability of puns to establish teasing parallels between different classes. Wealthy men may be vulgar; poets may be dependent for their success upon tailors, while grooms and coachmen may themselves be artists. While appearing to admonish the prospective punster ('we have not room to set down all the prohibited puns extant'), Hook offers him or her a brisk training and plenty of ammunition.

The fine line that the pun walks in the nineteenth century between social and anti-social behaviour, unconscious vulgarism and highly deliberate transgression of class rules, makes it a loaded trope. Hood exploits this delicate balance between pleasure and displeasure to the full, making the 'tied trope' central to his personal high wire act. 'Forcing' puns, in this context, can be part of the spectacle, adding further tension to the performance, and it is a mistake to assume, as some critics have done, that such 'forcing' is a mark of pitiable desperation. As both Lamb and Hunt suggest, the 'worst' puns may be the best: 'badness' has positive value in the jokework puns perform. Puns can deliberately act out the awkward conjunction of different emotional registers. Many of Hood's puns involve visual illustrations as well as verbal games, and play with phrases as well as single words. One such illustration is tellingly self-referential. 'A Double Meaning' depicts a woman who is beckoning a child winningly with one hand, while concealing a broom in the other, behind her back, with which to chastise him. This could stand as a type for the frisson generated by the pun in this period, with its composite yield of social pleasure dependent on the threat of social punishment.

The doubled consciousness that the pun invokes renders it a particularly suitable medium for exploring other kinds of doubled consciousness that society requires its members to sustain. Thus many of Hood's most effective phrasal puns take expressions that are innocuous social commonplaces and translate them into a context where they describe violent and anti-social acts (Fig. 5.1). 'I must come out next spring' describes not a young debutante but a lion escaping from a cage. 'Off By Mutual Consent' refers not to a broken engagement but to a monkey losing its head to a cannon, which it has mischievously ignited. 'More Billing than Cooing' (Fig. 5.2) depicts domestic violence – as husband and wife threaten each other with billhooks. 'White Bait' shows cannibals roasting a white man, while 'A Day's Sport on the Moors' illustrates white men pursuing black figures with guns. In all of these examples apparently 'refined' parlance proves surprisingly liable to 'barbarous' interpretation. Puns can explore the internal dialogue between the polite requirements of society and repressed antisocial feelings in a manner comparable to Hood's other wonderful technique of juxtaposing conventional sentiments with 'truth in parenthesis', where the speaker's outer expressions and inner reflections form a witty counterpoint:

OFF BY MUTUAL CONSENT.

WHITE-BAIT.

5.1 Hood, 'Off By Mutual Consent' (1839) and 'White Bait' (1827)

'What! must you go? next time I hope
You'll give me longer measure;
Nay – I shall see you down the stairs –
(With most uncommon pleasure!)'[46]

The pleasure of Hood's punning illustrations often involves a similar
counterpoint between an expected 'primary' and repressed secondary

5.2 Hood, 'More Billing than Cooing' (1834) and 'Civil War' (1837)

reading of the verbal characters presented: where the secondary reading is unexpectedly brought to the fore by the pun. One of the most brilliant of Hood's illustrated puns is 'Civil War' (Fig. 5.2). In this multiply punning picture soldiers attack each other in battle, but the words in their speech bubbles are capable of extremely polite reading. 'After you Sir', insists one soldier decorously as he pursues his foe . . . 'Don't rise', declares another, using his bayonet to suppress an opponent. Again here puns dramatize conflict between social and anti-social impulses, through equivocal expressions that can be read as self-deprecating or aggressive, humane or brutal. Punning in the nineteenth century can serve as a mode of acting out, in miniature form, the perpetual, ordinarily tacit, war between the 'civil' and 'uncivil' self.

Hood's children reported that, when he was bothered by the visits of a scandal-mongering old lady, he responded by sending her 'a mischievous peace-offering of those brown, wizzened, stony apples which go by the uncharitable title of "medlars"'.[47] This acted double-entendre once more suggests the 'cognizant delinquency' puns release, and their capacity to meld the social (gift-giving) with the anti-social (name-calling). In this case the insult is especially tart because the recipient is required to decode it, in a sense to produce it herself, acknowledging not only the visual resemblance between 'meddlers' and 'medlars' but between old maiden gossips and wizened, stony fruit.

Punning as a grotesque art

Hood's illustrations, like the 'medlar' incident, clearly demonstrate the continuity between verbal and visual punning. 'Cock of the Walk', for example, in the 1833 *Comic Annual*, draws on the verbal analogy between a proud man and a strutting rooster: the illustration, however, develops this into a visual pun, where the man's projecting coat-tails resemble tail feathers, his nose a beak, his stance that of a bird (Fig. 5.3). A similar illustration, 'A Strange Bird', is reproduced in Chapter 4 (Fig. 4.6). Recalling the definition of the grotesque as 'a mixed or hybrid form, like tragicomedy, its elements, in themselves heterogeneous . . . combining in unstable, conflicting, paradoxical relationships', it is evident that punning can be seen as itself a form of grotesque art.

John Clare's playful letter to Allan Cunningham, in which he describes Hood's punning, is full of the imagery of hybridity (giants, mermaids, two-headed girls, Siamese twins), seamlessly melding the idea of Hood's body ('his I's & his no's & his air's & his here's') and his language in terms of composite forms.[48] There is a long popular tradition, in which both Hood and Clare participate, of relating the mutability of the physi-

COCK OF THE WALK.

5.3 Hood, 'Cock of the Walk' (1833)

cal body to that of the body of language. Verbal-visual punning is a feature of Gothic art and architecture. T. Tindall Wildridge in his 1899 *The Grotesque in Church Art*, notes that memorials to a founder, builder, or architect were frequently incorporated into church decoration in the form of punning rebuses, such as the cocks representing Bishop Alcock in Henry VII's chapel, or the eye and slip of a tree for Bishop Islip, Westminster.[49] Hood frequently plays upon his own name in this way: some sketches, sent to Alfred Crowquill as hints for the cover of *Hood's Own*, include a smiling flower ('Monk's Hood'), and a man with one closed eye ('Hood wink').[50] Indeed, with writer-illustrators such as Hood, who meld word and image, there is often no secure distinction between 'verbal' and 'visual' punning.

An intriguing early prose work, 'A Dream' (*Whims and Oddities*, 1826), shows Hood thinking about the mechanisms by which the mind creates what we might now dub 'duck-rabbits': figures that combine features that can simultaneously be read in terms of two completely different frames of reference. Hood illustrates his meaning with a medley of human faces, where floating features belong in common to different visages, the eyebrow of one, for example, forming the mouth of another. In this picture, he explains:

> I have tried to typify a common characteristic of dreams, namely, the entanglement of divers ideas, to the waking mind distinct or incongruous, but, by the confusion of sleep, inseparably ravelled up and knotted into Gordian intricacies. For, as the equivocal feature in the emblem belongs indifferently to either countenance, but is appropriated by the head that happens to be presently the object of contemplation; so, in a dream, two separate notions will naturally involve some convertible incident, that becomes, by turns, a symptom of both in general, or of either in particular. Thus are begotten the most extravagant associations of thoughts and images, unnatural connexions, like those marriages of forbidden relationships, where mothers become cousin to their own sons, and quite as bewildering as such genealogical embarrassments.[51]

Hood's thoughts about dreaming are clearly influenced by Thomas De Quincey's *Confessions of an English Opium Eater,* recently published in the *London Magazine,* but Hood anticipates Freud in focusing on the 'convertible incident' that enables the embarrassing, incestuous union of ideas and images that would otherwise be kept separate. In one of the dreams recounted, the pit of the theatre where the author's play is being staged turns into the pit of Hell, peopled with fiends. The verbal pun on 'pit' is one of the equivocal features on which the theatrical fantasy turns; the eyebrow/mouth, meanwhile, is literally and figuratively an 'equivocal feature', a grotesque visual and verbal pun. Articles such as 'A Dream' demonstrate the links between Hood's punning, his grotesque imagery, and his interest in psychology. The nightcap, as Hood elsewhere asserts, is the mind's 'cap of liberty': the revolutionary subconscious finds means of evading the prohibitions of conscious thought.[52] Hood was fascinated by the mind's capacity for begetting 'unnatural connexions'; the pun is the 'convertible incident' par excellence that enables such forbidden couplings. In poems such as 'Lycus the Centaur', the exploration of the anxious continuity between human and animal flesh is made possible by the conjunctions of traditional myth: the doubled figure of the centaur and Circe's transformational world. In Hood's blackly comic poems the pun acts as the 'double-figure', the agent and product of grotesque combination.

In many of the poems we have already looked at as examples of Hood's grotesque art, the pun both detonates the violent actions that lead the body to fragment and recombine and mirrors those physical fissions and fusions in its own capacity to split and splice language. The anatomized lover in 'Mary's Ghost' complains:

> O William dear! O William dear!
>   My rest eternal ceases;
> Alas! My everlasting peace
>   Is broken into pieces.
>
> I vow'd that you should have my hand,
>   But fate gives us denial;
> You'll find it there, at Dr. Bell's,
>   In spirits and a phial.
>
> I can't tell where my head is gone,
>   But Doctor Carpue can:
> As for my trunk, it's all pack'd up
>   To go by Pickford's van.[53]

It is the pun that shatters 'peace' into 'pieces', revealing the susceptibility of language, like that of the body, to atomization. Puns constantly earth the ethereal in the material, insisting that even disembodied souls keep their soles firmly planted on the ground. Mary's figurative 'hand' may have been promised in marriage to William, but the fate of her actual hand is to float in spirits in a laboratory; Mary's 'trunk' is a commodified object little different from a suitcase. Hood is fascinated by the body as receptacle, a 'husk', 'trunk', or 'shell': the transferability of these words, their punning ability to contain different but related meanings is, for Hood, symptomatic of the ambiguous and transferable qualities of life itself. In 'The Supper Superstition' (*Comic Annual*, 1831), Jack Jupp appears as a ghost to warn his family not to eat the seafood on the table, because the fish has previously been dining off his drowned corpse:

> Those oysters, too, that look so plump,
>   And seem so nicely done,
> They put my corpse in many shells,
>   Instead of only one.[54]

The pun, 'shell' (carapace/coffin), is essential to the tenor of Hood's thoughts about the consumption of the human body, a consumption which is both comically unreal – accidental cannibalism is averted here as it is in 'A Legend of Navarre' or 'Ben Bluff' – and gravely real. Like Peter Fin in 'The Mermaid of Margate', Jack Jupp realizes that, within the cycle of consumption, the corollary of eating is being eaten. The conception of a single, unique self with absolute bounds is undermined through the realization that the 'single, self-identical sound sequence correlated with a distinct idea – the word' is at best a necessary fiction: words and people alike are organic composites, sharing elements with ostensibly 'lower' forms.

As we have seen, in 'The Dead Robbery' Peter Bunce narrowly escapes the fate of becoming a corpse in a medical laboratory, only to drive a thriving trade in the bodies of the doctors who would have bought him. The pun on 'subject' ('the actor that governs a verb' or 'a lifeless ana-tomical specimen') is integral to the role-reversal in which this poem delights. Puns effect the transformation from person to thing and back again. Likewise in 'White Bait', the illustration of cannibals roasting a man, the double meaning of the pun serves as a pivot for role reversal between human and animal. In 'A Waterloo Ballad', a poem in which a dying soldier on the field of battle announces his fate to his former fiancée, puns similarly disturb linguistic assumptions of difference and hierarchy:

> 'This very night a merry dance
>   At Brussels was to be; –
> Instead of opening a ball,
>   A ball has open'd me.'[55]

The pun on 'ball' enables the reversal of subject and object. Peter Stone, who was to have been active in life's drama, has become a victim of the role-reversing misrule of which the pun is lord. In the accompanying woodcut, 'War Dance: The Opening of the Ball', which depicts soldiers 'dancing' about as a shell explodes in their midst, the double meaning of 'dance' as well as 'ball' is illustrated. The body, which ought to be sportive, becomes the site of sport, as homonyms invert the syntactic power relationship between person and thing. A corollary of this reifica-tion of the body is its potential consumability, and this, too, is suggested through the double-vision of the pun:

> 'O why did I a soldier turn,
>   For any royal Guelph?
> I might have been a butcher, and
>   In business for myself! . . .
>
> 'Without a coffin I shall lie,
>   And sleep my sleep eternal:
> Not even a *shell* – my only chance
>   Of being made a *Kernel*! . . .
>
> 'Farewell, my regimental mates,
>   With whom I used to dress!
> My corps is changed, so I am now,
>   In quite another mess.'[56]

Peter, who might have been a butcher in business 'for himself', is now dead meat: a position emphasized by puns on 'shell', 'kernel', 'dress', 'core' and 'mess', all words associated with food or cookery. The vulnerability of the 'corps' to change, manipulation, and consumption is reflected in the metamorphic qualities of language. Indeed, chopping and changing words – particularly relishing the impact of each pointed pun – becomes a proxy form of violence toward the body in which author and reader can both legitimately participate.

Critics such as John Clubbe and Walter Redfern, who stress the defensive quality of Hood's punning, are, I believe, too apt to see Hood's puns, in a poetic context, as a form of padding, a recurrent emphasis on verbal dexterity that buffers and ultimately lessens the impact of the work's, frequently violent, narrative. Clubbe, who values above all Hood's humanitarian writing, asserts that in his earlier poems the 'serious' message is often 'hidden' under puns and layers of whimsy: 'Hood was, through puns, provided with a defense mechanism by which he could shy away from the full implications of his vision'; 'He had a pathological fear of being taken at face value.'[57] Walter Redfern takes up this phrase, implying that puns are a defusing mechanism.[58] Roger Henkle comments that 'the psychic charges of [Hood's] puns seem to travel rapidly through the reader, firing off into release before they can be absorbed in the consciousness, before they can be *experienced* in any way'.[59] In these readings the 'point' of the pun is often, in fact, to be, like a stage sword, pointless. It appears to mimic the operation of violence (firing off), yet its charge is blank: it does no harm, acting as a defense mechanism, not a means of attack.

But this view is challenged by the political context in which poems like 'A Waterloo Ballad' appeared. 'A Waterloo Ballad', although written for the 1834 *Comic Annual* (appearing in December 1833 to catch the Christmas market), was immediately reprinted in the *Political Soldier* for 14 December 1833. The *Political Soldier* was a radical, working-class paper, describing itself as 'a radical miscellany that seeks to disseminate sound republican principles amongst the soldiers. It advocates abolition of flogging and other forms of military torture.'[60] In its second issue 'A Waterloo Ballad' is reprinted on the same page as a serious and controversial piece entitled 'The Soldier Flogged'.[61] Evidently the compilers and readers of this paper saw no critical lack of fit between Hood's punning black comedy and more openly polemical work, nor felt a class barrier to printing two such poems on a single sheet. This suggests that, for a contemporary audience, the mordant wordplay in 'A Waterloo Ballad' did not exclude political readings. Some of the punning illustrations to the 1834 *Comic Annual* also have an undertow of violence which is open to political interpretation. 'Firing Shells', the tailpiece to

'A Waterloo Ballad', shows the skeletal figure of death discharging coffins (shells) from a cannon (Fig. 5.4). This pun captures a terrible truth of war: that armaments have their equivalent, and indeed the transactional return on their economic outlay, in human fatalities. The punning framework of Hood's war poems suggests the disposability of the male bodies involved; Ben Battle, John Day, Peter Stone are scarcely individuals: they are puns-in-waiting, their feats of arms bound to explode into severed limbs, their corps always liable to disintegrate into someone else's mess. Edmund Blunden recognized the imagery of Hood's poetry and illustrations as the same he encountered in the trenches in 1914–18. Hood is not writing anti-war protest verse of the kind that Siegfried Sassoon would pen during the First World War, but, by Sassoon's own admission, Hood is one of the authors who made his own work possible. 'A Waterloo Ballad' is folk ancestor to the grotesque jollity of Sassoon's 'The General', and Auden's 'James Honeyman'.

The very ubiquity of puns, their accumulation, can underline the banality of the process whereby subjects and objects are exchanged and transvalued. This is what happens in 'Miss Kilmansegg and Her Precious Leg', where the proliferation of puns is the precise analogue to the unstoppable, ultimately fatal proliferation of gold in the poem. The relentless violence of the refrain 'Gold, gold, gold', and of the inherent play upon guilt (gilt) bring us back to one of the possible etymological roots of 'pun', to 'pound' into pieces. Indeed the punning relationship, standard in Hood's period, between 'pun' and 'pound' (the unit of weight and of currency) underlies the mimetic link between the poem's unstoppable minting of homonyms and the Kilmanseggs' insatiable capitalism. Hood uses a tissue of puns to show the warped value system, inculcated linguistically through the commodification of virtue, into which Miss Kilmansegg is born:

> The very metal of merit they told,
> And prais'd her for being 'as good as gold'
>   Till she grew as a peacock haughty;
> Of money they talk'd the whole day round,
> and weigh'd desert like grapes by the pound,
> Till she had an idea from the very sound
> That people with naught were naughty.[62]

The poem is fraught with puns (mettle/metal; desert/dessert) that translate abstract qualities into literal and measurable quantities, mimicking the Midas-like power of commodification that the Kilmanseggs exert, as they move from an agrarian history (pigs) to a modern economy based on metals (pigs of lead). Brilliantly, in the above stanza, obvious

FIRING SHELLS.

FOOT SOLDIERS.

5.4 Hood, 'Firing Shells' (1834) and 'Foot Soldiers' (1831)

puns (mettle, desert) are surrounded by less self-evident puns also concerned with market exchange (told, pound, good) until we are led to examine the economic and moral values implicit in language itself (naught/naughty). When Hood comes to discuss Miss Kilmansegg's marriage he uses the opportunity to riff for several stanzas on the delights of doubleness ('There's strength in double joints, no doubt, / In double X Ale and Dublin Stout, / That the single sorts know nothing about – / And a fist is strongest when doubled'). His reflections on doubleness even incorporate the puns in which they themselves are couched: 'however our Dennises take offence, / A double meaning shows double sense'. But the poem simultaneously critiques the obsessive productivity it mimics. Its genius is to revel in the commerce it describes, persistently generating puns (doubling/Dublin) and products and emphasizing their power, while simultaneously insisting on the crash to which incessant reduplication is inevitably building: doubleness may also signify duplicity and division, and Miss Kilmansegg's partner will effect a final, profitable doubling of her own body that will kill her.

To examine fully the multiverse of linguistic play in 'Miss Kilmansegg' would require an essay in itself, but a few of the more suggestive puns are worth noting here. Hood considers that the golden leg might be put in the 'Stocks' ('N.B. – Not the parish beadle's!'), insinuating that the commercial marketplace and the public pillory for moral turpitude are meaningfully similar. Miss Kilmansegg is 'undermined' literally and morally by the golden leg, a 'member' which costs as much as a 'Member for all the county'. Miss Kilmansegg's extravagant limb supports only herself as an individual and asserts the rights of her class – MPs, Hood implies, are equally costly, and equally unserviceable to the greater part of humankind. The fact that this pun appears almost identically in 'Faithless Nelly Gray' (1826) ('The army-surgeons made him limbs: / Said he, – they're only pegs: / But there's as wooden members quite / As represent my legs!') underlines the continuity between Hood's early and later poetry and the social criticism frequently embedded in punning connections between the physical body and the body politic. In Hood's illustration 'Close Corporations' (*Comic Annual*, 1837) the overly cosy companies in question are depicted as two fat men, whose bellies touch conspiratorially in the middle of the frame. Squeezed between them hangs a picture of a starving whippet labelled 'Reform'. The puns construct a political allegory. The swollen corpuses of the men represent the greed and insider dealing of the corporations; unless they re-form, then 'Reform' will remain a mere hang-dog sign. The pun, with its own grotesque doubleness and indeterminacy, is, in this kind of political cartoon, at one with the message and the spirit of the critique. It enables the cutting comparison between the private and public body, subject and object, the concrete and abstract. Its own susceptibility to re-form, meanwhile, hints at the vulnerability of the bodies it describes: sooner or later, willingly or unwillingly, they will be changed.

Hood's punning, then, is intimately allied to other aspects of grotesque play in his writing and illustration. It adumbrates the instability of the body – its proximity to animal forms, its susceptibility to consumption, its reification within the insistently transformative world of the marketplace – that, as we saw in the previous chapter, is both a source of anxiety and of delight in his work. The proliferation of Hood's puns, which has irritated many critics, is the corollary of the insight that the individual pun per se unfolds: one word is never only one word; language is hydra-headed, and the more one seeks to resist its grotesque capacities to be more than one thing simultaneously, the more it will resist attempts at containment. This irrepressible exuberance is often joyful, appealing to the child in every reader through repetition, through excess, through composite words (such as 'sombamboozleism', Hood's portmanteau word for mesmerism) that defy ordinary linguistic limitations. But the proliferation of Hood's puns, as the discomfiture of so many critics attests, also contains an element of threat. The energy with which language multiplies, cat-calls, and evades capture in Hood's work evokes memories of the crowd. V.S. Pritchett is right to say that in 'Miss Kilmansegg' 'the puns give the poem a kind of jeering muttered undertone'.[63] Another of Hood's illustrations neatly exemplifies the political tension between possible pleasure and displeasure, harmlessness and threat that the grotesque pun can embody. 'A Radical Demon-stration' (*Comic Annual*, 1839) shows a farmer with a pitchfork encountering a many-headed monster, a horde of 'demons', which also resembles a fire with many tongues (Fig. 5.5). One can read this cartoon in different ways. Hood could be suggesting that radical incendiaries are indeed like demons. Or (more likely) he could be suggesting that they have been exaggeratedly demonized. The fact of our uncertainty shows the pun's own power – a mutability and multiplicity that aligns it with the radical demons in the picture.

Punning and pluralism

Hood is a pluralist by nature. His most stinging attacks on named figures are reserved for those who seek to place restrictions on public freedoms and common pleasures. One of his earliest protest poems, the 'Ode to H. Bodkin Esq., Secretary to the Society for the Suppression of Mendicity' (1825), critiques restrictions on public begging; his 'Ode to

A RADICAL DEMON-STRATION.

5.5 Hood, 'A Radical Demon-stration' (1839)

Mr Malthus'(1832) spoofs Malthusian enthusiasm for limitations on procreation; his 'Ode to J.S. Buckingham' (1835) lashes out at the temperance movement; and the 'Ode to Sir Andrew Agnew Bart.' (1834), 'Ode to Rae Wilson, Esq.' (1837), and 'An Open Question' (1840) – three of his smartest and funniest poems – take on the Sabbatarian movement and its desire to prohibit Sunday working and hence restrict public access to non-religious forms of recreation on the Sabbath. Hood's political espousal of a pluralist position and his punning are fundamentally related. Hood's puns are an acted form of pluralism, an expression of and advertisement for tolerance.

Hood himself makes the connection between linguistic and religious tolerance when he notes, in the preface to *Whims and Oddities* (1826):

> I am informed that certain monthly, weekly, and very every-day critics, have taken great offence at my puns: – and I can conceive how some gentlemen with one idea must be perplexed by a double meaning. To my notion, a pun is an accommodating word, like a farmer's horse, – with a pillion for an extra sense to ride behind; – it will carry single, however, if required. The Dennises are merely a sect, and I had no desire to please, exclusively, those verbal Unitarians.[64]

Puns, in Hood's metaphor-rich mind, are accommodating words, with backs generous enough to bear more than one interpretation. Anti-punsters, like the Augustan John Dennis, are the equivalent of a sect that insists upon a single, indivisible deity. Hood's broad linguistic church is open to all. Tolerance and imaginative flexibility are linked to the ability and willingness to see and embrace multiple meaning. It is, then, a perfect expression of Hood's opposition to what he regards as gloomy, selfish, restrictive legislation when words escape the bounds of unitary meaning and, refusing to stay still, cavort around the figures who would like to contain them. The Malthusian in 'Ode to Mr Malthus' is harassed by his own large family, which has evidently led him to take such a misanthropic view of population. The puns with which Hood peppers the 'Ode' and its accompanying cartoon are the equivalent of his numerous progeny, pulling his nose and generally resisting his attempts to control them. In the cartoon, Mr Malthus, ogre-like, sits below framed paintings of battle entitled 'Siege of BABYlon' and 'Skirmish with INFANTry'. The puns emphasize the ridiculous and one-sided nature of a war against children. Puns, which recall the pleasures of childhood play around the orality of language, are always on the side of the young. Their own irrepressible multiplication flouts the concept of state-sponsored checks on procreation.

Similarly, in the 'Ode to Sir Andrew Agnew Bart.' puns are essential to Hood's attack on parties that seek to restrict general freedoms in favour of a particular moral agenda. Andrew Agnew of Lochnaw (1793–1849) introduced a Bill for prohibiting Sunday labour that was presented four times to Parliament. Had Agnew's law been enacted, many popular aspects of weekend entertainment – from visits to the zoo to food-stalls, horse-hire, boat trips, and the rental of bathing-machines – would have been outlawed. Hood, attacking Agnew, evokes the importance of Sunday leisure to 'town-weary sallow elfs' who after a week of weaving artificial flowers need the opportunity to go and enjoy the real thing at Primrose Hill. Drawing on Shakespeare's portrayal of the renovating greenwood in *As You Like It*, he emphasizes that religious devotion should be spontaneous rather than enforced and is as likely to be inspired by Nature as by man. Agnew, like Malthus, is portrayed as a dour spoilsport, who is vainly opposing himself to the tide of natural impulses:

> Go down to Margate, wisest of law-makers
> And say to the sea, as Canute did,
>   (Of course the sea will do as it is bid,)
> 'This is the Sabbath – let there be no Breakers!'[65]

Just as the sea resists all attempts at human control, so words themselves cheekily refuse containment. The pun on 'breakers' is symptomatic of Hood's use of lexical pluralism to demonstrate the impossibility of enforcing monological imperatives on a diverse and restless population.

Hood's parting shot in the poem involves a dangerous pun that was well calculated to bring its target's fury to the boil:

> Religion one should never overdo:
> Right glad I am no minister you be,
> For you would say your service, sir, to me,
> Till I should say, 'My service, sir, to you.'
> Six days made all that is, you know, and then
> Came that of rest – by holy ordination,
> As if to hint unto the sons of men,
> After creation should come re-creation.
> Read right this text and do not further search
> To make a Sunday Workhouse of the Church.[66]

'I wonder what Johnson would have said of the man who could utter, not only so despicable, but so truly infamous a pun as that', thundered Rae Wilson, one of Agnew's fellow-Evangelicals, vilifying Hood's pun on 're-creation'.[67] The tenor of his response is revealing for the strength of feeling it exposes and the way that Wilson's objections to Hood's position and his objections to Hood's punning become fused. Wilson perceives the truth that Hood's punning and his politics are deeply intertwined. In the 'Ode to Sir Andrew Agnew Bart.' the culminating pun on 're-creation' is the political crux of the argument: the endlessly recombinant energies of the pun embody the play of a workforce that cannot forcibly be contained in any church, and whose restorative free time is vital to its well-being. Puns are words that pro-create and re-create themselves without permission: they are thus admirably well-suited to expressing the prerogative of the populace to do the same.

Levelling puns: the 'House of Commons'

Puns were often treated in the nineteenth century as a kind of commodity, making them particularly appropriate vehicles for describing the urban marketplace. Lamb argued that 'this sort of merchandise above all requires a quick return'.[68] Louisa Henrietta Sheridan, editor of the *Comic Offering*, published a cartoon depicting the arrival of a fresh shipment of puns in barrels.[69] Keats joked that he wished pun-making was as good a trade as pin-making, that branch of manufacture identified by Adam Smith as the archetype of capitalism.[70] Perhaps it is the materiality of the resemblance between words that causes puns to be identified with commodities; perhaps it is the replication of and within punning that suggests mass production. The accusation of acting as a 'literary merchant' is certainly part of the stigma that attaches to punsters, such as Hood, in the nineteenth century, yet it is the pun's commonness, as the embodiment of the cheap literary product, that underlies its popular appeal. It is around 1840 that Christmas crackers begin to be manufactured, at first containing a line of poetry (sometimes Hood's), and then, commonly, a pun. The cracker neatly illustrates the relationship between the commercial and the social function that the pun performs. Both harmless and explosive, it is a purchasable unit designed to pull apart: yet in doing so to celebrate a social bond.

Hood's poetry and prose use various techniques that create a familiar relationship with the reader. One of the most pervasive is a habit of domesticating the solemn and potentially sublime (St Paul's is likened to

THE HOUSE OF COMMONS.

5.6 Hood, 'The House of Commons' (1833)

a tea urn), but also of realizing and releasing the fantastical in the every-day. Puns work in both these directions. Where Mussulmen are domes-ticated into mussel men, roman cement is transubstantiated into romancement. 'High' and 'low' vocabulary, abstract and concrete forms of commerce, are equated. The pun is the cement that binds apparently disparate social groups. Some of Hood's most ingenious puns occur in the false bookcase he designed at the request of the Duke of Devonshire to decorate the shelves at Chatsworth in Derbyshire. Hood invented over a hundred spurious titles for this acted joke, which can still be admired today by unsuspecting visitors. Among the punning titles are: 'The Scottish Boccacio by D. Cameron', 'Debrett on Chain Peers', 'Cursory Remarks on Swearing', 'Johnson's Contradictionary', 'Cook's Specimens of the Sandwich Tongue', 'Lamb's Recollections of Suett', 'Pygmalion by Lord Bacon', 'Shelley's Conchologist', and 'Percy Vere' – in 18 volumes. While imaginary authors like D. Cameron literally domesticate the foreign, piers and peers are united via a cross-class chain of words. Charles Dickens also owned a false bookshelf with punning titles. The similarity between his sham volumes and Hood's is striking: Dickens's false bookcase of 1851 boasted titles including: 'Blue Beard in Search of a Wife by More'; 'Butcher's Suetonius'; 'Malthus' Nursery Songs'; 'Captain Cook's Life of Savage' and 'Burke (of Edinburgh) on the Sublime and Beautiful'.[71] In Dickens's false titles, as in Hood's, the pun brings high and low together: William Burke, murderer, and Edmund Burke, MP, are momentarily confused (a pairing Hood makes in 'Miss Kilmansegg and Her Precious Leg'); Suetonius is reduced to a lump of lard; Lamb and Bacon are similarly domesticated in the larder. Both Hood and Dickens relish the orality of words, shadowed in the refer-ences to literary meats and hints at cannibalism, taking literature back to its cousinage among less celebrated consumables. Some of the puns they employ were generally current in contemporary comic periodicals, in whose illustrations Lamb appears as a sheep, Shelley as a conch, and 'Madame De Stall' as a costermonger. Although Dickens uses puns more sparingly than Hood we can see similar processes at work in their punning. The figurative is literalized;[72] the abstract is insistently realized by the concrete and commercial; names (the Chuzzlewits are descended from the Lord No Zoo) are comically transparent. Puns are symptom-atic of an approach to language and to literature that refuses hierarchi-cal distinctions between the former and the latter. Puns' playful emphasis on outsides rather than insides also complements the larger joke that a false bookcase makes: signs may be no more than signs; language has the appearance of nomenclature, but that may be mere trompe l'oeil. This insight has social implications: words prove, in class terms, to be surprisingly mobile, and titles surprisingly superficial. Alderson notes that in the eighteenth century puns were part of the democratization of wit fostered by tavern and coffee-house culture.[73] In the nineteenth century, despite the vilification of anti-punsters determined to relegate them to the realms of cockneyism and poor taste, puns continue to suggest familiar bridges across discourse boundaries, and between literary and other forms of commercial production, while dukes, clerks, and apprentices alike can enjoy them.

Conclusion

William Empson, in *Seven Types of Ambiguity*, opened the door to a revaluation of the pun. Hood was among the writers who figured in his analysis and Empson proves sensitive to Hood's 'philosophical' punning on the body's mutability. But Empson couldn't resist distinguishing between different kinds of punning. He disliked what he considered 'trivial and undirected verbal ingenuity' and characterized the nineteenth-century punster as, rather like a dancing-master, catering to the 'daughters of the house' with something 'that cannot possibly go to their heads'.[74] Other critics inherited his tone of mild disdain for Hood's vulgar inoffensiveness, distinguishing particular puns (which they enjoyed) from punning as a literary tic. This chapter has argued that we ought to look at Hood's punning not merely as a repeated series of minor acts but as a way of seeing, speaking, and writing language – an attitude toward communication with large implications. As Catherine Bate has proposed, readiness to accept puns is an index of linguistic risk aversion.[75] By this measure, Hood is a pioneer.

Hood's puns belong in a wider framework of historical and social reference than has often been assumed. In choosing the pun as his signature trope, he is drawing on a tradition with political ramifications, siding with Swift and against Johnson in a debate about 'polite' language shared by others in the 'Cockney' cluster of writers that included Lamb, Reynolds, and Keats. The pun is associated with play and sociability and part of the live collaborative creativity of writers in this group. Its official proscription makes it a loaded trope, well suited to exploring the boundaries between social and anti-social sentiments and behaviour. Producing a frisson between unconscious vulgarity and conscious class transgression, it acts out patterns of tension and release between the civil and repressed uncivil self.

Punning is also itself a form of grotesque art, the agent and product of fissions and fusions that relate the body to the body of language. It is thus thematically bound up with the chief concerns of Hood's writing, mimicking the metempsychosis and morphology inherent in the chain of consumption; subject–object exchange; the obsessive replications and conversions of capitalism. Hood's punning is political in its pluralism and in its democratic implications for discourse. It points forward to Joyce, for whom puns – wayward, polysemous, ever suggesting trans-lingual cross-fertilzation – will represent resistance to monological impe-rialist readings of nation and of history.

Notes

1 John Clare, letter to Allan Cunningham (circa 1830), reprinted in P.M.S. Dawson, 'Clare's "Letter to Allan Cunningham": An Unpublished Prose Work', *John Clare Society Journal*, 20 (July 2001), p. 32.

2 Theodore Hook, 'Punning' in *The Choice Humorous Works, Ludicrous Adventures, Bon Mots, Puns and Hoaxes of Theodore Hook* (London: Hotten, 1873), p. 316.

3 Jack, *English Literature 1815–1832*, p. 152.

4 Pritchett, *Living Novel*, p. 59.

5 Ainger's 'Memoir' is prefixed to Thomas Hood, *Poems of Thomas Hood Volume One: Serious Poems*, ed. Alfred Ainger (London: Macmillan, 1897).

6 Alexander Wedderburn in Ruskin, *Works of John Ruskin*, vol. 29, p. 223.

7 Alfred Crowquill (A.H. Forrester), *Absurdities: In Prose and Verse* (London: Hurst, 1827). Hood can also be observed to play with the phrase 'lively Hood' as early as 'An Address to the Steam Washing Company' (1825), see *PW*, p. 22.

8 Poe, 'Thomas Hood', p. 274.

9 Walter Redfern, *Puns* (Oxford: Blackwell, 1984), p. 63.

10 Heath-Stubbs, *Darkling Plain*, p. 50, describes Hood's punning as 'fevered'; Kroeber, 'Trends in Minor Romantic Narrative Poetry', p. 290, refers to 'those hideous puns!'; Jack, *English Literature 1815–1832*, p. 152, claims that 'there is something pathological about Hood's punning'.

11 Jonathan Culler, 'The Call of the Phoneme: Introduction', in Culler (ed.), *On Puns: The Foundation of Letters* (Oxford: Blackwell, 1988), pp. 13–14.

12 Ibid., p. 5. I follow Culler in choosing not to discriminate closely between different forms of pun and related wordplay that Hood employs (e.g. paronomasia, antanaclasis, anagrams, portmanteau words).

13 Oliver Sacks, *An Anthropologist on Mars* (London: Picador, 1995), p. 52.

14 Jonathan Swift, *The Prose Works of Jonathan Swift*, ed. Herbert Davis, 6 vols (Oxford: Blackwell, 1957), vol. 4, pp. 263–6. The 'Dying Speech' is quite likely a pastiche of even earlier, traditional deathbed puns.

15 William Charles Macready, *Reminiscences and Selections from His Diaries and Letters*, ed. Frederick Pollock, 2 vols (London: Macmillan, 1875), vol. 1, p. 406.

16 John Keats, *The Letters of John Keats 1814–1821*, ed. Hyder Rollins, 2 vols (Cambridge, Massachusetts: Harvard University Press, 1958), vol. 2, p. 360.

17 Joseph Addison, *The Spectator*, ed. Donald F. Bond, 5 vols (Oxford: Oxford University Press, 1965), vol. 1, p. 263. This reprints *Spectator* no. 61, of 10 May 1711.

18 Olivia Smith, *The Politics of Language 1791–1819* (Oxford: Clarendon, 1984), p. viii. See also Richard Marggraf Turley, *The Politics of Language in Romantic Literature* (Basingstoke: Palgrave, 2002), especially pp. 70–96, which consider the political implications of the philological ideas current in the Hunt circle.

19 Simon J. Alderson, 'The Augustan Attack on the Pun', *Eighteenth-Century Life*, 20 (November 1996), pp. 8–9. Alderson observes that the practice of the 'pro-pun' and 'anti-pun' camps was in fact more fluid that their positions on punning might suggest. Johnson does indeed, as Hood jokingly claimed, sometimes pun vigorously.

20 Ibid., p. 13.

21 The very title of Hood's *Whims and Oddities* also flew a pro-pun flag. A 'whim' is an old word for a pun.

22 John Arbuthnot, Alexander Pope, Jonathan Swift, John Gay, Thomas Parnell and Robert Harley, *Memoirs of the Extraordinary Life, Works, and Discoveries of Martinus Scriblerus*, ed. Charles Kerby-Miller (Oxford: Oxford University Press, 1988), p. 127. In quoting this collaborative work Hood also seems to hint at connections between the socio-intellectual milieu of the Scriblerus Club and the *London Magazine* circle, whence many of the poems in *Whims and Oddities* emerged.

23 *Whims and Oddities*, 2 (London: Tilt, 1827), title page. Compare *Memoirs*, p. 128.

24 Bias is probably a confusion, by the Scriblerians, for the fourth-century philosopher Bion Borysthenites.

25 'Johnsoniana', CW, vol. 2, pp. 12–13.

26 Ibid., p. 13.

27 William Hazlitt, 'On the Conversation of Authors', in *The Plain Speaker*, 2 vols (London: Colburn, 1826), vol. 1, pp. 79–80.

28 'Literary Reminiscences', CW, vol. 2, p. 389.

29 Leigh Hunt, *Wit and Humour, Selected From the English Poets* (London: Smith Elder, 1846), p. 52.

30 See, for example, Cox, *Poetry and Politics in the Cockney School*; Greg Kucich, ' "The Wit in the Dungeon": Leigh Hunt and the Insolent Politics of Cockney Coteries', *Romanticism on the Net*, 14 (May 1999); and Nicholas Roe, *The First Life of Leigh Hunt* (London: Pimlico, 2005).

31 Roe, *First Life*, p. 238, p. 243.

32 Hood, *Letters*, p. 57. Inventing and transmitting this kind of punning riddle remained a form of current fun throughout the century. See, for example, Edward Lear's letter to Chichester Fortescue, Lord Carlingford, 13 September 1871: 'When may the Lanes and Roads have shed tears of sympathy?

When the Street's *swept*', *Later Letters of Edward Lear*, ed. Lady Strachey (London: Fisher Unwin, 1911), p. 140.

33 Keats, *Letters*, vol. 2, p. 92.

34 Charles Lamb, 'Distant Correspondents', *London Magazine*, 5 (March 1822), p. 283.

35 Keats, *Letters*, vol. 1, p. 303.

36 John Hamilton Reynolds ('Peter Corcoran'), *The Fancy* (London: Mathews, 1906), p. xvi.

37 John Clare, *The Prose of John Clare*, ed. J.W. and Anne Tibble (London: Routledge, 1951), p. 86.

38 Tim Chilcott, *A Publisher and His Circle*, p. 144.

39 Charles Lamb, 'Distant Correspondents', p. 284.

40 Samuel Taylor Coleridge, *The Collected Letters of Samuel Taylor Coleridge*, ed. Earl Leslie Griggs, 6 vols (Oxford: Clarendon, 1971), vol. 5, pp. 472–3.

41 For discussion of Coleridge's interest in punning see John A. Hodgson, 'Coleridge, Puns, and "Donne's First Poem": The Limbo of Phetoric and the Conceptions of Wit', *John Donne Journal: Studies in the Age of Donne*, 4, 2 (1985), pp. 181–200 and Michael West, *Transcendental Wordplay: America's Romantic Punsters and the Search for the Language of Nature* (Athens, Ohio: Ohio University Press, 2000), pp. 59–67.

42 Lamb, *Letters*, vol. 3, p. 8.

43 Philip Collins, ed., *Dickens: Interviews and Recollections* 2 vols (London: Macmillan, 1981), vol. 1, p. 35.

44 Hook, 'Cautionary Verses to Youth of Both Sexes' verses 1, 6, 9, in 'Punning', p. 321. Compare 'A Punster's Narrative' in the *Comic Magazine* (London: Gilbert, 1832), pp. 187–8, where the supposed speaker laments that he is 'cursed' with a facility for punning, which has led him into various mishaps, including a spell in the Fleet Prison. It is telling that Hook directs his youthful readers to Entick's dictionary, which offered schoolchildren pages of homonyms that they should learn to distinguish. As Michael West points out in *Transcendental Wordplay*, p. xi, such primers were a rich resource for budding nineteenth-century punsters, who began their career in the classroom.

45 Hook, 'Punning', p. 316. A razee is an armed ship whose upper deck has been cut away, reducing it to an inferior class: hence, here, an old wit *razee* is one whose firepower has been diminished.

46 'Domestic Asides; Or, Truth in Parenthesis', *PW*, p. 222.

47 *Memorials*, p. 270.

48 Clare, 'Letter to Allan Cunningham', p. 32.

49 T. Tindall Wildridge, *The Grotesque in Church Art* (London: Andrews, 1899), p. 173.

50 Huntington MS, FR123. Illustrations sent by Hood to A.H. Forrester ('Alfred Crowquill').

51 'A Dream', *CW*, vol. 5, p. 135.

52 Hood, *Tylney Hall*, vol. 1, p. 52.

53 'Mary's Ghost', *PW*, p. 77.

54 'The Supper Superstition', *PW*, pp. 285–6.

55 'A Waterloo Ballad', *PW*, pp. 279–80.

56 Ibid.

57 Clubbe, *Victorian Forerunner*, p. 16, p. 56.

58 Redfern, *Puns*, p. 63.

59 Henkle, *Comedy and Culture*, p. 192.

60 *The Political Soldier*, 14 December 1833, p. 1.

61 Ibid., pp. 10–11.

62 'Miss Kilmansegg and Her Precious Leg', *PW*, p. 571.

63 Pritchett, *Living Novel*, p. 65.

64 Hood, *Whims and Oddities*, 1 (1826), address to the second edition, reprinted in *PW*, p. 737.

65 'Ode to Sir Andrew Agnew, Bart.', *PW*, p. 464.

66 Ibid.

67 William Rae Wilson, *Records of a Route through France and Italy with Sketches of Catholicism* (London: Longman, Rees, Orme, Brown and Green, 1835), p. 11.

68 Charles Lamb, 'Distant Correspondents', p. 284.

69 Louisa Henrietta Sheridan, *The Comic Offering* (London: Smith Elder, 1834), frontispiece. See also *The Comic Offering* (London: Smith Elder, 1835), frontispiece, which shows a package of puns arriving as one of the postal deliveries brought by the 'Wag-on of Fun'.

70 Keats, *Letters*, vol. 2, p. 214. Falstaff's *New Comic Annual* (London: Hurst, 1831), p. 5, one of many imitators that sprang up in the wake of Hood's *Comic Annual*, insists 'a pin or pun, / Although mechanical the one, / The other, of a mental make, / Equal hands and minds may take'.

71 Harry Stone, *The Night Side of Dickens: Cannibalism, Passion, Necessity* (Ohio: Ohio State University Press, 1994), p. 9, p. 112.

72 For example, in Mr Jingle's grotesque story in *The Pickwick Papers*, the 'head' of the family is literally deposed when a mother on a coach is decapitated by a low bridge.

73 Alderson, 'The Augustan Attack on the Pun', p. 9.

74 William Empson, *Seven Types of Ambiguity* (London: Chatto and Windus, 1930), pp. 108–9.

75 Catherine Bate, 'The Point of Puns', *Modern Philology*, 96 (May 1999), p. 435.

6

Sine qua non-sense: work, play, and criticism

> there is, I am aware, a kind of nonsense indispensable, – or *sine qua non-sense* – that always comes in welcomely to relieve the serious discussions of graver authors, and I flatter myself that my performances may be of this nature; but having parted with so many of my vagaries, I am doubtful whether the next November may not find me sobered down into a political economist.
>
> (Hood, *Whims and Oddities*, 2 (1827))[1]

> As my works testify, I am of the working class myself, and in my humble sphere furnish employment for many hands, including paper-makers, draughtsmen, engravers, compositors, pressmen, binders, folders, and stitchers – and critics – all receiving a fair day's wages for a fair day's work.
>
> (Hood, 'The Lay of the Labourer', 1844)[2]

Three Victorian publishers – Moxon, Routledge, and Macmillan – issued Hood's work in two volumes, one labelled *Serious Poems* and the other *Comic Poems*.[3] Generations of readers were encouraged to view the greater body of Hood's humorous output as distinct from his contribution to the literature of social protest. This approach occluded a truth that still often escapes students of nineteenth-century poetry: that contemporary debate about the parameters of leisure and debate about the conditions of labour are inseparable. This chapter re-examines the relationship between Hood's engagement with the subject of recreation and his engagement with the changing face of work. Tracing connections between his comedy, his anti-Sabbatarianism, his essays on behalf of new copyright legislation, and his best-known 'protest' songs, I argue that it is Hood's playfulness that allows him to confront the issue of work, so central to his time, with such success. His play offers a counter-discourse, rooted in intimacy and childhood memory, to the inhumane rhythms of incessant and mechanical work. But Hood is not anti-capitalist or opposed, in Roger Henkle's phrase, to 'commodification of the poetic sign system'[4] via the literary marketplace: he is opposed to the exploitative and punitive aspects of industry and their destructive social consequences. Indeed it is his unusual candour and comfort in representing the writer as a worker among others involved in creating the book as material object that enables him to make common cause between reader and author in the campaign for fair legislation regarding both labour and recreation. The ludic in Hood is fundamental to his participation in debates about control, productivity, and value that surround division between work and leisure and remain live today. Hood's influence on later Victorian literature has been underestimated because of his status as a parlour poet; it is, however, precisely the domestic, the familiar, and the intimate in Hood that gives his output such scope and reach and continuing power to trouble critical orthodoxies.

The early nineteenth century saw a struggle over patterns and forms of recreation that reflected competing class interests and changing pressures on private time and public space that brought those competing interests, and the contested nature of the boundary between private and public life, into sharp focus. Industrial capitalism imposed long hours and strict work discipline: labourers in textile mills, among them children, typically worked twelve-hour days. Sunday was the only day of rest and, as Peter Bailey observes in *Leisure and Class in Victorian England: Rational Recreation and the Contest for Control 1830–1885*, 'By 1834 there were only eight statutory half-holidays in England, and the trade calendar of religious feast days and the celebrations of seasonal tasks or particular trades had been considerably pruned, both by the employers and the Church'.[5] It was only after the passing of the Ten Hours Act in 1847 and the gradual shortening of the Saturday work-day which ensued, that the erosion of free time by the new exigencies of employment began to be reversed. Enclosure of public land and increasingly crowded living conditions in the expanding cities also put pressure on traditional forms of recreation. George Offer, appearing before the 1833 Select Committee on Public Walks, reflected that Great Tower Hill, where he used to play as a boy, had been enclosed and only the upper classes permitted entry. Naked bathing in London, once a popular sport for working-class youths, now exercised the middle classes because, in a congested city, they were more likely accidentally to encounter it. In 1833 it was reported that naked bathing in the Birmingham canal, offensive to lady pedestrians, had been banned. Leisure for all classes was increasingly privatized. Legislators particularly sought to control customs that involved a degree of physical disorder ranging through the whole community, such as the Stamford Bull Running, suppressed in 1840.[6] Middle-class concern about disorder and its relationship to working-class leisure found expression in social reform movements particularly active from the 1820s to the 1840s, notably the Sabbatarian movement, the animal rights movement, and the temperance movement. Meanwhile, however, as Hugh Cunningham concludes in *Leisure in the Industrial Revolution, c.1780–1880*, popular culture remained remarkably resilient and the early decades of the nineteenth century saw the growth and commercialization of popular leisure and the influence of popular forms of entertainment on 'high' culture. The class-led contest over recreation had a number of different battlegrounds and significant incursions were made on both sides, but readers should recognize that, as Cunningham puts it: '[d]ecisions and arguments about leisure were decisions and arguments about power and about control'.[7] Play, throughout the period when Hood was writing, was a topical political issue; regulation of the boundaries between work and leisure was intimately linked to anxiety about the boundaries between private and public space and the threat of disorder.

Labour, discipline, and entertainment: sanitizing the street

Hood's writing, from his time at the *London Magazine*, is concerned with issues of public order and the growing number of restrictions on public behaviour in city streets. Difficult post war conditions – large numbers of demobilized troops, domestic unemployment, and market dislocation – had led to an increase in crime, poverty, and demonstrations of public disaffection. Among the volunteer societies that sprang up in response to these urban problems was the Society for the Suppression of Mendicity, founded in 1818, and dedicated to tackling the upsurge in street begging. This society, whose key activist and first secretary, William Henry Bodkin, had been a metropolitan overseer of the poor, hoped to add regulation of begging to the reponsibilities of police magistrates. It was feared that spurious beggars could earn more by deception than by honest labour; the Society aimed to end 'indiscriminate almsgiving' and enable distinction to be made between 'deserving' and 'vicious' petitioners. As M.J.D. Roberts argues: 'In this way the principles of the free market were to be extended from the world of business and of labour discipline into the world of charity . . . investors in monitored forms of charity would be assured of the morally profitable return of a grateful and self-reliant labouring population, so encouraging further investment.'[8]

Both Hood and Lamb situate themselves squarely in opposition to the kind of social control that the Society for the Suppression of Mendicity proposed. Lamb's *London Magazine* essay 'A Complaint of the Decay of Beggars in the Metropolis' (1822) challenges the Society's ideology by claiming that beggars constitute a form of moral show that is worth paying to see, and the feigners are no worse than actors, who are paid for their performances.[9] By shifting the ground from labour (beggars are unproductive) to pleasure (beggars – even fake beggars – are productive), Lamb destabilizes the economic terms of the debate. Hood's own intervention in the debate over begging, his 'Ode to H. Bodkin, Esq., Secretary to the Society for the Suppression of Mendicity' (1825) relates closely to Lamb's essay. It dubs the former overseer a 'Dog in office, set to bark / All beggars from the door', pouring scorn on him for dispersing cripples, many survivors of the recent war, whose rags are 'holy flags'. As in Lamb's essay, play is not only a means of ridicule but a counter-offensive against the Society's demand that all citizens should submit to its labour-based discipline. When Hood remarks of one beggar:

> Poor Jack is gone, that used to doff
>   His batter'd tatter'd hat,
> And show his dangling sleeve, alas!
>   There seem'd no arm in that! [10]

the uncomfortable pun plays around the ideas of deficit and embarrassment, shifting them from the beggar to Bodkin. Hood's later cartoon, 'Why Don't You Look Out for Work?', which features a fat bodkin with its hands in its pockets criticizing a thin needle who is supplicating for charity, also illustrates, via play, the intolerance involved in attempts to suppress begging.[11] Hood echoes Lamb in discrediting another form of street regulation, the banning of chimney-sweeps from public hawking or crying[12] (again, they represent this regulation of labour as equally a restriction of public pleasure) and in deploring the exclusion of the poor from Westminster Abbey and St Paul's Cathedral outside of service time by the imposition of a prohibitive entry fee. Lamb claims that the reason for the new two-shilling Westminster Abbey charge was ill-founded fear of public disorder in the building, official desire for social control manifesting itself as restriction on entertainment. On all these issues Hood, like his fellow *London*ers, opposes what Lamb calls the 'all-sweeping besom' that sought to sanitize the street.

This period was one of increased social policing, with new Foucauldian emphasis on symbolic forms of discipline and control. M.J.D. Roberts links the Mendicity Society to the Prison Discipline Society, also founded in 1818, which similarly aimed to promote public trust, by 'acquiring dominion over the mind of the offender' and securing a reformation of character that would allow their social reintegration. Hood considered, as well as the scathing Ode to Bodkin, including an ode to William Cubitt, the inventor of the treadmill, in *Odes and Addresses to Great People*. The treadmill, first introduced at Brixton prison in 1817, was designed to force prisoners to perform labour in a fashion that was strictly regulated and impossible to evade: ten prisoners were mounted on an open wheel that constantly revolved, forcing them to keep stepping or fall off. The treadmill makes its appearance in Hood's imaginary 'Poems, By a Poor Gentleman' (*Comic Annual*, 1834), where an imprisoned somnambulist recounts a dream of ascending endless steps, which he takes to be those of Jacob's ladder ascending to Heaven, until 'lo! I wakened on a sadder stair / Tramp – tramp – tramp – tramp – upon the Brixton Mill'.[13] As is often true in Hood's poems, most famously 'The Song of the Shirt', this poem turns involuntary labour into a wilful form of echolalia ('tramp – tramp') subversively transforming the rhythm of work into literary pleasure. 'Sonnet Written in a Workhouse' (also among the 'Poems, By a Poor Gentleman') likewise sets up an inner dichotomy between the recreative pleasures of imagination and the discipline of an establishment where repetitive and unrelieved labour is designed to suppress escape into 'blessed literary leisure'. The unfortunate inmate, when the 'vandal elf', the overseer, is gone, leaves his hemp unpicked and replaces his task with Cowper's *The Task*, his 'work' with the 'works' of Johnson, Sheridan, and Goldsmith. But the freedom of literature, represented by Thomson's *Castle of Indolence*, remains 'a castle in the air', as a return to forced labour curtails his reverie. 'Overseer' in Hood's work is always a term of contempt: the workhouse model of unnatural confinement, family separation, and forced labour represents, as in 'The Workhouse Clock: An Allegory', the callousness of a broader social system of punitive regulation.[14]

Hood's poems frequently use their own play to counterpoint the dogmatism of unremitting work and to undermine the position of those who place checks on harmless recreation. In the Preface to the 1839 *Comic Annual* Hood claims to have received a Christmas Address, which has been sent to him by his Parish Beadle. The humour surrounding the unimaginative beadle is redolent of Dickens's comedy and social concern on the theme of pompous parochial administration. In Hood's hilarious scenario, the beadle, lacking poetic originality, has simply replaced every fourth line of the quatrains in Gray's 'Elegy Written in a Country Churchyard' with a moral sentiment supporting his own didactic ends:

> Let not ambition mock their useful toil,
> Their homely joys and destiny obscure;
> Nor grandeur hear with a disdainful smile,
> *The Parish Beadle calling at the door!*

Far from the madding crowd's ignoble strife,
Their sober wishes never learn'd to stray;
Along the cool sequester'd vale of life,
They kept the apple-women's stalls away!

Yet e'en these bones from insult to protect
Some frail memorial still erected nigh;
With uncouth rhymes and shapeless sculpture deck'd
He never lets the children play thereby . . .

Large was his bounty, and his soul sincere,
Heaven did a recompense as largely send,
He gave to misery (all he had) a tear
And never failed on Sundays to attend![15]

The beadle's bowdlerization of Gray's 'Elegy' forms its own commentary on the shift between eighteenth-century sensibility and Victorian evangelism. The graves of the poor, far from inspiring the parish officer with humility, become a platform for delivering his own imperatives. Preventing the children playing by the graveyard, keeping the apple-women's stalls away, and enforcing Sunday church attendance are linked: the evangelical killjoy is determined to maintain social discipline both by regulating the forms of work and pre- and pro-scribing certain uses of leisure. As Hood drily remarks in his 'Ode to Sir Andrew Agnew, Bart.': '[t]o knock down apple-stalls is now too late, / Except to starve some poor old harmless madam; / You might have done some good, and chang'd our fate, / Could you have upset *that*, which ruined Adam!' Hood's comic verse flouts the imaginary beadle by itself playing on the grave stones of Gray's elegy and scriptural story in defiance of his prohibitions.

Anti-Sabbatarianism and protecting play

Hood, like Lamb and Dickens, believed that on Sunday, the only day when workers were at liberty, they should not be legally restricted to spending the day in worship or domestic rest. The Sabbatarian movement was prominent and powerful in early nineteenth-century Britain; it opposed Sunday labour and secular Sunday leisure pursuits that it associated with intemperance and impiety. Its middle-class cohort and improving aims had much in common with those of the Society for the Suppression of Mendicity or the Prison Discipline Society, but its adherents were more numerous and its proposals threatened to prohibit formerly popular Sunday entertainments throughout the country.[16] Unsurprisingly, many of the fiercest literary opponents of Sabbatarian legislation were those who had risen to a position where they enjoyed some free time from a class background where leisure was scarce. Dickens wrote a pseudonymous anti-Sabbatarian pamphlet, *Sunday Under Three Heads* (1836), while George Cruikshank produced *Sunday in London* (1833), which pointed out that Agnew's bill effectively placed no restrictions on the upper classes, as private coaches could be driven (while public transport could not be hired), and private clubs were exempt from the restrictions placed on public drinking and gambling.[17] Since Sabbatarian legislation disproportionately threatened working-class freedoms, its detractors included many radicals, such as William Hone and the chartist Thomas Frost. As Hugh Cunningham notes: 'leaders of Bolton protestors against sabbatarianism were veterans of the radical politics of the 1840s'.[18]

Hood's comic poetry, then, should be seen in the context of a heated contemporary political battle over recreation in the 1830s and 1840s; his anti-Sabbatarian poems make a particular case for play whose general tenets are inherent throughout his oeuvre. Forced labour and restriction on leisure are constantly equated. In the 'Ode to Sir Andrew Agnew, Bart.' (1834), he ridicules Agnew's bill for seeking 'to make a Sunday Workhouse of the church'; again, in the 'Ode to Rae Wilson' (1837), he condemns the 'statute-labour' which, he claims, Sabbatarian enforcement makes of worship. In 'An Open Question' (1840), which advocates the zoo being open on Sunday, he claims that:

> Our would-be Keepers of the Sabbath-day
>   Are like the Keepers of the brutes ferocious –
> As soon the Tiger might expect to stalk
>   About the grounds from Saturday till Monday,
> As any harmless Man to take a walk,
>   If Saints could clap him in a cage on Sunday –[19]

Playing with the resemblance between the animals in the zoo and the people outwith it, Hood highlights the Sabbatarians as would-be jailers of humankind. Legislation that the Sabbatarians would represent as promoting piety is laid bare as a punitive measure designed to enforce social control. As we saw in Chapter 5, word-play is integral here both to Hood's argument and to his process of engaging the reader. In this poem puns shadow Hood's comparisons between beast and bible-basher: the puma *preys* 'extempore as well / As certain wild Itinerants on Sunday'; the Pelicans, like Agnew, present their *bills*; the elephant has a sermon in his *trunk*. Words are naturally pluralist: escaping unitary definition, they shape-shift, resisting attempts at containment. In recognizing and enjoying this freedom, we entertain a liberal view that logically extends to people, who also resist confinement within a single, imposed doctrinal position. 'An Open Question' conveys the harmless delights of one kind of recreation (zoo-going) through another kind of recreation (reading comic verse). By inviting us to participate in one form of play, Hood pulls us toward sanctioning the other.

Writing childhood: play and protest

Hood's playfulness aligns him with the child reader and with the adult reader's memories of childhood. Although not primarily a writer of 'children's literature', Hood, by inventing the *Comic Annual*, with its small size, accessible verse, and liberal illustrations, laid a groundwork for later Victorian children's writers. His letters show that, like Lamb, Hood meditated contributing to a Juvenile Library; and with his wife he compiled a volume of stories and verse for children issued posthumously by his son and daughter as *Fairy Land; or, Recreation for the Rising Generation* (1861). These stories bear all the hallmarks of Hood's poetry: they are enjoyably grotesque, violent, with traditional folk features and modern twists. In 'The Three Great Giants' a character's eyes fall out and are found by children, who play marbles with them until they are put back in. The giants are defeated by successive showers of plum pudding, roast beef, and cutlery on the city of Toomeniaitchez. But the lack of food amongst the rest of the populace leads to each citizen becoming so thin that they are required to bear a descriptive label:

> So from that day the town was full of fluttering white papers, on which was written, as the case might be – 'A soldier' – 'I am a man' – or, 'This is a boy'. And some people, who did not know their grammar, put 'Me', or 'This is me;' for which infringement of the law the Mayor ordered them to be put into the stocks.[20]

As in so much children's literature, the tale ends with moral justice being served, but much of its pleasure derives from delinquence. Phonetic spelling (Toomeniaitchez) and bad grammar ('This is me') are part of a linguistic world where civic administrators crack down on inappropriate self-expression with glorious ineffectuality. In another tale, 'The Golden Armour', a spoiled princess is reformed by a mechanic, who kills the local giant by offering to become his cook. He fills the giant's meat with nails, his pudding with shot and finally blows the giant's head off with gunpowder pie. Again, the material is traditional, yet the terrorist mechanic has a roguishly modern edge.

The early nineteenth-century battle over recreation was partly fought in the nursery. Evangelical writers, such as the sisters Ann and Jane

Taylor, produced hymns and verses that overwhelmingly preached obedience, contentment, and industry. The Taylors' poem 'Dirty Jim', for example, admonishes naughty children who allow themselves to be indolent and grubby ('good boys are seen / To be decent and clean / Altho' they are ever so poor'); 'Contented John' relates that 'One honest John Tomkins, a hedger and ditcher, / Altho' he was poor, did not want to be richer; / For all such vain wishes to him were prevented, / By a fortunate habit of being contented'. 'The Horse. A Fable' tells of a horse that, wishing to be free from work and masters, runs away from home, but, as night draws on, regrets his departure and returns to the security of labour.[21] Hood's poetry instinctively resists the authoritarian discourse barely concealed in such nursery didacticism. His poem 'A Lay of Real Life' is, indeed, a parody of one of the Taylors' most famous poems, 'My Mother'. The fact that 'A Lay of Real Life' is a (hitherto unrecognized) parody of Evangelical nursery verse underlines the interrelatedness of Hood's play and his protest writing.

Ann Taylor's 'My Mother', like all of the Taylors' verse for and about children, is a poem that inculcates gratitude; Hood's parody 'A Lay of Real Life' (1835) points out that not all children enjoy the protection that engenders gratitude. 'My Mother' asks:

Who fed me from her gentle breast,
And hush'd me in her arms to rest,
And on my cheek sweet kisses prest?
                    My Mother.

. . . Who sat and watch'd my infant head
When sleeping on my cradle bed,
And tears of sweet affection shed?
                    My Mother.

. . . Who drest my doll in clothes so gay,
And taught me pretty how to play,
And minded all I had to say?
                    My Mother.[22]

The poem rehearses a catechism of maternal acts of piety and care, which the narrator promises to requite under the stern eye of God, who would 'look with vengeance' should (s)he ever 'dare despise' her mother. In Hood's 'A Lay of Real Life', by contrast, the narrator looks back on all those who were supposed to protect him but were actually exploitative and uncaring:

Who left me in my seventh year,
A comfort to my mother dear,

And Mr. Pope, the overseer?
>   My Father.

Who let me starve, to buy her gin,
Till all my bones came through my skin,
Then called me 'ugly little sin?'
>   My Mother.

Who said my mother was a Turk,
And took me home – and made me work,
But managed half my meals to shirk?
>   My Aunt.[23]

'A Lay of Real Life' is a remarkable and disturbing parody: its humour is extremely black. Noticeably, the workhouse overseer again appears as a tyrant figure, supplying paternal absence. While Ann Taylor's imaginary mother teaches the child how to play, the exploitative female relatives in 'A Lay of Real Life' make the child work. His stepmother makes him 'black shoes, clean knives, run far and wide'. When the catalogue of selfish relatives and friends is exhausted, the only person the narrator has to fall back on is 'Myself'. The social model Ann Taylor's poem assumes is one of happy dependence, where benevolent maternalism produces contented service. In Hood's poem the individual is failed by society.

Hood takes a comforting pattern common in nursery verse – short stanzas and simple rhymes, familiar shape and rocking refrain – and uses it to describe social abandonment; he uses play to evoke the want of play. Like Dickens's use of fairy-tale elements in *Bleak House* or *David Copperfield* to highlight the miseries of a childhood where play is withheld, Hood's combination of comic verse and social critique is potent in slipping under readers' defences, harking back to easy forms of poetry that recall childhood, while suggesting the deficits suffered by those denied social care. There is a strong element of parody of nursery evangelism in later Victorian children's writing: Lewis Carroll's 'Twinkle, twinkle, little bat' in *Alice's Adventures in Wonderland* parodies Jane Taylor's 'Twinkle, twinkle, little star'; his 'How doth the little crocodile' parodies Isaac Watts's 'Against Idleness and Mischief'. Hood is an influential forerunner, whose poems undercut an evangelicalism that, in the first half of the nineteenth century, was particularly associated with preaching the virtues of industry over the vices of idleness and with legislation inimical to working-class pleasures.

Another poem redolent of nursery verse that suggests the inextricability of Hood's play and his protest poetry is 'A Plain Direction' (1839). In this poem a man loses his way in London and to all his requests for directions receives only the oxymoronic answer 'Straight down the Crooked Lane, / And all round the Square'. A utopian vision of Britain is satirized, as all the man's enquiries elicit the same rebuff:

> I've heard about some happy Isle,
> Where ev'ry man is free,
> And none can lie in bonds for life
> For want of L. S. D.
> Oh that's the land of Liberty!
> But how shall I get there?
> 'Straight down the Crooked Lane,
> And all round the Square.'
>
> I've dreamt about some blessed spot,
> Beneath the blessed sky,
> Where Bread and Justice never rise
> Too dear for folks to buy.
> It's cheaper than the Ward of Cheap,
> But how shall I get there?
> 'Straight down the Crooked Lane,
> And all round the Square.'
>
> They say there is an ancient House,
> As pure as it is old,
> Where Members always speak their minds,
> And votes are never sold.
> I'm fond of all antiquities,
> But how shall I get there?
> 'Straight down the Crooked Lane,
> And all round the Square.'[24]

The form of this poem has many popular antecedents, such as the nursery verses where a traveller asks 'how many strawberries grow in the sea?' and is told 'as many red herrings as grow in the wood'.[25] Hood's traveller, similarly, in the final verse of 'A Plain Direction' asks about a 'pleasant land, / Where omelettes grow on trees'. But the pointed allusions to parliamentary and judicial corruption, and to the imprisonment of debtors – a subject painful to Hood, who had been driven to emigrate by a financial collapse that would otherwise have landed him in debtors' prison – turn 'A Plain Direction' from abstract whimsy to direct critique. The poem's childlike 'nonsense' renders it apparently innocuous, yet nonsense is central to its political charge: that the 'famous Land' of which patriots are proud is pure fantasy, for the real Britain bears no relation to its advertised self.

Samuel Butler's *Erewhon* (1872) and William Morris's *News from Nowhere* (1890) similarly adopt forms of tale familiar from childhood to explore a utopian vision that critiques contemporary Britain. As with Hood's 'A Plain Direction', the form is significant to the critique. First, it emphasizes commonality: forms of literature (and, primarily, oral culture) familiar from childhood constitute forms of shared experience, whose mutually acknowledged territory is a basis for creating solidarity and conjuring shared social visions. Second, since a principal target of nineteenth-century social critique is the effect on human lives of the labour conditions imposed by industry, and the vulnerable economy of the family itself, play represents a figured escape from and counter-discourse to those conditions. Hood's engagement with childhood and his appeal to the child in the adult reader are integrally related to his opposition to a culture where the liberty of the human body can be forfeit to 'want of L. S. D.' and the control exerted by an exploitative labour market threatens the native and commonly held freedoms represented by and expressed in play.

The working writer and the rights of labour: 'Copyright and Copywrong'

Hood is opposed to the exploitative and punitive aspects of industry and their destructive social consequences, but in my view he does not, as Roger Henkle suggests, oppose 'commodification of the poetic sign system' or regard the evolving literary marketplace as part of a 'redefining of art by the bourgeois capitalistic economy' that threatens individual subjectivity. Books, for Hood, are always, and were always, commodified objects: authors are workers among many others (engravers, binders, typesetters) involved in the material creation of literary products. When that process becomes exploitative – a consequence of booksellers' unchecked power rather than industrialization per se – it is not the author's selfhood but his livelihood that suffers. In acknowledging all literature as commercial and material in essence and focusing on the failure of legislation to protect the writer as a worker from profiteers, Hood's contribution to an evolving labour protest movement is rooted in the common cause he identifies between writers and other workers, cutting across class lines and distinctions between artist and artisan.

Hood is unusual amongst nineteenth-century writers in constantly representing to the reader the work involved in writing and in bringing books to press. In the introduction to his novel, *Tylney Hall* (1834), he 'dreams' of being trapped between two readers for printing-offices, one of whom finds his work too gloomy, the other of whom finds it too light-hearted. Rather than immersing the reader directly in fiction,

Hood's 'alienating' opening describes the vagaries of the publication process: the typesetters, the printers' devils. Similarly, in his introductions to the *Comic Annual*, Hood conveys the difficulties that have been overcome to set the work before the public for another year. The 1839 *Comic*, whose publication was dogged by illness, explains that:

> to account for the unusual lateness of the present crop in coming to market, it must be told how, at the eleventh hour, when all that ought to be cut was cut, and only a small portion wanted carrying, the labourers, one and all, master and man, were suddenly disabled by the same complaint, and confined to the same bed.[26]

The author, like a man working in the fields to bring in the harvest, is a labourer in Hood's rhetoric and shares in the community and vicissitudes of labour. Those vicissitudes were especially stark to Hood in the years between 1832 and 1840, when he was conducting the *Annual* from a situation of self-imposed exile on the Continent, while trying to retrieve himself and his family from financial collapse. His difficult sojourn in Germany and Belgium naturally led Hood to compare different systems of government and to reflect in greater depth on the political deficits that sustained social injustice.[27] The injustice he felt most keenly in his personal situation was legislative failure to protect authors' rights against profiteering publishers. During 1837 he contributed a series of 'open letters' (in fact highly polished essays) to the editor of the *Athenaeum* on the Copyright Bill, presented to Parliament by Hood's former colleague Thomas Noon Talfourd, which would have extended the term of copyright to sixty years after the author's death.[28] These letters are extremely revealing, both as Hood's most direct contribution to parliamentary politics and in highlighting contemporary debate about the relationship between writing and other kinds of labour.

Hood persuasively argues that the question of legislative protection for authors against piracy at home, unremunerated publication abroad, underpayment and misrepresentation is not merely financial. The legislature considering the Copyright Bill will also indirectly determine:

> Whether literary men belong to the privileged class, – the higher, lower, or middle class, – the working class, – productive or unproductive class, – or, in short, to any class at all.[29]

At present, Hood asserts, authors, 'like certain birds and beasts of difficult classification', go without any:

> We are on a par . . . with quack doctors, street-preachers, strollers, ballad-singers, hawkers of last dying speeches, Punch-and-Judies, conjurors, tum-

blers, and other 'diverting vagabonds.' We are as the Jews in the East, the Africans in the West, or the gypsies anywhere. We belong to those to whom nothing can belong. I have even misgivings – heaven help us – if an author have a parish! I have serious doubts if a work be qualification for the workhouse!

Hood's first poem of 'social protest' had been an attack on those who sought to control begging. Here, albeit serio-comically, he aligns authors with itinerants and vagabonds, those who have no secure social 'place' and hence no secure social entitlement. As in his 'Sonnet: Written in a Workhouse', he teasingly raises the notion of the book as a 'work' and questions its relation to the kind of labour prescribed by the authorities.

Hood was not alone in remarking the anomalous social status of authors in early nineteenth-century Britain. Douglas Jerrold quizzed: 'is the author, in these days of light, no longer considered an equivocal something between a pickpocket and a magician?'[30] Edward Bulwer Lytton in *England and the English* (1833) complained that, in England, authors 'hold no fixed position in society'.[31] As Clifford Siskin argues in *The Work of Writing*, the years to 1830 see progressive professionalization of writing, but that process of defining what kind of work writing is, and how it should be viewed in relation to other forms of work, is contested, and profoundly alters subsequent conceptualization and hierarchization of labour.[32]

Hood approaches the problem of defining writing as labour head on. In 'Copyright and Copywrong', he attributes the habit of undervaluing and underpaying authors largely to 'the want of any definite ideas amongst people in general' about how, why, and what authors write. Thus some believe that writing is easy, that it is primarily the fruit of unconscious inspiration, that writers are chiefly motivated by a love of antiquity or posterity, personal amusement, or self-improvement. In fact, he argues, all published writing is a form of poorly remunerated commercial productivity and those who twit 'a humble class of men, who live by their pens' as 'penny-a-liners', 'girding not at the quality of their work, but at the rate of its remuneration', are insulting Milton:

Why he was, as you may reckon any time in his divine Paradise Lost, not even a ha'penny-a-liner! We have no proof that Shakespeare, the high priest of humanity, was even a farthing-a-liner, and we know that Homer not only sold his lines 'gratis for nothing,' but gave credit to all eternity! If I wrong the world I beg pardon – but I really believe it invented the phrase of the *republic* of letters, to insinuate that taking the whole lot of authors together they have not got a *sovereign* amongst them![33]

The punning play that relates the impecunious nature of authorship to its democratic potential neatly follows the introduction of three figures whom Hood associates with writing's origination with and dedication to the 'common man': the republican Milton; the deer-stealer Shakespeare, whose 'socialism'[34] Hood revered; and the blind beggar, Homer. It 'has happened according to some inscrutable dispensation', he contends, that the foremost writers are likely to come of humble origins:

> Our poets have been Scotch ploughmen, farmer's boys, Northamptonshire peasants, shoe-makers, old servants, milk-women, basket-makers, steel-workers, charity-boys, and the like.[35]

Thus it is especially vital that the writer is accorded professional recognition and is enabled to make a good living that will not leave him[36] and his dependants to the uncertain mercies of charity. In valuing the writer materially, by ensuring he enjoys the profit he produces, legislation will also be ensuring that he is properly valued as a citizen. At present, Hood argues, few authors are 'forty-shilling freeholders' and thus entitled to vote, much less financially qualified for a seat in Parliament or the Lords. More authors should be in these representative positions: Hood, three years before the publication of Shelley's *Defence of Poetry*, asserts that writers should themselves be legislators.

Hood's defence of the writer as a worker is significant in various ways. By presenting his anomalous social situation, he aligns the author with several different classes at once. From one perspective the author is like a member of 'the privileged class', the gentry, in that, rather than from regular employment, he derives much of his income in perpetuity from 'estates' which can be 'poached': Hood points out the irony that, while common land is being enclosed by private landowners, the author's estates quickly revert from private to common property, threatening his means of supporting his heirs.[37] From another perspective the author may be a salaried professional akin to a vicar, but without a sign to proclaim his office. Viewed in yet another light, the author is a jobbing labourer, producing prose or poetry at fixed rate and quite likely to have a background in manual work (shoe-making, basket-making, steel-working). Hood doesn't fully answer the question he claims the legislature is posed as to 'whether literary men belong to . . . the higher, lower, or middle class, – the working class, – productive or unproductive class': but he is very clear that they are workers, that they are productive, and that, although they may stem from any one of the social classes, they ought to be able to participate in public affairs and in government at the highest level. The fruitful ambiguity of the author's class status allows him to occupy a range of situations and claim the allegiance of different interest groups, participating personally in the wider debate about how the labourer should be guaranteed fair remuneration and what share of the profits of his industry is rightly his. By insisting upon the question of authorial social status as shared, rather than individual, Hood asserts the claim of writing to level prior distinctions, conferring its own. Moreover, by presenting authors as a group that overwhelmingly struggles to make ends meet and literature as 'unprotected by the constable (that's the law), threatened by the beadle (that's the law too), repulsed from the workhouse by the overseer (that's the government), and denied any claim on the parish funds',[38] Hood voices not merely sympathy but solidarity with the dispossessed.

Hood's insistence on writing as labour, and on the text as material object, permeates his writing, constantly forging sympathetic links between the writer and other kinds of worker. 'Madame Hengler, Firework-Maker to Vauxhall' (1830) is the subject of a wonderful celebratory poem which urges her to:

Accept an Ode not meant as any scoff –
The Bard were bold indeed at thee to quiz,
Whose squibs are far more popular than his;
Whose works are much more certain to go off.[39]

In 'The Assistant Drapers' Petition' (1839) Hood establishes community with the weary shopman 'Selling from morn to night for cash or credit; / Or with a vacant face and vacant eye, / Watching cheap prints that Knight did never edit'.[40] Drapers were demanding a reduction in their working hours, which Hood supported. Via puns, he transforms the 'durable fabric' of the clothing industry to that of 'Shakespeare, Milton, Dryden, Locke', whom, he asserts, drapers should have time to 'lay in'. Hood's poem, making the material of drapers' work into the stuff of play, demonstrates the trade-off it wishes to see between labour and recreation. It is difficult to imagine another poet – Wordsworth, Coleridge, Byron or Shelley – writing about assistant drapers: to do so would represent too great a forfeit of caste. One of Hood's great strengths as a writer is that his willingness to relate his poems to other commodities, and his labour to that of other toilers struggling to win new legislative protection, creates the conditions for a new kind of bond between the author and the working reader.

Work songs: consolation and complaint

The bitter wit of 'Copyright and Copywrong' and the play of poems from 'Sonnet – Written in a Workhouse' to 'The Assistant Drapers' Petition' that pit work against literary 'works' are formative backgrounds to Hood's best-known protest poems, where he articulates the claims of labour. In 1844, responding to newspaper accounts of the sentencing of Gifford White, an agricultural labourer, to death merely for threatening to set fire to his master's ricks, Hood wrote 'The Lay of the Labourer'. In his introduction to the poem he announced:

> As my works testify, I am of the working class myself, and in my humble sphere furnish employment for many hands, including paper-makers, draughtsmen, engravers, compositors, pressmen, binders, folders, and stitchers – and critics – all receiving a fair day's wages for a fair day's work.

Critics now may baulk at Hood's insistence that he is 'of the working class', preferring to define him as 'lower middle-class'. Isobel Armstrong, as we have seen, considers Hood 'to some extent a ventriloquist for the working class'. Yet Hood's assertion is not disingenuous. It is, as Harriet Martineau notes, in Hood's period that the expression 'working class' becomes current. She thinks of it as according a mark of respect to groups previously defined by their subordination to other social groups ('lower classes').[41] By insisting that his literary 'works', produced by a range of hands including all those involved in constructing the book as material object, testify that he, too, is of the 'working class', Hood deliberately situates authorship within a community of labour. The poem that follows voices the claim of the labourer to employment and to a fair wage.

> Ay, only give me work,
>   And then you need not fear
> That I shall snare his worship's hare,
>   Or kill his grace's deer;
> Break into his lordship's house,
>   To steal the plate so rich;
> Or leave the yeoman that had a purse
>   To welter in a ditch.[42]

'The Lay of the Labourer' is, on the one hand, a poem designed to allay the fears of masters anticipating worker insurrection. In the voice of the labourer, it insists that, as long as he is provided with honest work and wages, he will be 'a willing drudge'. However, repeatedly calling for 'A spade! a rake! a hoe! / A pickaxe, or a bill!', it also draws attention to the implements of work that might potentially be raised in violent retribution, should the masters fail to heed the cry of labour; the poem cries 'woe to him / Who does their pay begrudge' and warns that those who dock wages will find themselves paying in the end, for the criminality engendered by desperation. Hood's cross-class position here is awkward but advantageous, allowing him simultaneously to threaten and to placate.

Indeed the plain forms and simple rhythms of Hood's late protest poems, in general, are both consoling and monitory, echoing the repetitive patterns of those caught in an economic cycle beyond their control. In 'The Bridge of Sighs' (1844) the body of the suicide, a 'fallen' woman, is rocked by the dactylic dimeters as if by a caring hand, but the relentless motion also echoes the rise and fall of the river that drowned her. In 'The Workhouse Clock: An Allegory' (1844), the insistent beat conveys both the hammer of work and the tramp of resistance:

> The Sempstress, lean, and weary, and wan,
> With only the ghosts of garments on –
> The Weaver, her sallow neighbour,
> The grim and sooty Artisan;
> Every soul – child, woman, or man,
> Who lives – or dies – by labour.
>
> Stirr'd by an overwhelming zeal,
> And social impulse, a terrible throng!
> Leaving shuttle, and needle, and wheel,
> Furnace, and grindstone, spindle, and reel,
> Thread, and yarn, and iron, and steel –
> Yea, rest and the yet untasted meal –
> Gushing, rushing, crushing along,
> A very torrent of Man![43]

The tight metrical formula suggests the quasi-hypnotic compulsion of the workhouse clock, symbolic of industry, which makes no adjustment for social needs. Yet the controlling rhythm of enforced work is converted, via the play of verse, and transformed. The mass, bearing down upon the workhouse and the overseer, who is setting the clock, with 'irresistible moral force', constitutes an alternative mechanism with 'Blood-power stronger than steam'. 'The Workhouse Clock', evoking the crowd's instinctive confluence, turns the march of machinery into an organic 'Human Movement' and collective chant. Similarly, in 'The Song of the Shirt' (1843), the poem both replicates the obsessive rhythm of unremitting work and converts it into a form of counter-labour that embodies the pleasure and respite the seamstress so desperately craves. These poems recall ancient traditions of 'work song', designed to mimic, to protest, and to allay the collective suffering of labour.

Like Dickens, Hood has been accused of being 'sentimental' in his protest verses: V.S. Pritchett complained that he preferred to 'let the poor or oppressed describe their lives uncouthly' than to 'attack the rich'.[44] But the consolation these poems offer is integral to the mediation they undertake. With many of the same devices (puns, monologue, grotesquerie) and strong metrical and formal characteristics as Hood's comic poems, they invite the reader to join in. Indeed everything about these poems, from their cumulative movement to the identification of shared objects (the shirt, the water, the clock) emphasizes familiarity. Hood's poems may be easier, in various senses, than modern critics could wish. But it was precisely this easiness that ensured their success. Hood could not have made such an impact with his 'protest' poems had his credentials as a comic poet not already been firmly established. Appearing in otherwise comic vehicles – the *Comic Annual*, *Hood's Magazine*, *Punch* – the 'protest' poems were inoffensive yet powerful, critical yet sufficiently enjoyable to reach a very large, mixed audience. The *Comic Annual*, appearing in the Christmas season and designed to be given as a present, had created a link between Hood and holiday, the intimacy of home and the generosity of gift-giving. Many readers, meanwhile, were aware of Hood's financial struggles and ill-health: his best-known protest poems appeared in the final years of his life, when these were most acute. Hood was, then peculiarly well placed to articulate both the miseries of sweated labour and the restorative value of recreation. His playfulness and the work accomplished by his writing are inseparable.

Mass appeal: intimacy and influence

Hood's appeal is rooted in the intimacy he establishes with the reader. His influence has been underestimated because of his academic status as a parlour poet; it is, however, precisely his association with the domestic, the family, and the 'minor' that enables his verse to form part of the cultural bridgework upon which future novelists and artists would build. The foremost example of this is 'The Song of the Shirt' (1843), which as John Dodds remarks, was 'perhaps of all poems in the decade the one to make the deepest impact on the largest number of people'.[45] As Lynn M. Alexander demonstrates in *Women, Work, and Representation: Needlewomen in Victorian Art and Literature*, public consciousness about the abuses of the dress trade had been raised by numerous articles in the early 1840s, culminating in publication in 1843 of *The Second Report of the Children's Employment Commission*, which revealed that there were fifteen thousand women employed as milliners in London, many under eighteen, working inordinately long hours at punitive rates of pay, with insufficient food and air, leading to early deaths.[46] Hood was not the first commentator on this topical issue, but his poem profoundly affected the form and iconography through which this kind of industry was represented and thus the form and iconography through which the reader or viewer encountered the vicissitudes of labour exploitation.

'Work – work – work!
  My labour never flags;
And what are its wages? A bed of straw,
  A crust of bread – and rags.
That shatter'd roof, – and this naked floor –
  A table – a broken chair –
And a wall so blank, my shadow I thank
  For sometimes falling there!

. . . 'Oh but for one short hour!
  A respite however brief!
No blessed leisure for Love or Hope,
  But only time for Grief!
A little weeping would ease my heart,
  But in their briny bed
My tears must stop, for every drop
  Hinders needle and thread!'[47]

Hood's needlewoman is atypical of her profession in that she is a solitary operator. But the loneliness Hood conjures is an effective element of the poem's strategy, as is his insistence on the seasons and scenes of 'blessed leisure' from which the needlewoman is excluded. The swallows 'brood' under the eaves, raising their young, while the seamstress's obsessive brooding over her production can end only in death: the enforced conditions of labour are contrasted with natural rhythms of growth, care, and respite. Hood deliberately chooses as his symbolic worker a lone woman, a figure intimate and vulnerable rather than threatening. As Alexander notes, all Victorian women sewed: it was a form of work that cut across classes, blurring the boundaries between domestic and industrial employment. In inviting compassion Hood also invites self-identification. Moreover, by placing his sickly seamstress in a garret, singing her dolorous song, he conjures an image similar to that of the tragic artist. In various ways, then, the poem succeeds in galvanizing support for the seamstress by its relocation of a public evil within a private, quasi-domestic sphere and by articulating a shared economy in which the reader is directly implicated. Via the common thread of clothing, Hood shows the causal connection between middle-class leisure, which helps to generate demand for dress, and sweated labour. Yet the poem also performs its own redemptive part in this economy, as the song metonymically substitutes itself for the shirt, discharging its own burden of 'work – work – work', offering itself as both product and gift.

In articulating and mediating the relationship between middle-class leisure and working-class labour, Hood provided a model for many other nineteenth-century writers and artists. The graphic simplicity and symbolism of 'The Song of the Shirt', doubtless affected by Hood's long experience as a designer of woodcuts, made it an iconic piece, whose lines and images were continually reproduced in various formats over the decades that followed. Richard Redgrave's painting *The Sempstress*, exhibited at the Royal Academy six months after the publication of Hood's poem portrayed a lone needlewoman in a bare attic and carried lines from the poem in its catalogue description. As Alexander points out, an 'iconographic vocabulary'[48] developed, such that subsequent paintings of the seamstress (for example Anna Blunden's *'For only one short hour'*, John Everett Millais's *'Stitch! Stitch! Stitch!'* and George Frederic Watts's *The Song of the Shirt*) almost all quote Hood, verbally and/or visually. Hood, apostrophizing 'Men with Sisters dear! / O! Men! With Mothers and Wives!' warns that 'It is not linen you're wearing out, / But human creatures' lives'. The shirt became the common symbol of an endemic problem that touched – literally – all men intimately. Condition of England novels of the 1840s and 1850s also drew on Hood's imagery and tactics as a touchstone, in narratives designed to illustrate the interdependent lives of workers and employers, producers and consumers, and to foster understanding between them. Camilla Toulmin's *The Orphan Milliners* (1844) prefaces her novel with an epigraph from the poem. Hood is the first named poet quoted in Elizabeth Gaskell's *Mary Barton* (1848) after the anonymous 'Manchester Song' and nursery rhyme that open her first two chapters: his poetry becomes part of the cultural weave strategically uniting high and low, literary and oral traditions. Gaskell's *Ruth* (1853) takes a betrayed seamstress as its heroine, while, in *North and South* (1855), Hood's 'The Lay of the Labourer' appears at the head of a chapter that concerns the suicide of an unemployed millworker. The plot of Charles Kingsley's *Alton Locke* (1850), which handles the injustice suffered by workers in the clothing industry, expands the idea inherent in 'The Song of the Shirt' that sweated labour is worked into the fabric of the garments the rich buy: the cloth is, in some sense, made of the poor as well as by them. One of the slopworkers in the novel remarks, 'stitch, stitch, stitch. – Somebody's wrote a song about that – I'll learn to sing it'.[49] Kingsley's protagonist, who wishes himself to become a poet, reads Hood and is advised by his mentor that 'True poetry, like true charity, . . . begins at hame. If ye'll be a poet at a', ye maun be a cockney poet . . . Shelley's gran' always gran'; but Fact is grander.'[50] By all these writers Hood's verse is referenced as a poetic analogue to the 'democratic art' the novel itself attempts, which dwells on common objects in order to emphasize common cause between polarized communities.

Novels such as *Alton Locke* and poems such as 'The Song of the Shirt' can seem to the modern eye tame palliatives that eschew direct political action against social injustice; yet contemporary readers did not perceive them as sops: Gerald Massey's account of the impact of Hood's writing, from a working-class perspective, is passionate. Massey, a chartist poet, was the child of manual labourers, who himself worked in Tring silk mill from the age of eight. Through writing and public speaking he escaped the misery of this early hardship, becoming an ardent advocate of Hood, and of Lamb, on whom he lectured in Britain and America:

> The 'Song of the Shirt' was the first summons of the army of the poor which had besieged the citadel of wealth. The very music of it was like the march of ten thousand men, who come, with dogged step, set teeth, and flashing eyes, to demand redress for their long sufferings and wrongs. It had an ominous sound. Men looked at one another, and for every poor one pale with want, there was a rich one pale with fear. The wealthy had not known, or did not care to know, what want and wretchedness existed around them, and how small a space they were from the gnashings of hunger, the effluvia of disease, and the seething fires of revolution . . . The 'Song of the Shirt' called forth a tide of feeling so strong and impetuous, that it threw down and overleaped many an ancient barrier that had so long divided the rich from the poor. It was an equivalent for the horrible poor law system, which severed the last human link between them . . . Who can compute the influence that these songs exerted for good, or how powerfully they contributed to bring about the many benevolent and noble schemes put forth and adopted, to alleviate the distress that existed? That it was great, we know – how great, we can never know.[51]

Allowing for Massey's enthusiasm, this remains a striking tribute. He credits Hood both with sounding a clarion call to action and with reviving cross-class sympathies that the New Poor Law of 1834 had fatally undermined. Certainly there is evidence that Hood's work circulated widely amongst working-class audiences, as well as amongst the middle and upper classes. James Hepburn's study of nineteenth-century broadside ballad finds that Hood is well represented in this cheap, typically pirated, popular form: Wordsworth and even Byron (admired for his radical sympathies, but represented only by a few short lyrics) did not enjoy such extensive circulation.[52] In *News from Nowhere* William Morris alludes to 'The Song of the Shirt' as a 'revolutionary song'.[53]

Versions of 'The Song of the Shirt' rapidly appeared in German, Italian, and Russian, while workers such as E.L.E., author of *Poems by a Sempstress* (1848), used Hood's poetry and *Hood's Magazine* as vehicles through which their own voice could be broadcast. Hood's accessibility and the informal register of his work meant his style was easily adopted and adapted. Siegfried Sassoon was out of the last poets to acknowledge Hood as a formative influence on his protest poetry. In *The Old Century and Seven More Years* he describes his reading of Hood's 'Bridge of Sighs' in the library as an epiphany that crystallized his desire to become a poet:

> Idly I pulled out a book which happened to be volume iv of Ward's English Poets. By chance I opened it at Hood's 'Bridge of Sighs', which was unfamiliar to me. I had always preferred poems which went straight to the point and stayed there, and here was a direct utterance which gave me goose flesh and brought tears to my eyes.[54]

The pithy, blackly comic address of some of Sassoon's best war poetry is indebted to Hood's style, unashamedly dramatic and alive with wordplay that mimics the breaking and reconstitution of bodies: the directness and familiarity of tone creates an intimacy with the reader that drives the betrayals of war home.

The collapse of Hood's reputation is linked to suspicion of this kind of familiarity. The modernist movement toward intellectualism, abstraction, and a cooler relation between author and reader rejected the output of poets like Hood as restrictively domestic and emotionally manipulative. John Heath-Stubbs describes, with distaste, being 'brought up on' 'Eugene Aram' and 'The Bridge of Sighs' in his schooldays in the 1920s, when they seemed to move in a 'gas-lit, fuggy world of sentimental pity and melodramatic terror' shared by 'the contemporaneous works of Dickens'.[55] Dickens's academic reputation recovered gradually during the twentieth century from the negative reaction to Victoriana; Hood, as I hope this book has shown, deserves similar reconsideration. Part of that reconsideration involves looking at inherited assumptions about the relation between poetry and a mass audience. W.H. Auden, Hood's last well-known poet advocate, warned readers in 1938 that, in undervaluing accessible, comic authors such as Hood, they were effectively rejecting the possibilities of cultural democracy:

> Light verse can be serious. It has only come to mean *vers de société*, triolets, smoke-room limericks, because, under the social conditions which produced the Romantic Revival, and which have persisted, more or less, ever since, it has been only in trivial matters that poets have felt in sufficient intimacy with their audience to be able to forget themselves and their singing-robes.[56]

Poetry that is both light and adult is, to Auden, the mark of 'a society which is both integrated and free'. Auden, who regards Hood as 'a major poet', primarily for his comic poetry, insists upon the high political value of the intimacy that verse dubbed 'light' reflects and generates between the poet and society. The dearth of such verse signals the end of poetry's popular, political role. Auden's claim remains live. Books of and about poetry now account for less than 1 per cent of publishing output; major presses have eliminated their poetry list as unprofitable; new poetry has failed to connect with the general reader in the twenty-first century. We are still, to a great extent, living in the partition state he identified in which highbrow poetry is culturally marginal and 'light' verse is intellectually suspect: that barrier, among others, needs to be eroded if students and other readers are to engage with the pleasures of poetry on a more regular basis.

One of the most acute challenges that Hood makes to academic critics is that the fact that analysing literature is our work may blind us to the elemental function of poetry as play. It has been noticeable to me, through many years of reading Hood, that he is better known outside the academy than within it. Hood's familiar, ludic style, developed in a society increasingly dominated by alienating labour discipline, challenges not only the work/play divide of his own time but that of ours. Britain remains locked into a culture of long hours and an unhealthy estrangement between work and family life. Universities, in the last twenty years, have become increasingly dependent on private sector funding and concomitantly dominated by industrial models of competitive tender and increase in measurable outputs as the yardstick of success. Imposed regardless of discipline, such models ignore and undermine the value of the Humanities as a source and reflection of human community, one of whose chief motives and ends is pleasure. Hood's poetry is not all comic, but it is all predicated on the primacy of play as a means of communication, of creating intimacy, sympathy, and – as a direct consequence of these – political solidarity. Academics will produce no telling critique of it until we absorb its telling critique of academics: our professional preference for depth over surface, mind over matter, the work we have made of literature as against the play it urges in us.

Notes

1 Address to the third edition of *Whims and Oddities*, 2 (1827), reprinted in *CW*, vol. 5, pp. 171–2.
2 Hood, *Hood's Magazine*, 1 (November 1844), p. 424.
3 See *Comic Poems of Thomas Hood* and *Serious Poems of Thomas Hood*, ed. S. Lucas (London: Moxon, 1867); *Comic Poems* (London: Routledge

1885) and *Serious Poems* (London: Routledge, 1886); *Poems of Thomas Hood Volume One: Serious Poems* and *Volume Two: Poems of Wit and Humour*, ed. Alfred Ainger (London: Macmillan, 1897).

4 Henkle, 'Comedy as Commodity', p. 306.

5 Peter Bailey, *Leisure and Class in Victorian England: Rational Recreation and the Contest for Control 1830–1885* (London and New York: Methuen, 1987), p. 25.

6 These examples of growing middle-class restriction on working-class leisure are taken from Hugh Cunningham, *Leisure in the Industrial Revolution, c.1780–1880* (London: Croom Helm, 1980), pp. 79–83.

7 Ibid., p. 12.

8 M.J.D. Roberts, *Making English Morals: Voluntary Association and Moral Reform in England, 1787–1886* (Cambridge: Cambridge University Press, 2004), p. 107.

9 Charles Lamb, 'A Complaint of the Decay of Beggars in the Metropolis', *London Magazine*, 5 (June 1822).

10 'Ode to H. Bodkin, Esq.', *PW*, p. 32.

11 Hood, *Comic Annual* (London: Baily, 1836), p. 137.

12 Charles Lamb, 'The Praise of Chimney Sweepers: A May-Day Effusion', *London Magazine*, 5 (May 1822); Hood, 'The Sweep's Complaint' (1835), describes 'poor starving figures' in cellars, dependent for income on sweeping and now effectively prevented from plying their trade.

13 'Sonnet – A Somnambulist', *PW*, p. 269.

14 See also the cartoon 'Looking Up to the Overseer', *Comic Annual* (London: Tilt, 1833), p. 153, where the pauper so exceeds the overseer in stature as to make the caption ridiculous.

15 Preface to the 1839 *Comic Annual*, reprinted in Hood, *CW*, vol. 7, pp. 290–2.

16 See p. 167 for Andrew Agnew's Bill for prohibiting Sunday labour.

17 James Wight and George Cruikshank, *Sunday in London* (London: Wilson, Hurst, 1833).

18 Cunningham, *Leisure in the Industrial Revolution*, p. 39.

19 'An Open Question', *PW*, pp. 561–2.

20 Thomas and Jane Hood (with additional material by Tom and Fanny Hood), *Fairy Land; or, Recreation for the Rising Generation* (London: Griffith and Farran, 1861), p. 82.

21 Ann and Jane Taylor, *Original Poems for Infant Minds*, II (London: Darton, Harvey and Darton, 1814). 'Dirty Jim' by Jane Taylor, p. 39; 'Contented John', also by Jane, p. 115; 'The Horse. A Fable', p. 47.

22 Ann Taylor, 'My Mother', in Ann and Jane Taylor, *Original Poems for Infant Minds* (London: Darton and Harvey, 1808), pp. 71–3.

23 'A Lay of Real Life', *PW*, p. 233.

24 'A Plain Direction', *PW*, p. 538.

25 In America traditional verses about the 'Big Rock Candy Mountain' describe a utopia, where food is free.

26 Hood, *Comic Annual* (London: Baily, 1839), p. v. In the preface to the *Comic Annual* (London: Tilt, 1831), p. x, Hood sincerely hopes that 'what is my Work may be the amusement and relaxation of others, in Town, in Country, and in the Suburbs'.

27 Always an opponent of the Corn Laws, which kept the price of bread in Britain artificially high, Hood's experience of customs duties made him an even greater advocate of free trade. He approved of the German experiment with universal free primary schooling and more enlightened German laws regarding debtors; like many expatriate Britons he benefited from Germany's less rigid class system but resented exploitative pricing of goods for foreigners and other aspects of a culture he came to regard as mercenary and intolerant.

28 Talfourd's bill aimed to extend copyright to sixty years after the author's death from the existing maximum of twenty-eight years or the life of the author, whichever was longer.

29 Hood, 'Copyright and Copywrong', *Athenaeum*, 15 April 1837, p. 264.

30 Blanchard Jerrold, *The Wit and Opinions of Douglas Jerrold* (London: Kent, 1859), p. 52.

31 Edward Bulwer Lytton, *England and the English*, 2 vols (London: Bentley, 1833), vol. 1, p. 148.

32 Clifford Siskin, *The Work of Writing: Literature and Social Change in Britain, 1700–1830* (Baltimore and London: Johns Hopkins University Press, 1998), pp. 104–9.

33 Hood, 'Copyright and Copywrong', *Athenaeum*, 22 April 1837, p. 286.

34 Hood states in his 'Review: Shakespeare, Library Edition, edited by C. Knight' reprinted in *CW*, vol. 8, p. 241, that '(Johnson) could not comprehend or value the Catholic toleration, the Socialism (a good word badly abused) which is the essential characteristic of Shakespeare'.

35 Hood, 'Copyright and Copywrong', *Athenaeum*, 29 April 1837, p. 305.

36 Despite his contact with women writers such as Hannah Lawrance, Mary Lamb, and Mary Russell Mitford, Hood conceives the writer primarily as male.

37 Chris R. Vanden Bossche, 'The Value of Literature: Representations of Print Culture in the Copright Debate of 1837–1842', *Victorian Studies*, 38 (1994), pp. 41–68, describes the use of the metaphor comparing landed estates with literary estates as a significant tactic among proponents of the copyright bill. The opposition contended that authors, like other workers, were paid an absolute sum as recompense for their labour, which then became the absolute property of the employer. The proposition countered that the publisher was more like a tenant, who paid to profit from the author's property under contract, than a buyer who thereafter owned the property in perpetuity. Authors, fighting for status, argued that they were not demanding better pay but were protecting their estates so that they could 'found a family' upon them. Talfourd's bill was rejected between 1837 and 1841, but a modified version (extending copyright to forty-two years from

publication, or seven years beyond the author's death, whichever was longer) was passed in 1842. For a fuller account of the issues at stake see Catherine Seville, *Literary Copyright Reform in Early Victorian England: The Framing of the 1842 Copyright Act* (Cambridge: Cambridge University Press, 1999).

38 Hood, 'Copyright and Copywrong', *Athenaeum*, 22 April 1837, p. 286.
39 'Ode to Madame Hengler', *PW*, p. 257.
40 'The Assistant Drapers' Petition', *PW*, p. 551. Charles Knight was a leading light of the Society for the Diffusion of Useful Knowledge, editor of cheap periodicals, such as the *Penny Magazine*, which made general information available to a working-class audience, and of affordable reference works and editions. Hood wrote a positive review of his 'library edition' of Shakespeare; see note 34.
41 Harriet Martineau, *History of England 1816–1846*, 2 vols (London: Knight, 1850), vol. 1, p. 46.
42 'The Lay of the Labourer', *PW*, p. 652.
43 'The Workhouse Clock', *PW*, p. 648.
44 Pritchett, *Living Novel*, p. 64.
45 John W. Dodds, *The Age of Paradox: A Biography of England 1814–1851* (New York: Gollancz, 1952), p. 210.
46 Lynn M. Alexander, *Women, Work, and Representation: Needlewomen in Victorian Art and Literature* (Athens, Ohio: Ohio University Press, 2003), p. 51.
47 'The Song of the Shirt', *PW*, p. 625.
48 Alexander, *Women, Work, and Reprensentation*, p. 222.
49 Charles Kingsley, *Alton Locke* (London: Cassell, 1967), p. 91.
50 Ibid., p. 86, p. 91.
51 Massey, 'Thomas Hood: Poet and Punster', pp. 326–7.
52 James Hepburn, *A Book of Scattered Leaves: Poetry of Poverty in Broadside Ballads of Nineteenth-century England*, 2 vols (London: Associated University Presses, 2000), vol. 1, pp. 42–3.
53 Morris, *News from Nowhere*, pp. 99–100.
54 Sassoon, *The Old Century*, pp. 217–19.
55 Heath-Stubbs, *Darkling Plain*, p. 49.
56 W.H. Auden, Preface to *The Oxford Book of Light Verse* (1938) reprinted in *The English Auden: Poems, Essays and Dramatic Writings 1927–1939* (London: Faber, 1977), p. 364.

Select bibliography

Alderson, Simon J., 'The Augustan Attack on the Pun', *Eighteenth-Century Life*, 20 (November 1996), 1–19.

Altick, Richard D., *Punch: The Lively Youth of a British Institution 1841–51* (Columbus, Ohio: Ohio State University Press, 1997).

Anderson, Patricia, *The Printed Image and the Transformation of Popular Culture* (Oxford: Oxford University Press, 1991).

Armstrong, Isobel, *Victorian Poetry: Poetry, Poetics and Politics* (London: Routledge, 1993).

Auden, W.H., *Nineteenth Century Minor Poets* (London: Faber, 1967).

Bailey, Peter, *Leisure and Class in Victorian England: Rational Recreation and the Contest for Control 1830–1885* (London and New York: Methuen, 1987).

Bakhtin, Mikhail, *Rabelais and His World* (Bloomington, Indiana: Indiana University Press, 1984).

Baldick, Chris, *In Frankenstein's Shadow: Myth, Monstrosity and Nineteenth-century Writing* (Oxford: Oxford University Press, 1987).

Bate, Catherine, 'The Point of Puns', *Modern Philology*, 96 (May 1999), 421–38.

Bauer, Josephine, *The London Magazine 1820–29* (Copenhagen: Rosenkilde and Bagger, 1953).

Blunden, Edmund, 'The Poet Hood', *A Review of English Literature*, 1 (January 1960), 26–34.

Brander, Laurence, *Thomas Hood* (London: Longman & Green, 1963).

Brantlinger, Patrick, *The Spirit of Reform: British Literature and Politics, 1832–1867* (Cambridge, Massachusetts: Harvard University Press, 1977).

Bratton, J.S., *The Victorian Popular Ballad* (London: Macmillan, 1975).

Broderip, F.F. and Hood, Tom, *Memorials of Thomas Hood* (London: Moxon, 1869).

Burwick, Frederick, *The Haunted Eye: Perception and the Grotesque in English and German Romanticism* (Heidelberg: Heidelberg University Press, 1987).

Byron, Glennis, *Dramatic Monologue* (London: Routledge, 2003).

Cadoux, Margaret, 'L'Angoisse dans la Poesie de Thomas Hood', in Christian La Cassagnere (ed.), *Visages de L'Angoisse* (Clermont-Ferrand: Université Blaise-Pascal, 1989).

Chilcott, Tim, *A Publisher and His Circle: The Life and Work of John Taylor, Keats's Publisher* (London: Routledge, 1972).

Chorley, Henry Fothergill, 'Review of Hood's Works 1827–38', *London and Westminster Review*, 29 (April 1838), 119–45.

Clubbe, John, *Victorian Forerunner: The Later Career of Thomas Hood* (Durham, North Carolina: Duke University Press, 1968).

Cox, Jeffrey N., *Poetry and Politics in the Cockney School: Keats, Shelley, Hunt and Their Circle* (Cambridge: Cambridge University Press, 1998).

Cronin, Richard, *Romantic Victorians: English Literature 1824–1840* (Basingstoke: Palgrave, 2002).

Cronin, Richard, Chapman, Alison, and Harrison, Antony H., *A Companion to Victorian Poetry* (Oxford: Blackwell, 2002).

Culler, Jonathan (ed.), *On Puns: The Foundation of Letters* (Oxford: Blackwell, 1988).

Cunningham, Hugh, *Leisure in the Industrial Revolution, c. 1780–1880* (London: Croom Helm, 1980).

Dagley, Richard, *Death's Doings* (London: Andrews & Cole, 1826).

Dart, Greg, 'Romantic Cockneyism: Hazlitt and the Periodical Press', *Romanticism*, 6 (Autumn 2000), 143–62.

Dilke, Charles Wentworth, *The Papers of a Critic: Selected from the Writings of the Late Charles Wentworth Dilke*, 2 vols (London: Murray, 1875).

Douce, Francis, *The dance of death exhibited in elegant engravings on wood: with a dissertation on the several representations of that subject* (London: Pickering, 1833).

Dyer, Gary, *British Satire and the Politics of Style* (Cambridge: Cambridge University Press, 1997).

Eliot, Simon, *Some Patterns and Trends in British Publishing 1800–1919* (London: Bibliographical Society, 1994).

Elliot, Alexander, *Hood in Scotland* (Dundee: Mathew, 1885).

Empson, William, *Seven Types of Ambiguity* (London: Chatto and Windus, 1930).

English, James, *Comic Transactions: Literature, Humor, and the Politics of Community in Twentieth-Century Britain* (Ithaca and London: Cornell University Press, 1994).

Erickson, Lee, *The Economy of Literary Form: English Literature and the Industrialization of Publishing 1800–1850* (Baltimore: Johns Hopkins University Press, 1996).

Fraser, J., 'Thomas Hood', *Westminster and Foreign Quarterly Review*, 1 April 1871, 337–54.

Gatton, John Spalding, 'Of Publishing, Polkas and Prudery – A Restored Letter by Thomas Hood', *Kentucky Review*, 2 (1981), pp. 89–97.

Gilmartin, Kevin, *Print Politics: The Press and Radical Opposition in Early Nineteenth-Century England* (Cambridge: Cambridge University Press, 1996).

Gray, Donald J., 'The Uses of Victorian Laughter', *Victorian Studies*, 10 (December 1966), 145–76.

Gray, Donald J., 'Victorian Comic Verse; or, Snakes in Greenland', *Victorian Poetry*, 26 (1988), 211–30.

Groves, David, 'Thomas Hood, London, and the Edinburgh Literary Gazette', *English Language Notes*, 27 (1990), 34–9.

Hall, Samuel Carter, *A Book of Memories of Great Men and Women of the Age from Personal Acquaintance* (London: Virtue, 1871).

Harpham, Geoffrey Galt, *On the Grotesque: Strategies of Contradiction in Art and Literature* (Princeton: Princeton University Press, 1982).

Harris, Michael, and Myers, Robin (eds), *Economics of the British Booktrade* (Cambridge: Chadwyck-Healey, 1985).

Harrison, Antony H., *Victorian Poets and the Politics of Culture* (Charlottesville: University of Virginia Press, 1998).

Heath-Stubbs, John, *The Darkling Plain* (London: Eyre and Spottiswoode, 1950).

Henkle, Roger B., *Comedy and Culture 1820–1900* (Princeton: Princeton University Press, 1980).

Henkle, Roger B., 'Comedy as Commodity: Thomas Hood's Poetry of Class Desire', *Victorian Poetry*, 26 (1988), 301–18.

Henley, W. E., *Views and Reviews: Essays in Appreciation* (London: Nutt, 1890).

Hollington, Michael, *Dickens and the Grotesque* (London and Sydney: Croom Helm, 1984).

Hood, Thomas, *Whims and Oddities*, 1 (London: Lupton Relfe, 1826).

Hood, Thomas, *National Tales*, 2 vols (London: Ainsworth, 1827).

Hood, Thomas, *The Plea of the Midsummer Fairies, Hero and Leander, Lycus the Centaur, and Other Poems* (London: Longman, Rees, Orme, Brown and Green, 1827).

Hood, Thomas, *Whims and Oddities*, 2 (London: Tilt, 1827).

Hood, Thomas (ed.), *The Gem* (London: Marshall, 1829).

Hood, Thomas, *Mathews and Yates at Home* (London: Duncombe, 1829).

Hood, Thomas, *The Comic Annual* (London: Hurst and Chance, 1830).

Hood, Thomas, *The Comic Annual* (London: Tilt, 1831–34).

Hood, Thomas, *Tylney Hall*, 3 vols (London: Baily, 1834).

Hood, Thomas, *The Comic Annual* (London: Baily, 1835–9).

Hood, Thomas, *Hood's Own* (London: Baily, 1839).

Hood, Thomas, *Up the Rhine* (Frankfurt: Jugel, 1840).

Hood, Thomas, *The Comic Annual* (London: Colburn, 1842).

Hood, Thomas, *Whimsicalities: A Periodical Gathering* (London: Moxon, 1843).

Hood, Thomas (ed.), *Hood's Magazine and Comic Miscellany* (London: Renshaw, 1844–5).

Hood, Thomas, *The Headlong Career and Woful Ending of Precocious Piggy*, ed. F. F. Broderip and Tom Hood (London: Griffith and Farran, 1859).

Hood, Thomas, *The Complete Works of Thomas Hood*, ed. Tom Hood and F.F. Broderip, 10 vols (London: Moxon, 1869–73).

Hood, Thomas, *The Poetical Works of Thomas Hood*, ed. W.M. Rossetti, 2 vols (London: Moxon, 1875).

Hood, Thomas, *Poems of Thomas Hood*, ed. Alfred Ainger, 2 vols (London: Macmillan, 1897).

Hood, Thomas, *The Complete Poetical Works of Thomas Hood*, ed. Walter Jerrold (Oxford: Oxford University Press, 1906).

Hood, Thomas, *Selected Poems of Thomas Hood*, ed. John Clubbe (Cambridge, Massachusetts: Harvard University Press, 1970).

Hood, Thomas, *The Letters of Thomas Hood*, ed. Peter F. Morgan (Edinburgh: Oliver and Boyd, 1973).

Hood, Thomas, *Selected Poems of Hood, Praed and Beddoes*, ed. Susan Wolfson and Peter J. Manning (London: Penguin, 2000).

Hood, Thomas, and Hood, Jane, *Fairy Land; or, Recreation for the Rising Generation* ed. F.F. Broderip and Tom Hood (London: Griffith and Farran, 1861).

Hood, Thomas, and Reynolds, John Hamilton, *Odes and Addresses to Great People* (London: Baldwin, Cradock and Joy, 1825).

Horne, Richard H., *The New Spirit of the Age*, 2 vols (London: Smith Elder, 1844).

Hudson, W.H., *A Quiet Corner in a Library* (Chicago: Harrap, 1915).

Jack, Ian, *English Literature 1815–1832* (Oxford: Oxford University Press, 1963).

Jeffrey, Lloyd N., *Thomas Hood* (New York: Twayne, 1972).

Jerrold, Walter, *Thomas Hood: His Life and Times* (London: Alston Rivers, 1907).

Jerrold, Walter, *Thomas Hood and Charles Lamb: The Story of a Friendship* (London: Ernest Benn, 1930).

Jones, Leonidas M., *The Life of John Hamilton Reynolds* (Hanover, New Hampshire: University Press of New England, 1984).

Jordan, John O., and Patten, Robert L. (eds), *Literature in the Marketplace: Nineteenth-century British Publishing and Reading Practices* (Cambridge: Cambridge University Press, 1995).

Kayser, Wolfgang, The *Grotesque in Art and Literature*, trans. Ulrich Weisstein (Gloucester, Massachusetts: Smith, 1968).

Kent, David A., and Ewen, D.R. (eds), *Romantic Parodies, 1797–1831* (Cranbury, New Jersey and London: Associated University Presses, 1992).

Klancher, Jon, *The Making of English Reading Audiences 1790–1832* (Madison, Wisconsin: University of Wisconsin Press, 1987).

Kroeber, Karl, 'Trends in Minor Romantic Narrative Poetry', in James V. Logan, John Jordan and Northrop Frye (eds), *Some British Romantics: A Collection of Essays* (Columbus, Ohio: Ohio State University Press, 1966).

Lamb, Charles, *The Letters of Charles Lamb*, ed. E.V. Lucas, 3 vols (London: Dent and Methuen, 1935).

Lawrance, Hannah, 'Recollections of Thomas Hood', *British Quarterly Review*, 46 (1867), 323–54.

Lemon, Mark, *The Sempstress: A Drama* (London: Dick's, 1886).

Lodge, Sara, 'Romantic Reliquaries: Memory and Irony in the Literary Annuals', *Romanticism*, 10 (Spring 2004), 23–40.

Lytton, Edward Bulwer, *England and the English*, 2 vols (London: Bentley, 1833).

MacFarlane, Charles, *Reminiscences of a Literary Life* (London: Murray, 1917).

Macready, William Charles, *Reminiscences and Selections from His Diaries and Letters*, ed. Frederick Pollock, 2 vols (London: Macmillan, 1875).

Marchand, Leslie A., *Letters of Thomas Hood from the Dilke Papers in the British Museum* (New Brunswick: Rutgers University Press, 1945).

Martin, Robert B., *The Triumph of Wit: A Study of Victorian Comic Theory* (Oxford: Clarendon Press, 1974).

Martineau, Harriet, *History of England 1816–46*, 2 vols (London: Knight, 1850).

Massey, Gerald, 'Thomas Hood: Poet and Punster', *Hogg's Instructor*, 4 (1855), 320–8.

Mathews, Anne, *Memoirs of Charles Mathews, Comedian*, 3 vols (London: Bentley, 1839).

Moody, Jane, *Illegitimate Theatre in London, 1770–1840* (Cambridge: Cambridge University Press, 2000).

More, P.E., *Shelburne Essays*, 7 (New York: Putnam, 1910).

Morgan, Peter F., 'John Hamilton Reynolds and Thomas Hood', *Keats–Shelley Journal*, 11 (1962), 83–95.

Myers, Robin G., and Harris, Michael H. (eds), *Development of the English Book Trade 1700–1899* (Oxford: Oxford Polytechnic Press, 1981).

Najarian, James, 'Canonicity, Marginality, and the Celebration of the Minor', *Victorian Poetry*, 41 (2003), 570–4.

Nemoianu, Virgil, *The Taming of Romanticism: European Literature and the Age of Biedermeier* (Cambridge, Massachusetts: Harvard University Press, 1984).

O'Leary, P., *Regency Editor: A Life of John Scott* (Aberdeen: Aberdeen University Press, 1983).

Oswald, Emil, *Thomas Hood und die soziale Tendenzdichtung seiner Zeit* (Vienna and Leipzig: Braumller, 1904).

Parker, Mark, *Literary Magazines and British Romanticism* (Cambridge: Cambridge University Press, 2000).

Patten, Robert L., *George Cruikshank's Life, Times, and Art*, 2 vols (Cambridge: Lutterworth, 1992).

Planché, J.R., *The Recollections and Reflections of J. R. Planché*, 2 vols (London: Tinsley, 1872).

Poe, Edgar Allan, *Essays and Reviews of Edgar Allan Poe* (Cambridge: Cambridge University Press, 1984).

Pritchett, V.S., *The Living Novel* (London: Chatto and Windus, 1946).

Redfern, Walter, *Puns* (Oxford: Blackwell, 1984).

Reeves, James, *Five Late Romantic Poets* (London: Heinemann, 1974).

Reid, J.C., *Thomas Hood* (London: Routledge & Kegan Paul, 1963).

Roe, Nicholas, *John Keats and the Culture of Dissent* (Oxford: Clarendon, 1997).

Russett, Margaret, *De Quincey's Romanticism: Canonical Minority and the Forms of Transmission* (Cambridge: Cambridge University Press, 1997).

Russett, Margaret, *Fictions and Fakes: Forging Romantic Authenticity, 1760–1845* (Cambridge: Cambridge University Press, 2006).

Saintsbury, George, *Essays in English Literature, 1780–1860* (London: Percival, 1890).

Schoenfield, Mark, 'Voices Together: Lamb, Hazlitt, and the *London*', *Studies in Romanticism*, 29 (Summer 1990), 257–72.

Scott, Patrick, 'From Bon Gaultier to *Fly Leaves*: Context and Canon in Victorian Poetry', *Victorian Poetry*, 26 (1988), 249–66.

Shelley, Henry C., *Literary By-Paths in Old England* (London: Grant Richards, 1909).

Smith, Olivia, *The Politics of Language 1791–1819* (Oxford: Clarendon, 1984).

Sinfield, Alan, *Dramatic Monologue* (London: Methuen, 1977).

Siskin, Clifford, *The Work of Writing: Literature and Social Change in Britain, 1700–1830* (Baltimore and London: Johns Hopkins University Press, 1998).

Stafford, Fiona J., *The Last of the Race: The Growth of a Myth from Milton to Darwin* (Oxford: Clarendon, 1999).

Stones, Graeme, and Strachan, John (eds), *Parodies of the Romantic Age*, 5 vols (London: Pickering and Chatto, 1999).

Talfourd, Thomas Noon, *Literary Sketches and Letters, Being the Final Memorials of Charles Lamb* (New York: Appleton, 1848).

Thesing, William B., *The London Muse: Victorian Poetic Responses to the City* (Athens, Georgia: University of Georgia Press, 1982).

Thomson, Philip, *The Grotesque* (London: Methuen, 1972).

Trodd, Colin, Barlow, Paul, and Amigoni, David, *Victorian Culture and the Idea of the Grotesque* (Aldershot: Ashgate, 1999).

Tucker, Herbert F., 'House Arrest: The Domestication of English Poetry in the 1820s', *New Literary History*, 25 (1994), 521–48.

Tucker, Herbert F. (ed.), *A Companion to Victorian Literature and Culture* (Oxford: Blackwell, 1999).

Turley, Richard Marggraf, *The Politics of Language in Romantic Literature* (Basingstoke: Palgrave, 2002).

Vann, J. Don, and VanArsdel, Rosemary T., *Victorian Periodicals and Victorian Society* (Toronto: University of Toronto Press, 1994).

West, Michael, *Transcendental Wordplay: America's Romantic Punsters and the Search for the Language of Nature* (Athens, Ohio: Ohio University Press, 2000).

Whitley, Alvin, 'Thomas Hood as a Dramatist', *University of Texas Studies in English*, 30, (1951), 184–201.

Whitley, Alvin, 'Hood and Dickens: Some New Letters', *Huntington Library Quarterly*, 14 (August 1951), 385–413.

Whitley, Alvin, 'Two Hints for Bleak House', *Dickensian*, 52 (September 1956), 183–4.

Whitley, Alvin, 'Keats and Hood', *Keats–Shelley Journal*, 5 (Winter 1956), 33–47.

Wicke, Jennifer, *Advertising Fictions: Literature, Advertising and Social Reading* (New York: Columbia University Press, 1988).

Wood, Marcus, *Radical Satire and Print Culture 1790–1822* (Oxford: Oxford University Press, 1994).

Wright, Thomas, *A History of Caricature and Grotesque in Literature and Art* (London: Virtue, 1865).

Young, G.M. (ed.), *Early Victorian England 1830–1865*, 2 vols (Oxford: Oxford University Press, 1988).

Index

Note: 'n.' after a page reference indicates the number of a note on that page